THE WATCHMAN

THE WATCHMAN

THE TWISTED LIFE AND CRIMES OF
SERIAL HACKER KEVIN POULSEN

JONATHAN LITTMAN

LITTLE, BROWN AND COMPANY

Boston New York Toronto London

Library of Congress Cataloging-in-Publication Data

Littman, Jonathan.
The watchman : the twisted life and crimes of serial hacker
Kevin Poulsen / Jonathan Littman.—1st ed.
p. cm.
Includes index.
ISBN 0-316-52857-9
1. Poulsen, Kevin, 1965– 2. Computer hackers—United States—
Biography. 3. Computers and society—United States.
4. Computer crimes—United States. 5. Computer security—
United States. I. Title.
HV6772.P68L57 1997
364.16'8'092—dc21
96-47168

10 9 8 7 6 5 4 3 2 1

HAD

Published simultaneously in Canada by Little, Brown
& Company (Canada) Limited

Printed in the United States of America

For Sherry Lue and Elizabeth Claire

CONTENTS

—■—

Prologue   3

PART I

Dungeon Master   11
WarGames   21
Play a Game?   27
Network News   33
Good Fellas   38

PART II

Top Secret   45
Star Watch   53
Identity Crisis   59
Command Control   67
Corporate Headquarters   75
Watchman   79
The Anti-Hacker   87

PART III

The Storage Locker   95

The Bust   102

Blindfolded   109

The Meeting   116

The Wiretap Machine   124

Home Shopping   131

Risky Business   137

Controlled Detonation   146

Classified   156

Tap Dancing   164

Kevin's Court   173

Grand Jury   180

Happy Birthday   187

The Indictment   192

PART IV

Blonds Have More Fun   207

The Giveaway   214

The Stakeout   222

The Chase   230

Unsolved Mysteries   240

Musical Chairs   250

The Office   256

Houdini   265

Epilogue   273

Author's Note   287

THE WATCHMAN

PROLOGUE

———■———

oday is the day he takes matters into his own hands. He fires up yet another in his series of old clunkers, this one a weathered Army transport van. He drives east on Hollywood Boulevard, past the motley array of check-cashing joints, dusty unleased storefronts, palm readers, and sidewalks imprinted with the names of yesterday's movie stars. The summer smog is thick as the L.A. morning commute, an hour that usually finds him fast asleep. He works nights, though few would consider what he does work, but today, to earn a living, he's changed his routine and struggled out of bed a little after dawn. He's in a black phase, except for the hair, dyed platinum to alter his appearance. Baggy black Levi's, black Reeboks, a black bowling shirt from Melrose Street, and one diamond stud in his left ear. His face and body are narrow and angular, his nose long. But it's the eyes. They light up at the most unpredictable times.

He's thinking about the second cup of coffee he would have liked with his Pop-Tart when the music stops. "Today is the day!" booms radio personality Rick Dees. "This is song number one, 'Escapade,' by Janet Jackson. If it is followed by 'Love Shack,' by the B-52s and 'Kiss,' by Prince, you could be caller number one-o-two and win a brand-new fifty-thousand-dollar Porsche!"

The greatest radio giveaway in the history of Los Angeles is spinning to a climax. It's Friday, June 1, 1990, the last day of the fabulous contest. Once a week for seven weeks running, KIIS-FM 102 has handed out Southern California's fantasy of steel, leather, and status. You can't live or work in Los Angeles without being caught up in the frenzy. The gleaming, candy red convertibles are plastered on nearly every billboard and bus in town. The station is ubiquitous, playing in cars, malls, businesses, restaurants, and homes. Office workers, housewives, clerks, students, struggling actors, and contest freaks jam the call-in lines with cellulars, auto dialers, even ordinary phones. It's so American, the craze, the combo of phones and fast cars. We may not be created equal, we may not all enjoy the same privileges, but we all have an equal opportunity to win. It's so simple, even a child can do it. Just be the 102nd caller the moment Prince stops singing, and drive home a brand-new Porsche 944 S2 Cabriolet.

Five minutes. That's all he's got, he figures, as he zips through the lights down the broad, crowded boulevard. The sequence of songs should last longer than five minutes, but if his partner's late, as usual, it will be close. He hangs a hard right at Cahuenga at the famous International Newsstand, dashes across the street to the unmarked door next to Casanova's Adult World, and trots up the red wooden stairs. But the tune slows him to a brisk walk. Just as he suspected, the disc jockey is toying with the audience. The second song isn't the B-52s' "Love Shack."

But it won't be long. Kevin Lee Poulsen knows that before the day is out he, and not one of the other hundreds of thousands of Los Angeles hopefuls, will be the happy winner. He's always wanted a Porsche, but the $50,000 car isn't really the point. Kevin's a computer hacker and phone phreak. Access is Kevin's game. He knows secrets the mob would like to know, secrets for which foreign governments would gladly pay, secrets that could get people hurt. And as he burrows further into his fractal world of computer nets and telephone switches, he knows that access is changing him, as the seminary changes a young man, as the military changes a recruit.

To Kevin, the FBI doesn't understand. They take away his job, his life, they paint him as a criminal when he believes his actions have always been beyond reproach. In his mind, they're the real threat to freedom and privacy in the information age: the things they do to hackers, they'll soon try to do to ordinary citizens. But it won't work, not with what Kevin has planned. One more hack and he'll be a legend in the underground.

They think it's all about money, but to Kevin it's a challenge. Who would believe that a half-million-dollar radio contest could be manipulated with a PC, a few telephones, and a hacker's ingenuity? Kevin Poulsen, the artist, is on the verge of his greatest public performance.

Danger is only part of the romance. Today, he just might prove the almighty system is wearing no clothes. Kevin is fighting for his kind. Hackers and phreaks are being hunted to extinction. So what if Kevin's creative, rebellious predecessors helped jump-start the high-tech revolution. In the last few months, Secret Service and state law enforcement have been making dozens of hacker raids around the country, publicizing arrests and seizing scores of computers in a nationwide effort to thwart the new "electronic menace." Operation Sundevil, they call it, but soon it will be known as the great Hacker Crackdown. To the feds, all hackers are outlaws, digital desperadoes who've lived beyond their time.

Kevin is unique even in this elite club. Kevin hacks, phreaks, scales walls, and picks locks. He's studied Ma Bell's secrets since he was thirteen, been raided by the authorities twice, and will soon be featured on the television program *Unsolved Mysteries*. He's twenty-four now, and for him the radio contest is a testament to his ingenuity. He runs ten phone lines into his Hollywood office from the telephone closet down the hall, "floaters," unused lines he turns on by hacking into Pac Bell's computers. Normally, he'd need two phone lines to seize one of the radio station's eight lines. Normally, he'd be satisfied with simply improving his odds from one in four to one in two. Today, Kevin isn't taking any chances.

A week ago, Kevin hacked Pac Bell's computers and diverted the station's incoming calls to a phone at his Hollywood office. He then dialed 72 #, the forward command, and entered the station's original number. Once Kevin hung up his loop was complete. Every contest call would first bounce to his control number and then forward back to the station. Kevin knew the loop was live, because his control phone rang once each time it forwarded a call.

The plan is ingenious, but fundamentally simple, a sting in the style of the great Redford and Newman flick. He enlists the help of his old fellow hacker Ron Austin, because even the legendary hacker can't possibly juggle eight phones by himself. Shaggy, with uncombed dirty blond hair, mismatched jeans and shirt, Ron is Kevin's antithesis. His square jaw and sinewy body fit; he's handsome and he knows it. But Ron isn't here for fun or show. He detests KIIS-FM. He's heard every pop tune the station plays dozens of times, and Kevin is getting on his nerves. Over and over again, out of the blue, Kevin turns and deadpans, "Stop! Hammer time!"

The lyrics from the M. C. Hammer rap "U Can't Touch This" are stuck in his head. The claustrophobia presses in. There's the sense they can never totally escape the cramped room, that leaving the building even for a few minutes is dangerous. When they're too hungry, they make a mad dash to the corner Jack In The Box, radios in hand, ready to run back if they hear Janet sing. They take turns knocking a single ball with an old putter across the tattered brown carpet into a coffee mug. Ron brought in the putter, but in no time Kevin is banking the ball off the walls, turning the room into a miniature golf course.

— ■ —

Kevin is chipping the ball over a book when he hears the first song's lyrics.

"With a smile ... Lookin' shy ... You caught my eye ..."

And the second song?

"I'm heading down the Atlantic highway ..."

Could it be?

"Don't have to be beautiful to turn me on ..."

At last, Prince's familiar wail! As the song ends the calls pour in.

"Caller number two! ... Caller five! ... Caller seven! ... Caller nine!" the station employees shout.

Kevin's control phone rings wildly, but he's patiently counting. If he takes over the station's lines too early they might be detected. At sixty rings Kevin picks up the receiver and taps the 72 #—killing the forward command. Now everyone dialing the station will get a busy signal. Everyone except for Kevin Poulsen.

Half the lines are on speakerphone because Kevin fears they won't be able to juggle so many. It's reflex and timing now. Wait to hear them shout out the caller number, then flash that phone's switch hook to hang up the line. No need to redial. Kevin's hacked into Pac Bell and programmed the phones so that they instantly reconnect to the station.

They flash the switch hooks like a couple of New York hustlers playing the shell game, all the waiting forgotten in the final electronic flurry. The eighth and final fiery red chariot is about to be awarded in the $400,000 KIIS-FM Porsche giveaway. But as the countdown nears ninety, one more hurdle remains. If Dees puts more than the last couple of callers on the air, he might realize they sound suspiciously like the same two young men.

Yet getting caught fixing a radio contest is the least of Kevin Poulsen's concerns. For other, far more serious crimes, his name is climbing near the FBI's Ten Most Wanted list. The feds say he's done it all—compromised national security wiretaps, cracked secure military computers, wiretapped, and committed computer fraud. They want to put him away for thirty-seven years. But first they have to catch him. Kevin Poulsen is the first hacker to live the cyberpunk fantasy, the first to choose the underground over federal justice.

Ron jams the phone toward Kevin.

Over the phone and the airways of Los Angeles, Dees's voice booms loud and clear.

"This is KIIS. You're on LIVE!"

PART I

DUNGEON MASTER

Born in the fall of 1965, Kevin Poulsen came of age just as the postwar high-technology boom began to spread beyond the defense industry and into the universities and schools and corporations. Kevin phreaked phones before he hacked, and like many of his generation he followed a tradition, a myth, a code. Society, technology, and even the laws would change, but Kevin held within his memory bank an image. It was romantic, and yet many parts of it were true. Phreaking wasn't about getting free calls, it was about *how* to get them, *how* to make them. It was about the process of *access*. Legend had it that the first phreaks were blind kids who whistled free calls, tuning in to the sounds of the vast machines and places they could never see. To phreak was to discover and master invisible electronic worlds.

Phreaks routinely complained about evil, monopolistic Ma Bell, but to understand the machine, the network, the telephone system—these were the true goals of the phreaks, a journey that would eventually lead to a better understanding of the world. The first computer hackers brought light to a closed world. Early computers were giant, cumbersome machines tended by a priesthood of technicians who processed punch cards, maintained massive air-cooling systems, and replaced the occasional melted vacuum tube.

The first hackers challenged the authority of the priesthood and began nudging the computers to life, teaching them to play chess, Ping-Pong, even music. They cleverly removed superfluous commands so computers would need fewer cards. Hackers at MIT toured telephone central offices and pumped switchmen and engineers for the secrets that would enable them to ride the telephone network for free. They studied lock picking to coax open university doors to examine the computers up close.

Hackers were making computers better, more powerful, easier to use, blazing a path the next generation could use to probe deeper. The process of hacking, the dedication, the abandon with which they hacked, formalized a code: question authority and demand access to information. Hackers would change the world, hack the machines into something that would improve the life of the ordinary man. Impure motives were impossible for the self-evident reason that by nature and training, hackers had superior ethics. Real hackers never hacked or phreaked for money. To do so would be to undermine the calling, to prove that you were not, after all, really a hacker.

———■———

The year is 1978, the birthdate of the test-tube baby. There's talk of DNA sequencing to cure disease and the emergence of a mysterious malady that destroys the immune system and slowly kills huge numbers of its victims. The first breeze of the microcomputer revolution is in the air, and sales of Steve Jobs's and Steve Wozniak's revolutionary Apple II personal computer are taking off.

But Kevin Poulsen is perfectly capable of entertaining himself with the pay phones at the mall. The thirteen-year-old purses his lips and lines up his cheeks with the steel in his mouth. His parents have no idea what he can do with those braces they foolishly thought were there to straighten his teeth. Too poor to own his own computer, Kevin is in secret training, practicing the telephone arts, studying to be a cyberpunk before the word, let alone the technology, exists. The mouthpiece is up close, like a rocker's microphone.

He whistles the pulse of a one.

"CLICK."

He whistles twice for a two and listens.

"CLICK."

One more whistle to finish dialing . . .

"KERCHUNK!"

He's there.

"BRRRRIIIIINGG!"

Kevin has just whistled the pulses Ma Bell recognizes as the number 121—the internal number for the operator in Blythe, California. Kevin is whistling at 2,600 hertz, the music that shuttles calls through Ma Bell's long distance network.

"Blythe," welcomes the operator.

"I'm calling from a testboard," Kevin intones as deeply as possible, trying to sound at least nineteen. "I need you to place a call."

Kevin rattles off the number of an L.A. operator, and in seconds, friendly "Blythe" bounces him back to his home city. Kevin repeats the sequence for another city, and another, and another.

"You'll have to speak up . . ." The last operator can barely hear him through the echoes, through the long telephone chain he has set up.

"Operator, can you connect me to 213-. . ." It's the number of the pay phone next to Kevin in the mall.

"BRRR—"

Kevin grabs it before the bell stops ringing, a phone in each ear.

"HELLOOO, KEVIN!" he shouts into one phone, then presses his ear to the other.

The sounds of distant switches and telephone static bubble up in his ears: "KERCHUNK, CLICK, BIZZZZ, KERCHUNK, FISSSSS, BUZZ . . ."

New York, Santa Fe, Chicago, Portland, Washington, D.C. . . . his words reverberate cross-country, broken with so much switching noise and telephone static that his name—no, he!—slips through the switches. Kevin has fallen down Alice's rabbit hole, his voice echoing, shrinking into infinity.

"Hellooooo, Keeeeevin, hellooooooo, keeeevin, hellooooooo, keeeevin . . ."

Kevin won't do his math and can't concentrate in school. He really does want to do well, it's just that junior high is too easy, too boring. And besides, Ma Bell isn't on the course list. He talks his frustrated parents into transferring him to Valley Alternative Magnet, a school for creative and problem kids. The thirteen-year-old is planning for his future—down the block is Cal State Northridge. Instead of playing ball with friends, the prodigy spends his afternoons in the college engineering library, poring over the dense Bell Labs technical histories of the hundred-year evolution of the telephone network, perusing the Bell technical journals that detail each new advance.

Soon it's time for hands-on field research. Pacific Telephone locks its dumpster at the nearby Cedros central office, hiding the secrets Kevin desires. But Kevin knows Master locks are sold with the erasable Master lock number written on them, a fact the phone company overlooks. Kevin scribbles down the number, bicycles to a hardware store, and has a key cut. Within the hour, he's knee deep in the dumpster, trashing for manuals, passwords, old equipment—whatever he can find. What Kevin can't read at the engineering library or fish out of the trash, he social engineers. It's a simple method really, a phreak term for an old con. Just phone up the neighborhood central office and trick them into thinking . . . "Yeah, this is Bob from Cedros," Kevin says. "I'm kind of new here, and nobody's around. There's this wire, and . . ."

Kevin can recognize a telephone switch by its ring and busy signal, and sometimes just by its telltale idiosyncratic clicks. Kevin has a complete mental picture of the inner workings of the phone network. He knows Ma Bell's national ranking of five classes of offices starting with the handful of regional offices and working all the way down to the neighborhood central offices. He knows how the old switches work— the electromechanical Step-by-Steps invented in the last century—and the Crossbars that replaced many of them in the 1930s. When he notices an internal line at the local central office that sounds different, he makes a few social engineering calls and discovers why. Switchmen light their phones with tiny neon lamps, pulling off enough electricity to warp the ring.

Kevin manages to get service for the number 764-0006 in his very own bedroom. Who cares if "zero" numbers are reserved for internal phone company lines? Kevin promptly installs his own Radio Shack neon lamp, dims the lights, deepens his voice. He's got his own central office.

"Zero six," Kevin answers in his official phone company style when his friends call.

Kevin buys his first touch-tone phone, tears it apart, connects and twists a few wires, and attaches a toggle switch. Kevin's exploiting a capability present in every phone, a ghost key column designed primarily for the military. Kevin flips the toggle switch and the right-hand column, 3, 6, 9, and #, magically turn into the military keys—Flash, Flash Override, Intermediate, and Priority. He dials directory assistance in Rhode Island, toggles to military mode, and holds down the # key—Priority—catapulting his call to a small switch dedicated to distributing incoming calls. Kevin presses a few more keys and enjoys a wonderful anomaly. He's snuck in the back door of Rhode Island directory assistance. He's a spider eagerly awaiting a fly.

"Directory assistance," Kevin answers in his bedroom.

"John Smith, please," requests the unsuspecting subscriber.

"For what city?"

"Providence."

"THWAT, THWAT, THWAT, THWAT, THWAT . . . THWUNK!"

Kevin flips through the Yellow Pages as loudly as possible, holding the pages up to the mouthpiece, licking his finger for the dramatic, single-page turns. It's like he's performing old-time radio drama, exaggerating the sound effects.

"You'll find it on page four fifty-two," Kevin says helpfully.

"What's the number?"

"We don't give out numbers," Kevin explains in his best Ma Bell bureaucratic tone. "We assist you in locating numbers."

———■———

"Sean from North Hollywood."

He pauses just long enough. He's cool, he doesn't sound like other thirteen-year-olds.

"Hey, I'm Kevin from North Hollywood."

It's a party "chat" phone line, one of the dozens that connect the young and awkward of Los Angeles in the late 1970s and early 1980s. They're a new reality, a place to find yourself and maybe someone else.

"So what's your IQ?" Kevin probes.

It's Mensa for teens.

She doesn't hesitate. Doesn't every thirteen-year-old know her IQ?

"One thirty-six."

Sounds cute, Kevin thinks. Got a brain too.

"Can I come over?" Kevin asks.

"Yeah, sure."

She senses what's coming. He's much more confident and intellectual than the other boys. He'll be tall, strong, and handsome, the "mature" love she's read about in books.

Kevin pedals furiously, still catching his breath when he swings off his Schwinn ten-speed. Sean is waiting for him out front, a blond pixie standing on the uncut grass before the window of her mother's run-down brown stucco apartment, the one with the air-conditioning unit sticking out.

Kevin is everything his phone voice isn't, painfully thin, hollowed features, a dull, brown mop of hair—and those braces. High-water Sears Toughskins don't help.

Those deep, sad eyes. Why won't he look me in the eye?

Kevin doesn't move. He just stands there, like a toy soldier on the lawn, several uncomfortable feet away, the silence growing longer until finally there's nothing to do but pedal down the long block of bleak apartment buildings, back to a number and a telephone.

"Hi, Kevin," she says, sprawling on her bed a couple minutes later, suspecting it's him before she answers.

It's easier for Kevin to relate to other people this way, electronically, invisibly. And so the two pals chat endlessly on the phone. Time is no factor, since like many of the L.A. kids who jam the chat lines, neither bothers much with school. Kevin is having trouble paying attention in class and Sean is thinking about quitting for good. But for all the phone time Sean logs, Kevin is not an easy boy to get to know. He lives in a pleasant working-class section of San Fernando Valley's North Hollywood, in a tidy house near the end of Teasedale Street: fresh white and yellow paint, a well-manicured garden of cactus, dwarf palm trees, roses, and potted plants, and a sign over the door proudly proclaiming "The Poulsens."

Kevin invites Sean to his room one day and she's surprised by its Spartan neatness. The walls are devoid of the usual boyhood heroes. There are no posters of baseball or football players for the most obvious reason. Kevin's got the ganglies—all limbs and no muscles or coordination. He hates football and thinks professional sports a waste of time. He cares little for music and hardly watches television. Kevin doesn't have a lot in common with his family. There are few family outings other than the required Sunday visits to the nearby Lutheran church. His pretty half sister is a typical Valley girl. Stepmom teaches as a substitute at public schools. Dad wields a wrench as an auto mechanic for the Los Angeles sheriff's department and loves country music. He's part of the System, a very small link in the chain. His hobby is restoring vintage junkers in the tidy Poulsen garage.

But Kevin's mechanical skills won't manifest themselves for years. Books are his first love, nonfiction mainly. Biographies. Everything from Howard Carter, the discoverer of Tutankhamen's tomb, to the legendary Harry Houdini. Kevin is amazed by Houdini's feats as an escape artist and magician, but he's even more intrigued by Houdini's second career as a debunker of spiritualists and exposer of frauds and charlatans. To Kevin, magic is the search for wisdom and justice.

———■———

"RADIO SHACK," beckons the plastic sign at the mini mall.

Kevin's adopted parents can't provide the one thing he desires above all else. He walks into his local techno McDonald's. What he wants is in back, plugged in, ready to go. He pecks the keys on the clunky Radio

Shack TRS model 80. Trash-80 is what the kids call the box, a reel-to-reel cassette for storage, fat, mushy keys, and a screen like a cheap black-and-white TV. But the computer speaks!

"HELLO, KEVIN POULSEN."

A crude, synthesized voice, a cheap version of Hal in the movie *2001: A Space Odyssey*. Kevin pecks a few more times, hearing his name over and over again. Pretty soon the manager is eyeing this kid who won't let anybody else try out the hot new toy. He asks him once, twice, then demands he leave. But Kevin just pedals down to the next mini mall. The itinerant hacker makes his Radio Shack rounds after school, sneaking spare minutes on the machines, studying the BASIC manual, tapping out his first tentative programs.

The boy who would one day become America's most feared hacker must wait, contenting himself with the game kids all over America are playing. Dungeons & Dragons is taking off, and it's not just any game. Kevin pores through the lengthy Dungeons & Dragons guide like it's a Pacific Telephone proprietary manual. It's a system too—just like the telephone network. Charts and rules are its frames and switches. Fate is the roll of the dice. The Dungeon Master is Ma Bell, the creator of each game, scratching out a medieval world on graph paper, drawing a dungeon with treasures, dragons, and hidden dangers.

Kevin chooses a character, usually a magician or a thief surviving through brains, defeating physically stronger adversaries through spells and arcane powers. He's working to be a wizard, to open doors magically with a wizard "lock spell," render himself invisible, and even detect evil. But the principle of "alignment" is what gives D&D teeth. Characters can have good or evil alignment, respect authority or welcome chaos. Kevin always casts his magicians and thieves in the "chaotic, evil" alignment mold, a dark philosophy based on freedom, randomness, and woe.

Several times a week, Kevin and Sean challenge each other for hours on end at Daniel's house; he's a nice kid who goes to school, earns good grades, and is a very dull Dungeon Master. Sean is just learning to be a Dungeon Master, but she isn't sure she wants to play like either of her friends. When Kevin's the Dungeon Master, his world appears a typical medieval land, more or less copied from the handbook's overwrought fantasy style. But once Sean and Daniel play, they realize Kevin is no ordinary Dungeon Master. Treasure chests explode in their faces. Walls split, disgorging horrible monsters. The ground opens and Sean and Daniel tumble into spike-lined pits haunted by hideous monsters. Whenever Kevin runs the game his dungeons are so elaborate and treacherous that Sean's or Daniel's characters are doomed to be killed over and over again.

Why stop at D&D? Kevin soaks up mysticism and the occult, any system that promises extraordinary powers.

One day Kevin asks to join Sean and her mother on a trip to the House of Hermetics, a quirky Hollywood store run by a woman who claims to be a witch. The woman sells herbs, oils, incense, candles, and volumes on witchcraft and the occult from her cluttered storefront. Kevin tags along, buys a few things, and soon is a budding expert on witchcraft. When the Randols introduce Kevin to an astrologer, he quickly learns the foundation of the ancient art. Soon, he immerses himself in the cabala, and talks at length with Sean about the ancient Jewish tradition of mysticism. Kevin bathes his tiny North Hollywood bedroom in the eerie glow of dozens of white candles, reading himself to sleep with the old books and incantations. None of it makes any sense to his horrified stepmother, Bernadine Poulsen. All she can think is he must have gotten the crazy idea from that kooky alternative school he insists on attending.

But Sean is trying to understand him. "I'm adopted, you know," Kevin reveals to her one afternoon on the telephone. "And Bernadine's not my first adopted mother."

No. Sean doesn't know. He tells her almost nothing about his family. The reception is fuzzy, but this rerun plays all too often in Kevin's head: memories of Isabelle, his first adopted mother, speaking French with her daughter, Debbie. And the day Kevin can't forget, the day Isabelle sent Kevin and his half sister to the neighbors' to play with their children. They were both very young.

When they came back, they found their mother dead.

WARGAMES

———■———

Kevin knows the hacker code like he knows his own name, but he also knows that history and reality are far more complex. Many of the hackers canonized as the leaders of the personal computer revolution walked a fuzzy line between exploration and crime. Steve Jobs and Steve Wozniak were high-tech pirates before they founded Apple Computer and amassed fortunes worth hundreds of millions of dollars. In the early seventies, Jobs and Wozniak read an *Esquire* article about the notorious Captain Crunch, an ex–Air Force man who'd discovered that the free toy in a box of the cereal issued the 2,600 hertz tone that controlled the long distance network. But what intrigued the budding entrepreneurs most was *Esquire*'s description of a blue box, an automated version of the toy whistle that made stealing phone calls a breeze.

Within weeks, Wozniak had built a digital blue box. Unsatisfied, the duo sought out Captain Crunch himself, picked up a few tips, and soon Jobs saw a business opportunity. Wozniak had circuit boards printed, reducing manufacturing time to an hour a box. They sold dozens of them at $150 a pop, but after a few purchasers threatened to turn them in, Jobs dropped out of the venture, fearing they might be arrested. He was right to be concerned. The Captain was caught and fined for his own blue-boxing, put on three years' probation, and struggled with his image as a lawbreaker. Phone company traces had divulged Jobs's number, but he and Wozniak were lucky to escape punishment.

A few years later, they hatched another scheme to cash in on new technology. They called it Apple Computer.

———■———

"I have this way of making free calls anywhere from any phone," Kevin declares on the phone. "No, it doesn't require using any codes. And it's not anything illegal."

Stumped, Ron Austin, an older, less experienced phreak, ventures a guess. It must be hardware. "So you've got a red box?" It's a logical explanation, a twist on Wozniak's and Jobs's blue box, only it emits the sound of coins dropping in a pay phone.

"Nope."

Soon, Ron runs out of guesses and it's trade time.

"OK, you first," suggests master Kevin.

Ron gives Kevin something real and useful—a company's working internal Watts extender number that will yield dozens of free long distance calls.

"Now tell me about the free calls."

"OK, you call an operator and make a collect call. Before the party answers, after one ring, you click the line and shout, 'Yes, I'll accept!'"

Ron groans. How is it Kevin always manages to have the upper hand? It's the puzzle that always brings Ron back. What does this squeaky-voiced trickster really want? Information? Mental combat? Or simply the joy of the phreak?

Though they met a few months earlier on the Hey Wow! chat line, Ron couldn't be more different from Kevin. Tall and crowned with a halo of blond curls, Ron has a girlfriend and a life. He grew up five blocks from the beach in a modest house on Second Street in Santa Monica, the son of an engineer who escaped from Lithuania during World War II. Ron is a loner, a surfer dude, but he's got a brain. Too smart for Santa Monica High, Ron is into phones because they're a challenge, because he loves solving problems.

Kevin too, loves to problem solve and outsmart adults. One day,

Kevin uncovers an ingenious method to turn a flaw in L.A.'s few remaining electromechanical Step-by-Step switches into free conference lines. The intricate plan requires finding obscure disconnected numbers and social engineering framemen into physically adjusting the contacts. Soon Kevin and Ron have built their own little Ma Bell telephone empire, chat lines with not two but six or seven incoming lines, so many free lines that, like merry Robin Hoods, they generously share them with other phreaks. They're practicing the hacker ethic, providing a service, sharing access that they believe should be free.

They keep a few disconnects to themselves, especially the handful that end in internal phone company numbers. That way, if a phone company employee questions Kevin's identity and demands a callback number, Kevin simply offers one of his working numbers. It never fails.

One afternoon, Kevin, Ron, and another friend get a call they've been hoping for.

"Cedros," welcomes Kevin, adopting the name of the central office the caller thinks he dialed.

"Hi, this is Charley," says the lineman. "I've got a problem with cable two, pair ninety-nine. Could you listen to it?"

"Hold on," snaps Kevin, pausing for a minute, all the while biting his tongue to keep from laughing. "Nope. No tone."

"Damn!" swears the lineman. "Let me try one thing more . . . OK. Could you try it again?"

Kevin waits another minute. "Nope. No tone."

"Shoot. OK. I'll check something else and call you back."

When Charley phones back, Kevin's friend quickly dials the real frame room on three-way and patches Charley through while the three listen in.

"Hi, can I talk to Kevin?" asks Charley.

"There's no Kevin here," responds the real Cedros frameman.

"What do you mean? I just talked to Kevin! He checked some pairs for me."

"Look, I'm the only one here."

"All right, I need a pair shoed. SAS shoes."

"SAS shoes?" repeats the stumped frameman. "Never heard of them."

"I'll bet Kevin knows what SAS shoes are. Forget it. I'll call back later and get Kevin to put them up for me."

But Charley's wrong. Even Kevin Poulsen, teeth bound with braces, fluent in switches and frames, has no idea what SAS shoes are. At the time, it seems a little thing. Kevin's got plenty of time. Kevin knows no telephone secret is safe. He's fourteen. Only a few years stand between Kevin and the ultimate phreak. The power to wiretap.

Anybody.

———■———

One morning, when his high school English teacher isn't looking, Kevin pencils another name into her roll sheet. The class is so large and the teacher so harried that at first she doesn't even notice. Kevin writes his story, then he writes another one for his double. What could be more creative in a creative writing class? He reinvents himself, pushing himself to develop a different style and voice. But being two students in the same class is pretty demanding. Kevin is juggling, trying to keep his own alter ego up in the air. He's fifteen years old, and he's already experimenting with his first alias.

On his sixteenth birthday, a few months before Kevin drops out of high school, his parents finally buy him a two-hundred-dollar TRS-80 Radio Shack computer and a modem. There isn't much Kevin can do on a Trash-80. He can read the manual and write little logic programs, but after he's done that a few times it's pretty boring. The one thing the plastic and silicon contraption is good for, it turns out, is to connect via modem to other pieces of plastic and silicon.

He dials the computer bulletin boards cropping up all over the nation. Most of them, like their chat line predecessors, are mundane, carrying practical computer tips. But then there are the outlaw boards, lorded over by The Cracko, Napoleon Bonaparte, or The Dark Lord. They'll laugh if he calls himself something weenie like "Kevin from North Hollywood." Or worse yet, banish him from some prized system.

Phreaking free calls isn't the game anymore. On the nets, well past the midnight hour, the old game of Dungeons & Dragons is turning digital—and real. It's time for a change of identity, an electronic make-over, a handle with attitude.

"Log in?" prompts Kevin's screen.

He scratches his head. Nothing comes to mind so he wanders through the house. His parents have a library of classics, from Shakespeare to Milton. Up on the bookcase is the volume he just read, Dante's classic, *The Inferno*.

Kevin returns to his computer, types in Dante, and hits return. "Invalid log in," complains the screen.

Kevin tries it again, and again. Finally, a message appears. A bulletin board operator, offering a phone number for Kevin to call.

"It needs a first name," explains the operator.

"I just want 'Dante,'" Kevin stubbornly insists.

"Sorry, it won't work."

Kevin thinks for a minute and can't come up with anything. He asks for suggestions, and after a couple of duds, they've got one that Kevin likes.

"How about Dark Dante?"

———■———

In the spring of 1983, *WarGames* hits the L.A. multiplex theaters, a blockbuster computer hacker movie starring Matthew Broderick and teen heartthrob Ally Sheedy. Suddenly computer hacking is cool. Up on the silver screen, a star is portraying a role Kevin dreams of living. And what about the law? Broderick's good deeds far outweigh the laws he breaks, and anyway, he's too young to go to jail. Shortly after the movie's release, Kevin confides to Sean Randol that the movie is pretty cool. And he really likes Ally Sheedy.

———■———

Broderick and Sheedy are alone in his bedroom. He warns her against touching the keyboard, but her fingertips can't resist touching the numbers on the screen. He's instructed his computer to dial other computers in Sunnyvale, California, to find a new video game he fancies.

"What about the cost?" Sheedy asks.

"There's ways around that," he says with a chuckle.

She warns him about what happens when you break the law.

"Only if you're over eighteen," cracks Broderick.

The hacker puts on a dazzling display, scoring an access number for a bank and then making plane reservations for two to Paris. Suddenly, the words "LOG ON" appear.

This time it isn't so easy getting in. After a couple of aborted attempts, Broderick has an idea. He's looking for a video game. He types "Help Games." Text flashes across the screen.

FALKEN'S MAZE

BLACK JACK

He turns to Sheedy and smiles.

GIN RUMMY

HEARTS . . .

AIR TO GROUND ACTIONS

THEATERWIDE TACTICAL WARFARE

THEATERWIDE BIOTOXIC AND CHEMICAL WARFARE...

GLOBAL THERMONUCLEAR WAR

PLAY A GAME?

——■——

GUEST

Invalid account name.

ANONYMOUS

Invalid account name.

Dark Dante types in vain. Cax, the computer he's trying to crack at UCLA, is proving stubborn. It's the summer of 1983, and he's tried all the obvious account names. What about the University of California at Berkeley?

He punches in the initials "UCB," and the screen flashes a full menu of options. This is it! Kevin can fly inside the Net—just like in *War-Games*—and roam the real-life Dungeons & Dragons of nuclear games: Lawrence Livermore Labs, Los Alamos, White Sands, and the Ballistics Research Lab. He jets into UCLA's data banks and finds there's nothing to stop him from surfing others.

And Kevin can always dupe Ron out of information too. Ron, though still a neophyte, has learned of ABERTAC, a toll-free Arpanet dial-up located at a Chesapeake Bay Army base. Dark Dante wants to trade. To make his bartering chip seem more valuable, Dark Dante casts a spell on the "UCB" account, changing the password to a nearly unbreakable random series of letters and numbers. And finally, to greet his fellow hacker, once he cracks the password, the old Dungeon Master plants the seminal line from *WarGames*, when the deadly computer welcomes the young hacker to a dance with nuclear war.

GREETINGS, PROFESSOR FALKEN.

SHALL WE PLAY A GAME?

———■———

Kevin Poulsen is only seventeen, but he's already toying with the future, experimenting with a phenomenon that most of the world won't glimpse for a decade. He doesn't know it, but the roots of the computer network he's exploring go back to U.S. Defense Department R&D. In the late 1960s, ARPA, the department's Advanced Research Projects Agency, oversaw the development of spooky, futuristic weapons. ARPA officials figured America might make better bombs if the agents of the nation's military establishment could all tune in to the same cable channel. They called it the Arpanet, a giant electronic chat line, a massive computer network that strung together hundreds of military facilities, universities, think tanks, and defense contractors throughout the world. The Net, as the hip call it, is a new dimension, a new mode of communicating, as revolutionary as the telephone. In a few years they'll call it the Internet.

———■———

Everything is a game to Kevin, including his manipulation of Ron. Online, Ron complains that the Dungeon Master is intentionally trying to keep him in the dark:

> **RON:** WHAT IS THE KEY FOR THIS FILE?
> **KEVIN:** 'ZAPHOD'.
> **RON:** AND I WAS SUPPOSED TO KNOW THAT?
> **KEVIN:** OF COURSE ISN'T IT OBVIOUS? WHO WOULDN'T GUESS THAT?
> **RON:** AND THAT'S WHY YOU LOGGED OFF IMMEDIATELY AFTER SENDING IT?
> **KEVIN:** I WANTED TO WATCH THE REST OF BARNEY

Ron thought things would cool down once he and Kevin graduated from phreaking to computer hacking. Kevin appears cooperative, freely volunteering half of the access commands of some new system, and then, abruptly, in midsentence, drops off-line.

"You know, 'Zaphod,'" Kevin teases Ron later in a telephone call. "It's that character in *The Hitchhiker's Guide to the Galaxy,* Zaphod Bebblevax."

Attitude. It's Kevin's hacker style, and Ron finds it contagious. He too can be sneaky.

KEVIN: WHY ARE YOU USING BETTY?
RON: I CAN'T TELL YOU.
KEVIN: COME ON. WHY ARE YOU USING BETTY?
RON: I CAN'T TELL YOU. LET'S NOT TALK ABOUT THAT.
WHY DO YOU GIVE ME BULLSHIT KEYS (ZAPHOD)
. . .

Ron is fighting back. He's consumed a manual for the Unix operating system, the cryptic language of the Net. He's staking out new territories, amassing new accounts. On August 30, at 8:54 P.M., Ron commandeers a UCLA account and remotely logs into the Naval Research Laboratories in San Diego. Ron changes the password to "Zeppelin" and opens an operating manual file for the navigation system of an A-70 attack aircraft. Three days later, at 4:11 A.M., Ron reads a file titled "Fiscal Year '84, Financial Status," listing programs currently under development at "NRL." Ron finds it all intriguing. How many kids know what million-dollar war toys the Navy plans to buy next year?

———■———

Why would someone be logged in as UCB?

Dave Dalva, a UCLA grad student, is reading his e-mail when he notices the strange password and even stranger activity. UCB is examining a file that lists all the users on the system. Dalva dashes off a message to the system administrator, and within days, he finds half a dozen compromised UCLA computer accounts.

There's a new mood on the Net. *WarGames* has just warned the world that computers are vulnerable to attack. Computers are connected to the establishment, to the military—even to the missiles. Dr. Terry Gray, director of UCLA's Computer Center, does what comes naturally to a seasoned Dungeon Master. If the hackers wish to visit his dungeon, then let them come. He'll be ready. Gray's best and brightest grad students eagerly join the hunt, hacking out the secret code for the UCLA computer.

On August 2, 1983, the game imperceptibly changes. When the hackers return that evening, they don't notice the invisible trap laid by UCLA's supreme Dungeon Master. They can still seize accounts, peruse private material, and "chat" about their exploits. They can still fight.

KEVIN: WHO IS THIS?
RON: RON. RONALD MARK AUSTIN 396–8836 244 SECOND STREET.
KEVIN: DON'T BE STUPID. YOU WERE JUST BETTY, RIGHT?
RON: YES.
KEVIN: WHY WAS OSHER ON AT THE SAME TIME, ON ANOTHER DIALUP?
RON: WHAT???

— ■ —

Ron sits in his darkened bedroom, bathed in the eerie glow of his Texas Instruments computer. His parents are fast asleep. It's 3 A.M., September 19, 1983. Classes are already in full swing at UCLA.

But the sophomore physics major isn't studying particle physics, wave physics, magnetism, or even computer science. Super-users are his new target, the one or two systems administrators with "root" privileges on a major computer system. Super-users with root powers can wipe out files en masse, delete entire disks—or in Ron's case, wreak a little revenge, say change the password of one of Kevin's seized accounts to Zaphod.

Throwing names at a system doesn't work with the random passwords chosen by super-users. Instead, Ron tricks the system into revealing its hand. His trap is named after the mythological Trojan horse, and operates in much the same fashion. Ron buries the Trojan horse program in the directory of a target computer. Each time someone logs in, the Trojan horse invisibly sucks up his or her password, and then allows the normal log-on routine to continue.

That September night, Ron Arpanets to a Stanford University computer known as Shasta, finds an account for "Jim Miller" that's never been used (and therefore has no password), and transfers his Trojan horse into the operating system. Ron can sleep now. The Trojan horse will work steadily through the night, depositing any captured passwords into Miller's account.

———■———

Brian Reid, a Stanford professor of electrical engineering, notices his log-on is slow. Later that morning, one of his grad students tells him why—a phony "set terminal" has been planted in the local directory.

That afternoon, "Miller" returns, unaware that he has been traced to Indiana's Purdue University by a program Reid and his staff have written. Purdue faculty members complete the gumshoe work, tracing Miller's initial Arpanet entry to an access node a couple of football fields from Reid's office. Purdue was simply a guise, a detour to cover the hacker's tracks.

"Miller" returns the following afternoon to find his trap empty, and hastily departs. Reid seals Shasta off from the Arpanet. He memos campus users that the machine—though disconnected from the Net—will remain open.

But wait! Somehow "Miller" is back in. Reid anxiously traces the network connections. Miller has hacked into a computer in an adjoining building and leapfrogged over the campus network to Shasta. Time to pull Miller's plug again. He hits the kill command.

Reid is about to call it a night when he sees it on his terminal. Miller is back.

—■—

Kevin is exploring UCLA's computers the evening of September 21, 1983, but the systems are responding like a car that has lost its power steering. Kevin knows it can't be explained by simple heavy use.

"Something's up," he warns Ron on the phone.

Yeah, tell me about it, Ron thinks. He jumps to another UCLA computer, and there's the same guy signed on—somebody he's never heard of—Doug Trainor. Is there a Doug Trainor on every computer, or is this guy on his trail?

>
> **RON:**   HEY, IS THERE SOME SORT OF MANHUNT UNDER-
>   WAY?
> **TRAINOR:** I'LL GET BACK TO YOU.

There's still time. Grab his on-line bag of hacker's magic tricks crammed with Arpanet passwords. Ditch it in the Net thousands of miles from UCLA.

Disconnect.

But Ron is tired. He's just getting carried away by his imagination. Who really cares about a teenager hacking a few harmless Arpanet accounts? He plants a few Trojan horses on some UC Berkeley computers and crashes early—a good three hours before dawn.

Kevin isn't so easily mollified. He tries to engage someone in chat mode on UCLA's computers, hoping to puzzle out what's up, but like the individual who tailed Ron, this guy isn't providing answers. Kevin types:

WELL, GOT TO SIGN OFF NOW, THE FBI'S KNOCKING AT MY DOOR.

NETWORK NEWS

———■———

The time is a little before 7 A.M. on September 22, 1983. Lieutenant Duane Trump of the Los Angeles district attorney's office pulls up outside a single-story stucco house on Second Street in Santa Monica and raps on the door.

The door opens and Mrs. Austin appears in a nightgown. There's quite a crowd outside. Trump has brought along a fellow D.A. investigator, a couple of UCLA campus cops, and an FBI agent. Her son, the one they came to talk to, is fast asleep. Trump leads the way to the room. He wades through the mess—dirty clothes, a Frisbee, roller skates, a stereo, and a tennis racket, stuff you'd find in any teenager's bedroom, and then something still novel at the time: a small personal computer and modem. Trump, a tall, square-jawed man with a linebacker's build, gives the boy a shake.

"What's going on?" grumbles Ron, as he lies in bed rubbing the sleep from his eyes, and peering up at four big guys that look an awful lot like cops.

Trump sits Ron down at the kitchen table and asks him how he turned an ordinary personal computer and modem into a summer adventure. Trump finds Ron abrasive and defensive, but soon he has the boy describing the technical feats he's learned from his even younger friend. Ron has no idea that he's recounting his story to someone who already knows much more than he could imagine. Ron and Kevin had thought they were invisible, slipping into UCLA's dungeons through other Arpanet sites, never leaving a clue to their true origins. But the hackers' exploits had attracted the attention of the FBI. Reid at Stanford had called in the Bureau and convinced them to trace "Miller's" calls. When the phone company bungled the trace, UCLA's Terry Gray and his team of hackers ultimately proved the more skilled Dungeon Masters. Gray's boys deftly recoded UCLA's computers to print out every word the hackers typed on-line. In August, after weeks of playing cat and mouse with Kevin, Ron made the fatal mistake of mentioning his parents' address on-line. Campus cops called the D.A.'s office and seized the phone records of Ron and then Kevin.

That late-September morning, as Ron talks to Lieutenant Trump in the kitchen, the other investigators and the G-man carefully log the evidence they are confiscating. There's the Texas Instruments home computer Ron's parents gave him a few months before, a standard black GTE phone, a Vic modem. But it's the files and printouts they really want: dozens of printouts and hand-scrawled notes listing the phone numbers of Arpanet sites around the country, manuals and articles strewn around the room, excerpts from *Cheating at Cards*, *Credit Card Fraud*, and a *Newsweek* article, "Beware, Hackers at Play."

Tucked under a loose piece of carpet in Ron's crowded closet, the investigators find something they didn't expect: a manila envelope with round-trip airplane tickets to New York and London. A few feet away, hidden under the carpet at the foot of the bed, they turn up eight crisp hundred-dollar bills. Within days, Trump learns the tickets had been ordered on someone else's MasterCard and delivered to a ghost mailbox for which there was no corresponding apartment.

———■———

At nearly the same moment Trump searches Ron's bedroom, three men approach the front porch of the little yellow house in North Hollywood and step under the sign that reads "The Poulsens."

"Kevin, there's some people here to see you."

Kevin hears his mother's gentle knock and then rolls over.

"KNOCK. KNOCK. KNOCK. KNOCK."

"Open up, Kevin!" a man yells. "It's the D.A.'s office."

Terry Atchley, a wiry, chain-smoking Pacific Telephone investigator with wide brown eyes and slicked, wavy hair, takes in the skinny, awkward boy in pajamas and braces. Atchley has seen his kind before. He's worked cases against the legendary Kevin Mitnick, as well as "Roscoe," Susan Thunder, and several other L.A. phreaks and hackers. He likes his work, and he's good at it. But he knows Pac Tel and the D.A.'s office have got a problem. The kid looks even younger than usual, and Atchley soon learns his suspicion is correct. They'll have to throw this one back—at seventeen Kevin doesn't measure up for prosecution.

But just because they can't bust him doesn't mean they can't shake him up good. Atchley and the investigators box up Kevin's collection of Pac Tel manuals, printouts, cassette tapes, and the Radio Shack computer his parents gave him on his sixteenth birthday. One investigator asks Kevin what interests him besides computers.

"Is there anything else?"

———■———

Kevin and Ron may be the first to hack the Internet, but they're also part of a larger trend, a nation's youth challenging the powers that be. By the summer and fall of 1983, the nation's headlines ring with dramatic tales of teen hacker attacks on the nation's computers. The 414 gang, named for their area code, cracks the computers of the Memorial Sloan-Kettering Cancer Center in New York City, and from the pages of *Time* a doctor warns that the young mischief makers could have seriously hurt someone. But the attack reveals as much about the establishment as it does about the hackers. The respected New York hospital admits that it has virtually no security to protect its computerized patient records or treatment programs.

In the wake of the attacks, *Time* and other publications ask whether the nation is becoming dangerously dependent on computers. It's a valid question and the answer is troubling. The hard, tedious work of security hasn't kept pace with the rapid, expansive new use of computers. Technology is making it easier to access information, but it is also making it easier to cripple phone networks and power grids, to steal money and intellectual property, and to threaten national security.

Never before has so much of society's wealth been so vulnerable. The electronic priesthood's monopoly over access has disappeared, and so has that simpler, safer era. While past generations locked away their nation's jewels in offices, filing cabinets, or secure giant computers, in the 1980s networked computers run everything from banks, air traffic control, and the space shuttle to perhaps, one day, Reagan's Star Wars. Now a kid might prove that maybe, just maybe, we should think twice about putting so much power in something as intangible as software.

Time magazine speaks of a dramatic "war of nerves" waged between the feds and "thousands of teenagers" abusing federal networks—a federal "crackdown" no less serious than the war on drugs. Phone taps and electronic "sting" operations are used to "trap" the suspects. And though some worry the government's heavy-handed tactics risk turning the kids into heroes, others warn that apocalypse may be just around the corner. Adam Osborne, chairman of Osborne Computer Corp., the first portable computer company, tells *Newsweek* that it's only a matter of time before a disaster strikes the financial world. "If this is what kids can do on a lark," he says, "can you imagine what people are doing who are serious about this?"

———■———

Early on the morning of November 2, 1983, Trump and his compatriots from the D.A.'s office make a surprise return visit to Ron's bedroom, read him his rights, handcuff him, and drive him to the Los Angeles County Jail.

Ron's head is spinning. The jail is so overcrowded that he shares a windowless twenty-by-twenty-foot room with two dozen hardened criminals. A sheriff's deputy comes to see him in the afternoon.

"There's press people to see you."

"About what?"

"Oh, this is getting a whole lot of publicity. It's in today's papers."

Just then, Ron notices another deputy reading what appears to be the *Los Angeles Times* and looking at a photograph.

"Hey, this is you here!" exclaims the deputy.

"Yeah, that's me."

The deputy brightens. He shares something in common with the celebrity hacker. "You know, I went to UCLA too!"

Ron's accommodations immediately improve once they realize he's important enough to make the front page of the *Times*. They transfer him to Highpower, where his cell adjoins that of Angelo Buono Jr., the legendary Hillside Strangler, convicted earlier in the week of torturing and sexually assaulting an eighteen year old girl before strangling her to death.

Ron wonders where Kevin is right about now.

———■———

"Super Computer Caper: War Games II or Simple Fraud?" blasts the *Los Angeles Herald*'s banner headline. England, Japan, Spain, Norway. Newspapers around the world are running articles about Ron and Kevin's hacking spree, and the story appears to have legs. The *Herald* quotes L.A. district attorney Robert Philobosian saying Austin cracked "sensitive records" and may be facing a six-year jail term. The *Los Angeles Times* publishes articles three days running, and Ron even earns a mention on network news. He owes his newfound celebrity to the D.A.'s press conference. There's a war going on and the bad guys are America's brainy teens. Philobosian lays out the contents of Austin's bedroom like the evidence of a sinister conspiracy. Even Ron's black-and-white TV is included as potential evidence of the crime.

News trucks and camera cables clog Second Street in Santa Monica. Television newscasters and reporters for national papers jostle for position outside Ron's home, pestering his parents for interviews. But a few in the press sense that a tremendous error has been made, that the authorities have arrested the wrong man. UCLA's Dave Dalva, one of the student investigators, bluntly volunteers to the *Los Angeles Herald*, "The juvenile [looked like] the smart one."

GOOD FELLAS

∎

"**I**'m with Tom Hayden's office," says the slender, well-dressed blond woman standing at Ron's front door. "He thinks you're getting a raw deal. He'd like to talk to you."

Out on a $2,000 bail bond put up by his parents, Ron makes the trip alone in his Mustang to the posh house Tom Hayden and Jane Fonda share in north Santa Monica. Hayden, the famous sixties activist, is Ron's local state assemblyman. The maid opens the big oak door. "I don't think you've done anything that serious," volunteers Hayden, taking Ron by the shoulder and thrusting him into a crazy scene. Enormous, woolly dogs tear about the sprawling house, at each bound threatening to upend a lamp or an antique. Ron takes refuge in a chair.

"You know I've been in trouble with the law myself once," the celebrated left-wing politico confides in the young hacker. "Ever hear of the Chicago Seven?" Ron shakes his head, and Hayden tells how he, Abbie Hoffman, Jerry Rubin, and other antiwar crusaders were harassed after they disrupted the 1968 Democratic convention. "Ron, I think they're trying to do the same to you. They're looking for a scapegoat. You're going to get railroaded."

But Ron is distracted. Jane Fonda is coming down the stairs. He's seen her before in a wet suit at the beach, never actually surfing, just holding her board and gazing out at the waves. Tonight, she's dressed in jeans and a sweater, looking even better than she does in her movies.

She smiles but doesn't introduce herself as Hayden continues. "They're going to try to turn it into something bigger than it really is! You weren't hacking for money, it was an attempt to learn!" Ron is about to agree, but the Santa Monica assemblyman doesn't give him the time. "There was nothing to read on their computer files! That $200,000 damage charge, that was ridiculous!"

Ron nods in agreement. A dog spins a vase like a bowling pin. "If I can help with your legal defense just let me know," Hayden promises. "Let's see, who else might be good on this," he begins, rattling off names of state and national politicians.

Throughout the rambling monologue, Jane Fonda sits across the table, wearing a sympathetic face. "Would you like some tea?"

Kevin's seen the pitch on TV. *Control Data Institute, high-paying careers in computers and programming! Enroll in our technical courses, and you're guaranteed a job in the exciting, new computer industry!*

Soon after being raided by the district attorney, Kevin decides to clean up his act. He dials the 800 number displayed on the screen, makes an appointment, and drives to the nearby office to take the aptitude test with a roomful of hopeful potential students.

When Kevin aces the deductive and inductive logic test, Control Data is thrilled. His test scores indicate he's perfect for a career in programming. But they have one question.

"Kevin, what kind of formal, higher education do you have?"

"Well, I went to a junior college for a few months."

Suddenly, Control Data Institute reverses its spin. "How about our computer operator class, Kevin?"

It's the option generally offered to those who score poorly.

"But I want to be a programmer."

"We understand that, Kevin. The problem is you don't have enough post–high school education for our programming class."

Kevin thinks about mentioning his advanced fieldwork, but decides to keep it to himself. Hacking the Arpanet and having his computer seized by the D.A. probably wouldn't impress the folks at Control Data.

"But you just said I was perfect for a career in programming."

"Well, you know about our money-back guarantee. Once you've graduated, if for any reason you can't find a programming job, we refund your tuition. Without college experience, Kevin, we wouldn't be able to offer you that guarantee."

But the hacker is thinking fast. "I'd be willing to waive that guarantee," Kevin generously offers, neatly solving the logic problem.

"I'm afraid we couldn't do that. It would mess up our statistics."

◾

Control Data Institute may not be in the stars for Kevin, but someone else is watching out for the young hacker.

"Table for three, please."

Goodfellow is his name. He leaves his BMW 635i with the valet and his $10,000 Grid portable computer locked in the trunk, but he's packing his clunky cell phone. Geoffrey Goodfellow never goes anywhere without his cell phone.

Kevin protested the choice of restaurant but Goodfellow insisted. He never eats anywhere that doesn't take American Express. Tonight it's Le Petit Moulin in Santa Monica, just a sea breeze away from the palm-lined Pacific Ocean cliffs.

"A booth, please."

Kevin's quiet, watching, evaluating. Goodfellow is old for a hacker, around thirty, though he looks twenty-five. He's got a trim build, a schoolboy's haircut, humorless eyes, and floppy ears. Well-shaven, he wears a sweater, casual slacks, and brown suede shoes. When he gets keyed up, he talks fast, like he's speed typing and the keys stick. Sometimes he repeats a word.

Goodfellow's heard how Ron and Kevin hacked SRI, the company he works for in Silicon Valley. He sees two bright guys he might recruit who know a little about Unix and the Arpanet. Goodfellow's famous for tracking down that kind of talent.

"The wine list, please."

Goodfellow positions his Motorola "Brick" at the center of the table like an icon. Kevin and Ron are impressed: Bricks cost about $4,000, and cell phones are so new even drug dealers aren't using them. "We need a waiter," Goodfellow grumbles, huffily punching the fat buttons on his Brick.

Kevin catches Ron's eye with a questioning smirk. What is Goodfellow up to?

"Hello. We're over here in the booth," Goodfellow motions, waving his Brick above his head in the crowded, white table restaurant. The befuddled maître d' cranes his neck, looking for the pushy diner.

"Can you get the waiter to step on it?"

After impressing Kevin and Ron with a pager that receives e-mail, Goodfellow does most of the talking, breaking the ice by describing how much they have in common. It seems Goodfellow too began as a hacker, breaking into SRI when he was younger than Kevin. Once inside, he e-mailed the system administrator and told him if they gave him access he would plug in some software and improve the system. It was a pretty exciting prospect for a sixteen-year-old. SRI did a lot of military projects and groundbreaking work on the Net. They invented the computer mouse, the optical disk, and the ink-jet printer. A think tank with branch offices all over the world.

"They invited me over, gave me a door key, a building pass, and an account, and said, figure out how to do it, how to break security," Goodfellow excitedly tells his dinner companions. "I hung around there for nine months. Sat smack in the machine room right next to the central processor. They needed someone to burp and diaper their mainframe on the weekend, a system janitor, you know, to mop up the bits.

"So I dropped out of high school. You did too, didn't you, Kevin?"

Kevin nods, and Goodfellow looks pleased. He asks Ron why he thinks he needs to finish college.

"Because I'll have a better chance of a job when I graduate."

Goodfellow didn't need school and he doesn't see why anyone else should. His technical accomplishments are numerous, including the first radio network for transmitting computer data and the first e-mail pager. He has a high-level security clearance and he's testified before

Congress on telecommunications security and privacy. And he's got some novel ideas about how to deal with hackers. He believes all they need is a little attention, a little respect, and a challenging job.

———■———

Goodfellow orders wine, an appetizer, a salad, and an entree, while Kevin and Ron order Cokes and salads. Goodfellow believes no meal is complete without dessert. If more than one tempts him, he'll order two. Three is his limit. Goodfellow is devouring crème brûlée, while Kevin and Ron sip their sodas. Apart from their taste in food and Goodfellow's pricey tech toys, they've got a lot in common. They all share the same arrogance, wit, and humor. And they've all hacked SRI's computers.

"I've got this theory about hackers," Goodfellow announces. "You know *Star Wars:* Darth Vader and the Jedi Knights. Hackers need to be turned to the good side of the Force. If you guys worked for SRI you could hack for a living."

Kevin tallies up Goodfellow's toys: the new BMW, the $10,000 Grid portable, the $4,000 Motorola Brick, and the luxury cars Goodfellow mentioned, among them a rare vintage Jensen Intercepter. Is there really this much money in legitimate computer hacking?

"You know I'm really proud of you guys," Goodfellow gushes as he motions for the bill. "Yup, you guys are following right along in my footsteps." Then, the patron saint of hackers pulls out one more gizmo he hasn't shown his young friends. A plain old pocket calculator. "Let's see," he says, rapping the buttons like a keyboard. "Ron, you owe ... and Kevin you owe ... "

PART II

TOP SECRET

—■—

In 1984, hackers finally get some good press. Author Steven Levy celebrates the hackers who launched the computer industry and inspires a national outpouring of hacker pride with his runaway bestseller, *Hackers: Heroes of the Computer Revolution*. Veteran hackers rise up and protest the bad rap they've been getting from newspapers and the government. Levy reminds the world that without hackers there would be no Apple Computer, no IBM PC, no revolution in computing. Embracing the good in hackers, acknowledging the criminal roots of many of the industry's legends, Levy cites the young protagonist in *WarGames* as an example of a "Third Generation hacker who, having no knowledge of the groundbreaking feats of Stew Nelson or Captain Crunch, broke into computer systems with the innocent wonder of their Hands-On Imperative." He ends his book reveling in how today's hackers defy authority, their "triumph of the individual over the collective dispirit." Levy is giving the kids of the 1980s a second chance, an opportunity to rise to their noble calling.

Kevin Poulsen, too, is getting a second chance to prove that like Jobs and Wozniak he merely flirted with illegal hacking. He hasn't been arrested. He's got a chance to go legitimate and create a new, positive identity. And so one day he shows up unannounced at the home of his childhood friend Sean Randol with the exciting news. A big Silicon Valley company has hired him to work as a computer programmer, and Kevin couldn't be more proud.

———■———

Kevin fills out the questionnaire: his education, every place he's ever lived, where he's gone on vacations. His answers are shorter than most. Next, he has a chat with the security officer. After assuring him he's not a communist, drunkard, drug addict, or homosexual, he's rewarded with a security clearance.

Dedicated to the Peace and Prosperity of Mankind, reads the sleek stone monument at the main entrance to SRI's several suburban blocks of two-story, brick, concrete, and glass 1950s buildings. Behind the security desk at SRI International's Building A, Pentagon-style clocks display the time in every major city in the world. A large sign lays down the law: "In accordance with Department of Defense contractual requirements . . . briefcases, handbags, packages, etc., are subject to inspection."

Every morning just before 8 A.M., he walks straight to Building E, past the receptionist, down the corridor, and to the glass door he opens with his key. One flight down, he takes a left turn, past security, fifteen paces down the K wing, where he smiles at the security camera and picks up the phone next to the vault.

"I'm going into the Tank."

It's the fall of 1984, and once more Kevin is ahead of the game. Ron may be facing trial, but Kevin has a security clearance and a job. Goodfellow arranged for an account for Kevin on the Arpanet via a Navy host computer, and Kevin proved a fast learner. Perhaps most surprising was not that Goodfellow got Kevin a job at SRI as a computer operator and junior system administrator, but that he did it so easily. Top SRI managers, many of whom were internationally recognized experts with Ph.D.s in computer science, trusted Goodfellow's judgment, and saw no conflict in hiring a computer hacker and high school dropout to do classified military computer work. Only Donn Parker, a world renowned SRI computer security expert and author of numerous books on computer crime, protested Kevin's hiring. Parker had interviewed hundreds of hackers and computer criminals, and was the nation's most quoted authority on hackers and computer crime. He didn't believe hackers could be rehabilitated.

Kevin signs the "OPEN" side of the sheet hanging on the wall next to what looks like a bank vault. He knows the combination by heart. He twirls the dial to the last digits, spins the bars counterclockwise, and rolls back a massive steel door heavy enough to crush a man.

The chamber. Fluorescent ceiling panels give off the only light. He repeats the cycle with a second steel vault. Beyond that chamber another padlocked door, the third and final room, a tiny box not much more than seven feet square. He approaches the locked filing cabinet and spins the dial to the last combination he has memorized. Inside, he opens a little box and finds a tiny message like the fortune in a Chinese cookie.

The crypto device looks as if it were left over from the Vietnam War. Circuit boards and electronic gizmos hang in metal racks—six feet tall and three or four feet wide—with metal sides and a door. Kevin toggles the panel's switches to prepare the device to load the next key. He opens the door and pulls out an electronics board with levers that look like dimmer switches keyed to the alphabet along the side. He flips them up or down to match the letters of the key. It takes time. There are nearly thirty letters, thirty levers to slide, and no room for error.

Ten minutes later, Kevin snaps the card back inside and restarts the Vax 750 minicomputer. The whole setup is called a PLI, or private line interface, and connects to the Air Force's Strategic Air Command over the Milnet, a military subnet of the Arpanet. It's all part of a much larger SRI defense contract funded by the Department of Defense's Advanced Research Projects Agency.

DARPA wants a network that can truly survive a nuclear attack: distributed computer databases on planes, in mobile military vehicles, in ships, on bases. If Arpanet's leased lines are bombed, the mobile packet radio units can keep the network up and running. "SAC" is how the SRI staff refers to ARPA order 4715, "Command Control and Communications Testbed for the Strategic Air Command." In October of 1984, the same month Kevin is hired, the Emergency War Order, Nuclear Weapons Report is added to SAC. This is no video game. The crypto device ensures that secret, classified files can be sent without danger of interception to the Strategic Air Command at Offut Air Force base in Omaha, Nebraska. The rules are clear. Classified data can only be handled in the tank.

SRI's SAC software designers work in the tank room next to the crypto device. Tomblike, the room is lined with metal to absorb magnetic wave emissions from the terminals. Cables and power lines from the handful of computer terminals are filtered to protect against leakage. Crisscrossing copper wires under the floor soak up any straying emissions. The phones have standard military "cut-off cards" and "squeeze buttons," making it difficult to use bugs or other means to eavesdrop. Until Kevin changes the day's key, Offut Air Force base in Omaha, and other defense contractors on the project, can't "talk classified" to SRI. And on every third day, Kevin descends to the Tank with another Defense Department–cleared individual, snaps the lighter kept there just for the task, and ignites the paper keys in the urn, watching them curl to ash.

Just as Goodfellow did before him, Kevin is working his way up. He's been tapped by the Advanced Technology and Development Department, a hundred-strong group that routinely garners major computer and networking defense contracts. Kevin has passed the DOD standard security clearance background check with flying colors. He has no criminal record. His renown as a computer hacker is his credential. Kevin even augments his "secret" level clearance with a COMSEC cryptography addition by taking a DOD-certified SRI crypto class. His security briefing covers the dos and don'ts of handling and transporting secret documents; operating SRI's secure phone; "scrubbing" classified computer disks; running the DOD program that scatters every byte on a computer disk to zeros and ones and then shotguns them into a random sequence. Kevin signs the pages on the lengthy security manual, acknowledging that he's read and understood the Department of Defense policies.

Kevin finds SRI a big, exciting place to be. SRI appears to have every amenity imaginable in a high-tech R&D center. A three-story warehouse nearly a football field long where the company transforms vans into mobile military computer communication vehicles and fabricates its own routers and bridges for military networking projects. A machine shop with an amazing array of mills, lathes, and drill presses. An industrial-sized satellite dish. A radio physics lab, toxicology lab, and physical sciences lab. SRI also boasts one of the world's most advanced lasers. Then there's Building A, where scientists blow things up, and years later someone will die in a cold fusion experiment gone awry. Add to the mix a company robot stationed down the hall from Kevin that acts on spoken commands and delivers or retrieves documents from around the campus. The robot too is on the Net, tuned in to packet radio.

People aren't meant to stay where Kevin works, hunched on a stool, eyes inches from the flickering screen, engulfed by two large Vax 750 minicomputers and massive, whirring tape drives. The droning air conditioners keep the temperature a steady sixty-five inside SRI's third-floor computer room, a high-tech fish tank with a wall of glass peering out at the corridor. It's just the computers and Kevin—no desk, no partition to personalize, no corner to mark his identity. Apart from his morning coding routine, Kevin is a glorified computer operator, performing routine backups or "dumps," for an annual salary in the high teens. Dumps aren't exactly challenging. Line up the tapes, issue the Unix commands, and wait twenty or more minutes for the files to be copied. If after ten or fifteen minutes, something malfunctions, Kevin starts over again. And on top of it, he has to coddle the users, secretaries, and other novices.

But Kevin is in heaven those first few weeks, wearing his jacket to avoid catching a chill, guzzling Coca-Cola from morning till night. SRI contains everything a hacker could ever want: the latest computers, the source code to the machines, the manuals. He spends his days and most of his nights alone in the computer room, except for the dinners he can't afford with Goodfellow and his friends. Goodfellow rents him a room in his condo half a block from SRI, and Kevin dives into his new world, learning everything he can about Unix and programming. That's his deal with Goodfellow. Hack his way out of the freezer into a programming job.

Donn Parker of SRI, the revered SRI staff expert on hackers, computer security, and crime, requests a formal interview with Kevin for one of his research projects. Kevin considers it an honor since the security expert only interviews the best hackers and computer criminals, only those who have gone to jail or achieved a measure of fame. Kevin feels like a spy coming in from the cold, confessing his Arpanet exploits to this enormously tall, quiet, bald man whose poker face gives no clue to his impression of his subject, no clue that he alone considers Kevin's hiring a terrible mistake.

———■———

Kevin is sitting in the tedious weekly system support meeting when his ears perk up. "Oh, that's another NPA."

Did his boss just mention a familiar old acronym? Did Bob Gilligan just casually refer to an area code as an NPA, a numbering plan area? Kevin is stunned by the answer. His boss is a phone phreak.

Kevin would never have guessed. Bob Gilligan was one of the first people he met at SRI, and Kevin figured Gilligan would help straighten him out. The tall, blond, well-mannered Gilligan had already spent three years toiling on military projects at SRI. In his mid-twenties, Gilligan seemed the ideal, responsible boss—polite, receptive, organized, tidy in appearance and thinking.

But Gilligan, like so many creative members of the computer revolution, had a colorful past. As a boy, the same *Esquire* article that captured Wozniak's and Jobs's imagination had inspired Gilligan to phreak, build blue boxes, and mess with telephones. He blue-boxed his way into loop-around and conference circuits and chatted it up with other phreaks, but he was generally well behaved. At the University of California at Berkeley, Gilligan studied electrical engineering and computers. But what still intrigued and excited him was phones. He'd phreak international calls, set off alarms in some remote New Mexico central office, dial all the 800 numbers in Washington, D.C. (there weren't as many in those days), and scour old Bell System technical journals in the engineering physics library for secrets. At night, after studying at the library, like Kevin, he rifled the trash of local central offices.

The more they talk, the more Kevin and Bob learn how much phreaking they have in common. Soon, the system support segment of the weekly meeting is dispensed with in a few minutes to make way for the phone phreak nostalgia hour. They talk 2,600 hertz, whistling off tandems, loop arounds, Steppers. Bob gets almost emotional about this stuff. He teases Kevin with tales of the phone switch ESS dial-ups he toyed with at Berkeley, modem numbers he could dial that landed him inside the control console of a switch and enabled him to do whatever he wanted.

Kevin is impressed and full of questions. He knows he's in the right place. It's what makes SRI great. Got a question, just walk down the hall. Someone is sure to know the answer. And the person who loans you the book with all the answers will probably be its author, and more than likely the world's expert on the subject. So it is that Gilligan brings in a manual from his phreaking days with the very dial-up commands he's described, marches Kevin over to an SRI Xerox machine, and copies it cover to cover.

——■——

There's a certain irony in Kevin's boss encouraging him to phreak. Protected by the campus-like culture of SRI, they're oblivious to the sea change taking place around them. The federal crackdown is continuing, and Kevin's mentor, Goodfellow, is finding increasing resistance to his pro-hacker policy.

Just as he did for Kevin, Goodfellow has arranged for Ron to study on the Arpanet. But when a Navy officer discovers the account, he goes ballistic and e-mails Goodfellow: *"I trust that Ron Austin does not really have an account on a Navy machine that is used for security tests with real classified data. And that he is not actually using that machine as a base to collect information on how to break into other military systems."*

Goodfellow defends himself, pointing out there shouldn't be secret or classified data on any Internet host, and argues that Austin is using the Navy Internet account to study how to write programs, just like another notorious hacker who's turned out fine. *"Kevin now has a full-time job at SRI . . . He even has a clearance . . . we now have a shining star on the way to becoming a first rate UNIX wizard."*

The Navy officer isn't interested in Goodfellow's hacker philosophy and issues a warning. He's not going to let Navy computers be used for a hacker rehabilitation program. But the spunky Goodfellow fights back, standing by his hacker principles. *"I feel people are unfairly looking at Ron thru the pejorative label of 'bad hacker' of past actions. . . . I justify Ron's access in the same category as my own . . . learning about and improving the computing environment of our facilities at zero cost to anyone. Result: Improved tools and system for everyone. Immediate Past Example: Kevin Poulsen."*

But Goodfellow's bosses don't agree and order Goodfellow to cut off Austin's account immediately. They see a controversial hacker awaiting a highly publicized trial fooling around on a Navy host computer, a Department of Defense disaster in the making that could cost them millions of dollars of lost military contracts. They may sympathize with Goodfellow's point, but they can't ignore the government crackdown of the last two years. Kevin Poulsen aside, SRI isn't—at least officially—in the business of rehabilitating hackers.

At one minute after midnight, Goodfellow reads the depressing e-mail from his boss on his home terminal. Ironically, he's carrying on two conversations: one on his computer and the other on the phone with Ron Austin. Goodfellow's done all he can for the hacker and the cause, but he's outnumbered. Ron will have to disconnect. He dashes off a response to his boss, throwing in the towel and ending on a sad note.

"It is really quite sorrowful to see idle cycles go to waste."

STAR WATCH

—■—

Kevin is back in Los Angeles for the weekend, taking a little R&R away from the stress of SRI, squeezing in a little celebrity surveillance with his old partner in hacking. They sit patiently in the late-model white Buick Skylark, the air thick with the smell of hot grease, staring past the lighted Pioneer Chicken sign. The Buick, borrowed from Kevin's dad, resembles an unmarked cop car. They've got a clear view of the ordinary suburban home and the movie star's gray VW Rabbit. When will she come out to play?

Kevin doesn't worry that SRI might consider his behavior inappropriate for a rehabilitated hacker. Nor does he think much about how the company would frown upon his continued association with a celebrated hacker awaiting trial. The pull of Los Angeles and the past is strong on Kevin, and Ron offers something he's missed up north, a trusted accomplice and appreciative audience, someone who understands his need for adventure.

The whole escapade starts on impulse, because it's possible, because Kevin knows from her unlisted phone records that she lives in the Valley about a mile from where he grew up. He's read all the articles about her middle-class past and her sudden rise to stardom. He's just taking the next step.

They introduced themselves earlier, though she doesn't know it. "Is Scott there?" Ron asked when she answered the phone.

"There's no Scott here," she said.

"Sorry. Must have dialed the wrong number."

It's a phreak thing, claiming your star by making a wrong-number call. Kevin repeated the trick, asking for Scott, apologizing, and then hanging up.

Star surveillance, like bird-watching, requires patience, but Kevin and Ron are lucky this North Hollywood evening. Before long a woman and man leave the suburban house and get into the car, and Kevin tails his suspect. A few minutes later, on Ventura Boulevard, Ron gets a clear view of the occupants of the Rabbit.

"That's not Molly Ringwald" Ron sighs. "It's just some old lady."

Kevin shoots a look. "Crap."

Then he takes a closer look. "Wait a minute! She's just incognito."

Ron does a double take. "You're right!"

Molly Ringwald is doing her best to disguise herself, wearing spectacles and wrapping her hair in a frumpy spinster's bun. Kevin keeps up the tail, following Molly to the parking lot of the multiplex at Van Nuys and Ventura, staying behind her through the crowded ticket line.

The ticket booth cashier is waiting. "Which movie, sir?"

Kevin hedges.

What movie did she choose?

"Sir?"

"Yeah, two please."

"To what?" asks the cashier.

"Whatever it's called," blusters Kevin.

"What do you mean?"

"The movie . . . the movie SHE bought tickets for."

Molly and her companion take an aisle seat near the front for the evening showing of *Mask*. As Kevin takes an aisle seat right behind Molly, they notice her drape her purse along the back of the adjoining seat. Kevin's a phreak and a hacker, but there are limits to how far he'll go. He'd never steal Molly's purse. This is a virtual-reality game, proof of how a hacker can begin with the most basic on-line intrusion and safely flirt on the periphery of a celebrity's life.

Madonna and Sean Penn enter, and everybody, including Molly Ringwald, turns to look. They're in street clothes, but they've come to perform. They sit in the back, and once the film rolls, the famous couple begin making out. Half the audience prefers watching them over Cher up on the silver screen.

"Look, there's Sean Penn and Madonna!" mocks Ron, loud enough for everybody to hear.

Kevin can't resist joining in the fun. "Don't be ridiculous," Kevin bellows a couple of feet from Molly Ringwald's ear. "No celebrity would ever come to this theater!"

———■———

Kevin's boss, Bob Gilligan, has ordered Kevin to take an SRI field trip. Palo Alto's last electromechanical central office is giving tours before it closes its doors forever.

Kevin wanders off from the crowd, down the linoleum-tiled aisles under the long fluorescent bulbs, glancing up at the endless racks of brass crossbars and butterfly magnets that click like a thousand mechanical crickets. Everything is bigger than life.

"LOOK UP!" read the red letters, a big arrow pointing up. The plastic sign dangles from a great wooden ladder, itself hanging from rails in the concrete ceiling. How strange, Kevin thinks of the sign, but then he gets it. The ladders are sixteen feet high. You could easily grab one without noticing somebody on the top rung.

But who needs to climb? The switch envelops him. Row after row of gadgetry—a two-hundred-foot-long playground, consuming an entire floor. It's sort of like when he's working in the computer room. But Kevin is walking *through* a computer. He can see the moving, mechanical parts, hear the calls switching from one trunk to another, see the magnets flutter.

Kevin chats up the old switching supervisor who conducts the tour. Kevin impresses him with his knowledge and friendliness. He even knows how Steppers work. "So you figured out the old disconnects?" the old-timer says with a wry smile.

Soon, Kevin and Gilligan are both sitting in the switchman's office, listening to the old-timer's Stepper secrets. "Here, let me draw it for you."

It's better than Kevin could imagine. Not only does the switchman gladly chat away for a couple of hours, he even sends Kevin away with a Stepper diagram.

Next stop, the frame room. Cables rise like bamboo out of the concrete footings at the base of the massive sixteen-foot frames, wires sprouting like vines up the steel skeleton in a rainbow of colors, each pair a phone line, a place, a person, a small link in the Net.

Kevin is talking to Melvin, the frameman. Kevin's done it before, of course, but always with a computer and modem. And always, always from the outside. He strides right up to the terminal, flicks his fingers across the keys and fishes up the record for his boss's home phone number, displaying the calling features active on his line, his name, service address . . .

Kevin smiles at Melvin. "I used to work for the phone company."

On the way out, Gilligan secretly jots down a number next to a modem in the switch room. It's just like he promised Kevin. A direct dial-up into the switch. At home, Gilligan dials the switch with his SRI modem and they watch the cryptic codes flash by on his terminal. Later, at his apartment, Kevin also dials the switch with his SRI modem and terminal and sits transfixed, watching the messages flow like an electronic river, telling himself that it's not hacking if he just watches, if he issues no commands.

———■———

"They're tearing the old Steppers out of the Palo Alto CO!" Gilligan tells Kevin over the phone.

Finally, a chance to see the oldest switch, a Stepper! Kevin is ecstatic, but then he reminds himself. He has to sit at his terminal, finish the dumps.

"I order you to leave! I'm your boss. You have to go!"

Kevin logs off, scopes the hall for managers, and walks briskly to the back stairwell. Seconds later, he screeches out of the SRI parking lot in his Dodge Dart, all the while thinking of the souvenirs Gilligan says he "scored" earlier, but by the time Kevin pulls up, the workers are gone. He returns with Gilligan under the cover of night, and when he arrives, it's almost as if he were invited. Friendly Pac Bell has left a door slightly ajar. He's afraid at first, and then suddenly the adrenaline kicks in.

Kevin sweeps the flashlight. It's surreal, a huge frame of the switch abandoned in a bizarre, gigantic still life. A few emergency lights silhouette the looming skeletons of mechanical equipment. The crickets are silent. Like Pompeii, as though everyone had fled, leaving everything exactly where it had been—a half-empty ceramic coffee cup, handwritten maintenance notes, dusty, antiquated teletype machines, and amplifiers draped with gray dust covers.

There's even an old recorded announcement machine, a drum less than a foot in diameter with sixteen magnetic heads for playing up to sixteen different recordings. Kevin plugs his lineman's test set into the line and plays his favorite, the one most people will never hear. "We're sorry, due to a natural catastrophe, your call cannot be completed at this time."

Through the dim light Kevin sees it—the ultimate souvenir. Nailed over the doorway it must be forty years old. Hand painted on wood, the cracked sign says it all.

SWITCH ROOM.

———■———

Gilligan could be a mentor to Kevin. Bright, engaging, he could lead his impressionable young disciple to a brilliant and productive career in Silicon Valley. But Gilligan is no Goodfellow, he doesn't have the benefit of his experience or the wisdom of his years. Technology is power and Gilligan and Kevin want it no matter the price.

Soon after the late-night Palo Alto tour, Gilligan and Kevin case a Mountain View CO and notice Pac Bell has again been kind enough to leave a door ajar. Together, they walk inside, listening to the twitching brass bars and fluttering magnets of a crossbar switch in full force. But Gilligan suddenly freezes and makes a run for it. Kevin listens until the echoes of Gilligan's footfalls on the old linoleum fade. To Kevin the step he's about to take is small, but in the eyes of the law he's committing one of the oldest crimes on the books. There's no ambiguity or technology to cloud the issue. Kevin is breaking and entering.

He continues down the aisles, walking far enough to see a bookcase. Could they be Cosmos manuals, some of the secrets of this very real game of telephone Dungeons & Dragons? Seconds later, Kevin charges back into the parking lot, clutching an armful of Cosmos manuals, his heart pumping. Kevin can't believe it. He's finally taken a bold physical risk to increase his on-line access. Standing there with Gilligan in the parking lot, still shaking from the excitement of breaking into his first working central office, the experience overwhelms Kevin. His initial fear and sense of danger have changed into something pure, a power that seems to be pumping through his veins. Kevin feels a rush of exhilaration, and it's more than just the manuals. Taking the risk was a kick, a high like nothing he's ever felt before.

IDENTITY CRISIS

———■———

$\mathbf{R}$on has high hopes for his trial in the summer of 1985, but his parents can only afford to pay a defense attorney for a few days' work, not nearly enough to call and prepare witnesses. His attorney recommends that he waive his right to a jury trial, thinking Ron might get a fairer shake from a judge than a jury that has been inundated with hacker stories. But as testimony begins, Ron fears it's bound to end disastrously. The brief trial turns on the largely unchallenged testimony of one prosecution witness, a UCLA student, and Ron finds himself wanting to interrupt his attorney as he seems to play right into the prosecution's argument that he was a malicious, dangerous prankster.

Neither the damage claims of $200,000 nor the "sensitive files" cited by the district attorney are proved, but after closing arguments, the judge asks, "Is that all?" and promptly finds Ron guilty of twelve counts of computer fraud. Stunned, Ron writes the judge an angry letter, saying his crimes have been wildly exaggerated by the media and that he and his family have already been punished enough. It's not the penitent attitude the judge wants to hear. He sternly warns him not to play with "grade A double sized eggs" and orders him to undergo psychiatric evaluation at the California Institute for Men in Chino. The psychiatric evaluation is one hour with a psychiatrist and several weeks of hard prison time. Ron returns to court, his nose broken in an attack by three inmates, disgusted by the legal system. The judge orders him to perform six hundred hours of community service and sentences him to three years' probation. And throughout the whole ordeal, Kevin never writes one letter to his old hacker buddy.

———■———

"Read the source code! Read the source code! Read the source code!" Kevin chides the coworkers he's supposed to assist. No one spoon-fed it to him. Why should he volunteer anything?

On January 7, 1986, Kevin arrives at work and proudly reads his name on a list of promotions broadcast on the Net. Kevin Poulsen, all of twenty years old, is now a junior programmer. Goodfellow couldn't be more proud. Slowly but surely Kevin is becoming the responsible Unix "wizard" he always knew he would. Yet for all of Kevin's success, his basic duties have not changed. Routine backups and coddling users remain his responsibility, and he still must descend to the Tank every three days and change the codes.

Bored with the routine, Kevin phone hacks for his fellow workers to pass the time, betting coworkers that he can guess what number they're dialing by just listening to the touch-tones. When he learns that the same number to call "Time" in Los Angeles has not been assigned in the Bay Area, he convinces a coworker who lives in the correct prefix to order service in the number and then secretly forwards the incoming calls to his apartment. Kevin buys a Radio Shack talking clock, a couple of relays, and an answering machine. As if on cue, visiting Los Angelinos dial the local number several times a day, expecting to hear an automated voice recite the time. Sometimes they get Kevin's talking clock, sometimes they just get Kevin. "The time is—hold on a second. My watch is a little slow," Kevin jokes. "It's around four. No wait a minute, maybe it's closer to four-thirty."

Kevin seems to be having trouble growing up. Over the Christmas holiday, he surprised Sean one night at the Los Angeles restaurant where she was waitressing and offered her a ride home. She remembered it as a wild, weaving ride around Los Angeles in which she had to beg Kevin frantically to take her home. Kevin saw it as a perfectly normal evening, other than his admittedly impulsive and erratic driving. But on another occasion, Kevin was hardly normal. He dispatched his sister to the North Hollywood supermarket where Sean was working, and Debbie Poulsen popped up in the checkout line snapping photos of the puzzled girl, explaining, "They're for Kevin."

Even Goodfellow's enthusiasm for his young wizard is beginning to wane. Too often, Kevin's seat at Goodfellow's weekly pricey dinners is vacant, and when Kevin does show, Goodfellow wonders why he seems so distracted. One afternoon, Kevin offers Goodfellow a chance to win a dollar. He bets him he can make one of SRI's pay phones go dead, and Goodfellow takes him up on the offer.

Kevin promptly lifts the handset to demonstrate it has a dial tone and then trots down the hall. A couple of minutes later he returns with a smile.

Goodfellow wonders what Kevin is up to. Why isn't he working on his career—working on becoming the president of SRI?

"Now try it."

Goodfellow lifts the handset. The phone is dead.

———■———

Kevin isn't playing games anymore. He flips on David Letterman and methodically practices taking apart the lock on his apartment door. When he's done he puts it back together. Soon, he doesn't have to take his eyes off Letterman. It's all in the hands, in the feel.

Kevin has no real friends. He's too shy for girls. He doesn't have the money or the inclination to go to concerts or clubs. So he spends his evenings getting a feel for locks in his sparsely furnished studio apartment overlooking a parking lot. Scattered around are a few mismatched SRI furniture castoffs, lock picks, and a terminal linked to the company's computers. The bare walls are interrupted by a poster from the David Bowie movie *The Man Who Fell to Earth* and a lonely print of two antique gas pumps at a beach on a cloudy day, titled "Sea Pumps."

One night, Kevin squeezes the bolt cutters and snaps off the padlock from the metal gate at the nearby central office. Back at home, Kevin slices the lock open with a hacksaw. Since Pac Bell makes its own custom key blanks, Kevin must also modify a standard blank with a fine grinder, widening grooves, reshaping the edging. Thirty minutes later, Kevin's handmade blank fits the lock.

Kevin places his new blank in the cylinder, watching the lock's seven pins push up. He has to shape it so the pins align with the top of the cylinder. Kevin files the key carefully, then puts it back in to see where the first pin aligns. He files a little more until it's flush with the cylinder. Six more pins and Kevin gets lucky. When he returns, the key also fits the central office front door.

Around midnight a couple of evenings later, Kevin stuffs his backpack with his lock pick set, plug spinner, powdered graphite, and latex surgical gloves and sets out for a ten-minute fire drill beside a dark central office door. He slips on the gloves and dabs in a little graphite to loosen up the tumblers. He likes the physical touch, the fine grains of graphite, the beads of sweat that tickle his brow. But that's not what he loves most about picking locks. While his fingers twist the pick, his mind visualizes the internal workings. It's like phreaking an old Stepper switch or hacking the Net.

In no time at all Kevin has made or stolen keys to two dozen central offices along a sixty-mile stretch of the San Francisco Peninsula. He knows what time the last technicians leave with the night's computerized billing tapes. If Kevin can't pick a lock in a few minutes, he finds a window left ajar or climbs a drainpipe to enter a rooftop door.

He's unstoppable.

———■———

TO: KEV@SRI-SPAM
DATE: 29 APR 86 16:02 PDT (TUE)
FROM: KEV@SRI-SPAM

How do you reslove [sic] *yourself to having done something really stupid.*

Kevin is confessing his sins to the System, admitting the price of nightly central office crashing. Kevin doesn't return home until two, three, sometimes four in the morning, and then he can't sleep. He's like a cartoon-strip character stuck repeating the same ridiculous antics. His alarm doesn't ring, and he rolls out of bed late and races out the door. Speeding in his car, he hears the sirens. The guy with the dark glasses leans toward his window. "Do you know how fast you were going?"

It happens over and over again. Kevin may be an ace hacker and social engineer but he couldn't talk his way out of a speeding ticket if his life depended on it. The infractions and court appearances begin piling up. The penalties double and triple. Soon, his driver's license is suspended. And then it gets worse.

"Hey, Dwight, it's Kevin," he says casually one night on the phone.

Dwight Hare is one of Kevin's mentors at SRI, a skilled senior programmer with a secret clearance. He likes Kevin, considers him a talent.

"Dwight, I was wondering if you could bail me out?"

"What happened?"

"Traffic stuff. I'll tell you about it when you get down here."

"Where are you?"

"Redwood City Jail. Dwight, I need four hundred dollars to make bail. I'll pay you back tomorrow."

Dwight pauses to think. He doesn't trust Kevin with money.

"Where's your ATM card?"

"It's at home."

Hare bails him out with the ATM card, but Kevin forgot one little detail. He didn't have the money in the bank to cover the bail and his outstanding checks. Like the rest of Kevin's life, his finances are spinning out of control. His corporate American Express card and Macy's account are in collections, the credit union won't approve the loan he needs to dig himself out, and his boss delivers his last option. Sign a note with SRI for the amount due, and set up a payment schedule to have the money deducted from his paycheck.

But the night in jail and mounting debt aren't Kevin's only problems. His boss e-mails him about being late to key the crypto in the vault.

TO: KEV@SRI-SPAM.ARPA
SUBJECT: LATE KEYING OF THE KG AND ADMINFS SUPPORT
DATE: 08 MAY 86 14:58:00 PDT (THURS)

... the records show that you have been consistently late with getting the key installed ... you promised that you would get here on time in the morning ... This does not appear to be the case ...

Kevin feels he's getting a bum rap. He fires back an e-mail, defending himself, but Kevin's boss's superior simply cites another dissatisfied user.

TO: CONE@SRI-SPAM
SUBJECT: KEYING TIMES
DATE: 27 MAY 86 18:32:33 PDT (TUE)

Don,
Here is yet another complaint about the keying times not being met for your file.... We can no longer afford to lose this valuable time when the other contractors and/or clients need access to our machine.
... Kevin seems unable to manage his time to meet this obligation. It seems very inconsistent to me that he is so conscientious about the security issues in the vault but chooses to ignore the security [timing] requirements associated with the PLI.... This has to change immediately....

———■———

TO: KEV
DATE: 08 JUL 86 14:34:34 PDT (TUE)
FROM: KEV

Kevin Alexander Locke
3:15 Friday

Though it seems a puzzle, Kevin's memo to himself provides a clue to his future. Kevin has just finished reading *The Shockwave Rider,* a sci-fi tome that reads like a futuristic version of his life. The Shockwave Rider is sold by his mother as a "rent-a-child" until he's finally "requisitioned" by the Secretary of Defense and packed off to a bizarre behavioral center for "bright, deprived kids" to undergo unconventional, accelerated learning. He never lets himself "become deeply engaged in anything. It would be dangerous, as dangerous as coming to love somebody."

One day the Shockwave Rider does the unthinkable—he punches a new identity into the Net from a phone to become the person he chooses to be "instead of the person remembered by the computers." He cycles through personae as if he's changing clothes: utopia designer, gambler, computer-sabotage consultant, systems rationalizer. Kevin too seems to have half a dozen personae. Just as Kevin keys memos to himself on the Net, the Shockwave Rider updates his brain banks with "memos to selves." And Locke is the Shockwave Rider's alias.

In Kevin's mind, the System forces him to take a radical, illegal step to resolve the problem of his suspended license. Oblivious to the consequences of his actions, like a child playing in a grown-up world, Kevin doesn't see that his games have graduated from harmless phone pranks to picking locks and compulsive, nightly Pac Bell break-ins. And why should he? Until now, Kevin's virtual world has held him in good stead. His on-line crimes have won him a job, his boss has encouraged his phreaking, and he's more or less managed to separate his nighttime obsessions from his daytime duties.

In a strange sense, Kevin's lack of self-knowledge may be an advantage in the journey he's about to take. The hacker is preparing to take his fantasy role-playing to another level, readying himself for the ultimate cyberpunk magic trick. Kevin starts with his own birth certificate, ordering a photostat at a print shop and obliterating all the pertinent information and names, including his own, with a black felt tip photostat pen. Ironically, his original birth certificate is incomplete. Birth certificates for adopted children are reissued after adoption, with the new parents' names typed in but the signatures missing. Kevin is going to make his fake certificate look more authentic than his real one.

He slides the photostat into an old-fashioned typewriter and types in his new name and new birthdate using white correction tape. Then he places the correction tape across the document and signs for his new parents. He makes ten copies of the photostat on high-quality, thick bond paper, neatly cutting them to size. He soaks one for a few minutes in Lipton tea for a faded, twenty-year-old look.

Next, he visits a print shop to get it embossed with a phony California state seal. The first place sends him packing, the second store makes him a seal—no questions asked. The Department of Health stamp is a little tougher. First, he copies the back side of his birth certificate, then he finds a shop that doesn't ask questions. Twenty dollars later he's got the stamp.

Kevin is proud of the finished, authentic-looking product. He's thought everything through, right down to modeling his new identity after his past in case he's ever questioned. Kevin Alexander Locke was born at the UCLA Medical Center in Los Angeles and raised in Van Nuys. His father, John Norman Locke, was a schoolteacher just like his adopted mother.

Kevin gets knocked a few points for excessive speed but passes his driver's test easily. The DMV clerk hands him a temporary license in the name of Kevin Alexander Locke, one blue-eyed, brown-haired, five-eight, 130-pound male. Kevin's permanent license will arrive at his mail drop in a few weeks. He can drive. He can be whoever he wants to be.

COMMAND CONTROL

—■—

Intercontinental nuclear missiles wipe out half the nation's major air bases. Nuclear fallout will soon engulf several more. By the time our bombers limp back home, where will they be able to land? Which air bases will have spare parts and fuel?

The date is July 16, 1986. SRI has sent Kevin to man a Sun workstation at Offut Air Force Base in Omaha, Nebraska, home of the Air Force's long-range atomic strike force. The first attack lasts forty-five minutes, the second an hour and a half, the third four hours. NATO dubs the simulcasts "Global Shield." Kevin is living the ultimate hacker dream. The U.S. military is paying him to play computer war games.

That morning he checks in with the base's military police station to get his colored pass, and listens to the required security briefing advising him on the use of red "secret" pouches and computer scrub downs. The base is enormous: four thousand acres of fields, grassy knolls, and pavement, punctuated by olive drab buildings and a two-mile-long runway strip.

Kevin's job is simple. Make sure there are no computer glitches during the nuclear catastrophe. Keep the systems up and running. On the Net, SRI emphasizes the computer's ability to make wartime decisions "much quicker and easier than humans":

The system [involves] three other sites operating on a secure subnet across the United States. . . . The "Advisor" function [notifies] . . . selected command personnel of aircraft launch activity, aircraft reentering the US, and aircraft redirection caused by events that disabled destination bases. . . .

This is the beginning of artificial intelligence in command control systems.

In the past year or so, Kevin has flown to simulations at military bases in New York, Washington, Texas, and Florida. Sometimes there are actual planes in the sky or soldiers on the ground, and sometimes it's a pure simulation. Algorithms compute the immediate damage of intercontinental nuclear strikes, graphics pinpoint planes, ships, and nuclear weapons, while minute by minute, the screens map the ominous spread of nuclear fallout.

SRI, with Kevin doing his small part for God and Country, is dabbling with the prototype of real computer war games. The System doesn't drop the bombs yet, but this is only the first version of the software. Kevin knows he's come a long way from the day when the D.A. knocked on his door. Among the authors of SRI's 1986 report "Command Control and Communications Testbed for the Strategic Air Command" is one Kevin L. Poulsen. His role in the U.S. military's program for survivable nuclear war is logical. Who could be better qualified than a hacker to write the section on security?

———■———

Just as Kevin has become a member of the computer security establishment, federal laws criminalizing hacking have finally come to pass. The Computer Fraud and Abuse Act of 1986 makes it a felony, punishable by five years in prison, to access or enter a "federal interest computer without authorization" and obtain "anything of value." Damaging or disabling a nonfederal computer, network, or program is a crime too.

"Access devices" have been rendered illegal too—credit cards, codes, account numbers, electronic serial numbers, and other keys to money or valuable services. It's a felony to steal $1,000 worth of access devices, or to possess fifteen of them fraudulently. And penalties for access device or computer fraud offenses can reach as high as twenty years in prison.

Unauthorized computer access is now considered more serious than physical breaking and entering. A joyrider who accidentally impedes the use of a critical computer program could face a sentence of several years. Law enforcement has new powers in tracking cybercrime too. The Electronic Communications Privacy Act authorizes eavesdropping on portable phones and certain pagers and requires telephone companies to hand over subscriber or toll records to the FBI without judicial review. So deeply is the FBI engaged in electronic surveillance that it is granted congressional approval to hire independent contractors to intercept communications.

There's a war on and the enemies are hackers and digital thieves. The Secret Service estimates electronic funds fraud exceeds half a billion dollars a year and the Justice Department acknowledges widespread vulnerabilities. Meanwhile most banks continue to transmit their customers' secret account numbers over unprotected telephone lines that *USA Today* says even a twelve-year-old hacker could tap.

———■———

The date is September 10, 1986. There's been a hacker break-in at nearby Stanford University. Excited by the prospect of combatting a real threat, Kevin e-mails his Stanford counterparts.

> *Boy, you really have problems with crackers over there.*

> *Could you send me the details of the initial attack? Did they come up with something new, or just use an old bug? Has the L.A. Times news wire gotten the story yet?*

Kevin has even adopted the lingo of the establishment. He's a hacker, while the intruder is a common, lowly cracker. In honor of Computer-

Security Week Kevin demands passwords be assigned even on unused SRI accounts, and inserts code to track failed log-ins. He e-mails his superiors and fellow workers, warning that they shouldn't permit users of one system to have access to all the other SRI systems. He knows the risk because like any top security expert he's been attacking SRI to pinpoint weaknesses.

> *In my opinion this is easily our greatest vulnerability ... our password file is also readily accessible to anyone in the outside world. ... The last time I tried, I think it took about five hours for a simple program ... to check a single encrypted password against the dictionary.*

———■———

Kevin shifts effortlessly between his selves. One day he works for the military, the next he hacks for fun. Within days of the Stanford "cracker" attacks, Ron sees a campaign ad for the "Toxic Water Caravan" and reads how Jane Fonda and her celebrity pals plan a California bus tour rally for Proposition 65, the 1986 Clean Water Initiative. Kevin is intrigued when he learns Ally Sheedy has promised an appearance. After the phone call to introduce themselves, they bang out business cards on their computers.

The last weekend in September, Jane and about sixty celebrities pile into a bus and head north, trailed by a press bus packed with writers from *Time*, *People*, and countless newspapers, a blond photographer, and "Kevin A. Locke," a writer/photographer for *Health and Fitness Magazine*. It's dicey from the outset. When L.A. district attorney Ira Reiner takes the podium at the press conference to kick off the tour, Ron ducks to avoid being spotted. The risks are part of the fun. At a party on the Universal Pictures lot, Ron clicks away as Kevin slips behind Judd Nelson, Michael J. Fox, Rob Lowe, Roseanna Arquette, and Whoopi Goldberg. Ron tires of the tour, but Kevin continues without him, riding the whole four hundred plus miles north to San Francisco, mistakenly thinking Ally Sheedy will make her promised appearance.

Things aren't going quite so smoothly for Kevin at work. His performance review in early October isn't what he expected. Kevin knows they're wrong. He's proud of his security modifications to SRI's computers and his role in several military projects. His mistake was thinking he could work from morning to night, without a personal life. He e-mails his superiors:

> *. . . Unfortunately this single-mindedness took it's toll later on. I recently discovered that everything that I had neglected by way of my personal obligations had snowballed into an immense mountain of problems. . . . In addition, I've always had some trouble sleeping and my anxiety led to chronic insomnia. Consequentially, I began having more trouble getting to work on time in the morning. This impacted my ability to key the "PLI" security device in a timely manner, and made me unavailable at times when I was expected to be able to answer questions from staff members. . . .*

Any schedule problems Kevin may have had are a thing of the past. And the critical things his managers say about him simply aren't true. They say he is not a team player. Not so. Kevin is simply someone who doesn't need help.

> *The fact is, I rarely encounter a technical problem that I'm not able to handle without seeking aid. Most of my tasks are not even close to the limits of my own ability. . . .*

— ■ —

In the fall of 1986, Kevin's ex-boss Gilligan returns from a year at Brown University, and he and Kevin quickly pick up where they left off. Gilligan has taken a job at Sun Microsystems, the high-flying computer company, just a short, convenient drive from SRI.

It's just like the good old days, when the boss encouraged Kevin's nightly exploits. Gilligan knows where the keys are. They wait until midnight, scan the fleet of white pickups, and find one without SRI's brown logo on the door. Kevin drives the pickup out of SRI's main entrance, continues up to the bustling main avenue, El Camino, stops for gas, and makes a left down San Antonio. Peering through the chain-link fence, Kevin can't believe his eyes. Scores of defunct 1960s long distance operator consoles are scattered across the central office parking lot, bulky metal and plastic slabs used to patch through long distance calls. They look like control decks off the Starship *Enterprise*, and Kevin can't resist hauling one of the three-hundred-pound hulks home.

———————————— ■ ————————————

TO: GILLIGAN@SUN.COM
DATE: 15 OCT 86 10:14:36 PDT (WED)
FROM: KEVIN L. POULSEN

Yesterday was a nightmare. The first thing Joan said to me was "you look like you didn't get ANY sleep", plus some comment about my mental state that I can't remember. I had to leave work early at around 2:00, but I didn't want to go to sleep till nine or ten so I could get back in synch. I wound up lying down "just for a second", and waking up four hours later. Then I had to go to bed a couple hours after that. Groan.

Kevin.

The old partners in phreaking are back in business. One evening at their favorite Santa Clara central office, their usual second floor balcony door entry is locked. Kevin spies a heavy steel grate, wedges it aside, and unearths a twenty-foot drop to a six-by-six-foot concrete tomb and what looks like a door at the bottom. It's too far to jump, but back at the trash bins Pac Bell has left 50 feet of twenty-five-pair phone cable. Kevin wraps the colored cable around a nearby tree and tosses it down. He's played this role before, the thief in Dungeons & Dragons. Hand over hand down the thick, sinewy cable. Sneakers slap the concrete, twenty feet under.

"So . . . is it?" Gilligan whispers.

Kevin smiles upward in the dark. The door swings open.

They've got the fever. Three or four crazed nights a week they crash central offices, examining switches, perusing manuals, taking pass-words and test trunk sets, collecting discarded Crossbars, once even pry-ing a pay phone off the wall. When Kevin's not inside Pac Bell's offices, he boots up his computer, turns on his modem, and roams the phone company's electronic ordering database—Cosmos, or Computer System for Mainframe Operations. Studying those manuals he swiped has opened up worlds he didn't know existed. Kevin can do just about any-thing he wants in Cosmos: start or modify phone service, add or remove custom calling features, check for lines marked for repair, look up un-listed numbers. Kevin loves remote call forwarding or RCFs. For kicks, Kevin bounces calls around the Bay Area, trying to see how long a chain he can create.

Kevin and Gilligan fire e-mail back and forth, trading discoveries and comparing notes on everything from trunk lines and intricate Pac Bell calling options to tips on how to apply forty-eight volts to jolt the relays on their Crossbar switches to life. It's a strange mix of practical phreaking knowledge and phone trivia, the messages both giddy and conspiratorial, laced with reminders to call from a secure phone and bring tennis shoes and Levi's.

Kevin believes his adventures are innocent. This is the phone com-pany, after all, once the world's biggest monopoly. He can't imagine how his hobby could possibly threaten such a giant, powerful bureauc-racy. The phone company is practically invincible. He's just a kid swing-ing on the giant's shoelaces, going for a ride.

———■———

Gilligan lives near the San Francisco Soviet consulate, infamous for its satellite dish and forest of rooftop antennae aimed like ICBMs at Sili-con Valley. One of just three Soviet missions in the United States—the others are the embassy in Washington and the United Nations—the consulate is of huge strategic importance to the Soviet Union. The FBI estimates a third of the thirty-five- to forty-member delegation attached to the San Francisco consulate are intelligence officers. Against that cold war backdrop, Gilligan e-mails Kevin about how cool it would be to get a number similar to the Soviets' and snare some fascinating wrong numbers. Then Gilligan follows up his message with a note about how reality seems to have anticipated his fantasy.

TO: KEV@SPAM.ISTC.SRI.COM
SUBJECT: THE FBI
DATE: 28 OCT 86 09:45:38 PST (TUE)
FROM: GILLIGAN@SUN.COM (GILLIGAN GILLIGAN)

It looks like the FBI had the same idea as I, but earlier. Did you hear on the news about this guy, a former Air Force enlisted man, who was arrested yesterday for spying? Well the news stories said that he phoned the Soviet embassy in San Francisco and told them that he had some secrets to sell. Unfortunately for this guy, the news story went on, the FBI "intercepted his telephone call" and staged a meeting with an undercover agent, who this guy mistook for a Soviet.

I wonder what kind of arrangement they have? The embassy phone number (922) is definitely in the [central] office that serves the area where the embassy is located. Perhaps the FBI just has the lines run through their offices and always acts as "receptionist" for the Soviets. I wonder what the entry for that line looks like in Cosmos?

Obsessed, Gilligan drives by the consulate and urgently e-mails Kevin that all the windows on the first floor aren't windows at all but really one-way mirrors. But what intrigues Gilligan is how the FBI caught the spy. Does the FBI screen the Soviets' calls, and if so why wouldn't the Soviets catch on? Gilligan suggests the hackers find out for themselves.

"I think we should just give them a call and ask whoever answers who they are—FBI or embassy staff," Gilligan e-mails Kevin. "What do you say? We could do it on 3-way."

CORPORATE HEADQUARTERS

———■———

Kevin arrives just before 10 P.M., south of Market Street, near San Francisco's financial district, the imposing art deco skyscraper rising out of the mist like a vision from Gotham.

The date is February 15, 1987, and Kevin is about to enter territory that will forever separate him from those who pretend to be warriors of the electronic age. There's something surreal about the enormity of the risk he's willing to take. Before Kevin looms 140 New Montgomery, corporate headquarters for Pacific Bell. He raps lightly against the locked door and presses his ID to the glass. The guard unlocks the door and Kevin follows him across the marble floor to the streamlined desk. He's walked it countless times in his mind.

"*G. S. Holt,*" he signs, writing a random room number into the log book.

The guard hands back his laminated Pac Bell ID card, the one Gilligan suggested he try. Excited by his success, Kevin rides the elevator to the sixth floor, stops briefly, and continues to the top floor. He takes in the city lights and the tiny cars slipping in and out of the fog far below. Within minutes, Kevin finds an empty office and a phone.

"I'm in," Kevin phones Gilligan. "I'll keep you posted."

Kevin takes his time, methodically casing each floor. On the eighteenth, he notices a door with smoked glass and a chipped sign. Kevin reads it and muses, *Security.*

Picking the lock won't be easy, but he quickly sees he won't have to try. The old-fashioned transom window above the door is unlatched. Kevin drags over a thick cardboard box, gingerly steps up on it, and wiggles up and through the opening.

Kevin Poulsen has Pac Bell's corporate security offices all to himself. He wants to be the best, and what better way than to go to the source? Walk straight into the guarded, multibillion-dollar headquarters of one of the world's most technologically advanced phone companies and find its deepest secrets.

Kevin flips on the lights and gets down to work.

"I'm in security," Kevin updates Gilligan.

"Don't forget to bring back souvenirs," his former boss reminds him.

———■———

Kevin has been collecting lots of souvenirs lately. A few weeks before, during his Christmas break, Kevin hacked Cosmos and ordered an extension off Sean Randol's phone to be activated at his parents' house on Teasedale. "Bridge lifter" was the technical term, though secret party line was more like it. Kevin and his tape recorder became the third, uninvited party on Sean Randol's calls. He saw nothing wrong with his intrusion. As a hacker, Kevin knew that corporations and private detectives frequently violated people's privacy. He didn't see why he shouldn't too. Besides, Kevin simply had to know for certain. Sean had told him countless times that she wasn't interested in men, but Kevin couldn't be satisfied until he could hear the evidence live.

Ironically, Kevin played the wiretap recording for Ron a few nights later while they were sitting in Kevin's Dodge Dart on Old Victoria Road in Malibu, waiting to follow Ally Sheedy. As Ron listened to the wiretap, it was clear that Sean was uninterested in Kevin. Ron heard the two lovers fantasize about living together, and then he and Kevin joked as the girls described a couple of porno flicks. But to Kevin, the funniest part was when the line cracked and popped. The girls wondered what it was, and then Kevin heard Sean Randol say, *"It's probably Kevin Poulsen listening in."*

Listening to the wiretap, Ron wondered about that evening's target. More than the star of *WarGames*, Ally Sheedy was the sexy girl in black in *The Breakfast Club*, a Brat Packer and teen temptress to millions of American boys. Ron knew that Kevin was obsessed with the star, watching even her worst films over and over again, religiously hacking her latest unlisted phone number and address, and often joking to Ron in the lingo of a B-movie psycho, "I'm going to take this beauty away from all that."

Last summer Kevin had called Ron saying he'd somehow learned that Sheedy was going to be at a Malibu celebrity nightclub. Ron had tagged along, figuring it might be amusing. When Kevin pulled up outside the club on Trancas Street in West Malibu, Ron realized Kevin had only told him part of the story. Though they didn't see Sheedy that night, Kevin spotted her black Jeep next to a market. He parked his car a ways off, made the trip solo, opening the Jeep's passenger door and reaching into the glove compartment. A minute later, he was back in the Dodge Dart with Ron, showing off the vehicle registration he'd stolen from Sheedy. Ron had been surprised by the theft. Kevin really was becoming a stalker.

———■———

Scouring Pac Bell's eighteenth-floor security offices, Kevin helps himself to a secret Bell Lab security memo and another memo titled, "Compromising of Customer and Tel Co." He scans the files on various investigations, and makes sure to take the one on the notorious phone phreak Susan Thunder. Next, he picks a file cabinet in an adjacent, locked office, grabbing a stack of Pac Bell ID blanks, enough to provide a change of identity for every day of the week.

The phone rings.

"Security," Kevin boldly answers. It's Gilligan, asking what souvenirs he's found.

"Hold on," Kevin whispers, crouching down behind a security

officer's desk as he hears keys jingle outside the door. "I can hear the guard walking by."

The guard doesn't spook Kevin, but huddled behind the desk, whispering to Gilligan, he realizes he may have a problem. He's already collected a thick manila envelope full of documents from his evening's work. If the guard downstairs notices he didn't come in that night with the envelope, making a run for it will be out of the question. The front door is locked.

But on this cool Sunday night, a few minutes before 3 A.M., G. S. Holt strolls out of the eighteenth-floor security office with the manila envelope tucked under his arm, calmly takes the elevator down to the lobby, and signs out at the front desk of Pac Bell's corporate headquarters, as if he's done it a thousand times.

WATCHMAN

——■——

You know, Kevin," Goodfellow begins, "there's a reason I haven't kept in touch."

The mentor and his disciple are meeting for lunch at a Menlo Park restaurant. It's been a long time since the two have talked.

"You've been up to some of your old tricks again, Kevin."

Kevin smiles broadly. "OK, I've been going into some phone company buildings."

Kevin figures he's just doing the same stuff he's done since he was sixteen. Maybe he's a little more serious, but the way he sees it, that's nobody else's business, certainly not Goodfellow's.

Goodfellow doesn't buy it. "Kevin, I think you need an *attitude* adjustment."

Kevin knows the rules. You get a job, you stop hacking. Simply by being employed by SRI, anything you do in your private life can ultimately embarrass your employer. But maybe Kevin's past makes it hard for him to see that his mentor is making one more effort to help him. Didn't his real parents put him up for adoption and his first stepmother commit suicide? Why shouldn't Goodfellow abandon him too?

——■——

Instead of reaching out to Goodfellow, Kevin seeks out an old friend he's manipulated once before. Mark Lottor is subletting Goodfellow's condo, and he hasn't spoken to Kevin in over a year, not since he swore off the hacker for getting him into trouble. When Kevin reads a note on SRI's network that Lottor needs a roommate, he e-mails his interest. But Lottor puts him off, saying he has other people lined up.

A shy, bright young man with an impish grin and unruly hair, Lottor studied math at Carnegie-Mellon and had a hacker's distrust for authority. At SRI, Lottor oversaw the annual counting of hosts connected to the Net, the closest thing to an Internet census. Lottor and Kevin got along well at first, occasionally meeting at Goodfellow's lunches and dinners, sharing a mutual fascination with computers and phones. But then there were the dark parking lots Kevin drove him to, the telephone poles and fire escapes they climbed, the break-ins that Lottor later regretted, the compulsion that Lottor admitted he could only control by cutting off all contact with Kevin.

But when his other rent prospects fade, Lottor changes his mind. He decides to come straight with Kevin, to explain why he finds him fascinating and dangerous. He doesn't hate him. It's just Kevin's annoying ability to convince him to do things he doesn't want to do. Sure, maybe he could have restrained himself, but Lottor found it easier just to stop being friends. Now that he's learned what to avoid, Lottor hopes they might be able to be friends again. If he can just resist getting in the same car with Kevin, he's certain everything will be fine.

A few days after Kevin receives the rambling e-mail, he promises not to coax Lottor into a car, and formally begins moving into Goodfellow's pad with his expanding cache of swiped, salvaged, and purchased switches, antique phones, test sets, and other telephonic collectibles. The following week, Kevin e-mails Lottor and jokingly asks if he too admires the "aesthetic perfection" of the ridiculously large TSPS console he lifted from the central office parking lot with Gilligan. "Personally I think it would look awesome in the living room," suggests Kevin of the three-hundred-pound electronic carcass. Lottor can't help but agree.

———■———

Before long, Kevin is once again pulling Lottor into his vortex. Within a few weeks of moving in, Kevin talks Lottor into a weekend drive south along the coast on Highway 1, and a stroll on the Santa Cruz boardwalk. On the return trip, Kevin takes a shortcut through the Santa Cruz Mountains and suddenly veers off the highway. "Hey," Kevin says mysteriously, "I wanna show you something neat." Minutes later, dressed immaculately in white like a comic book superhero, Kevin picks a telecommunication trailer's lock on a remote mountain road and lures his friend inside.

It's only the beginning. Lottor soon finds himself drawn into Kevin's activities, and watches as his condo becomes a laboratory for phreaking and hacking. Kevin scavenges a pay phone from a central office and hooks it up in the condo, routing the calls through a wire closet in a Palo Alto building so they can't be traced.

Kevin is refining his wiretapping skills, trying to eliminate the noise from the Radio Shack recording device that made Sean suspect he was listening in. Kevin sets up a bridge lifter tap in Cosmos on a coffee shop pay phone in downtown Palo Alto so he can route his outgoing calls from his condo pay phone and tap the public. Kevin looks upon the downtown pay phone as communal property. He's willing to share. Once when Kevin's chatting on the line with a friend, someone at the coffee shop pay phone is surprised to pick up the receiver and hear a conversation. "Sorry, I'm just finishing up," Kevin apologizes, getting a kick out of the bizarre twist. "I'll hang up now."

———■———

Kevin is reading the *Watchmen* comic series, a bloody, apocalyptic story that resembles a novel more than a picture book. The main character is Walter Kovacs, the disturbed son of a prostitute who was abandoned by his father. When Kovacs blinds one of his boyhood tormentors, he's packed off to a children's home and then a sewing sweatshop. A woman orders a strange spotted dress and when she never picks it up the quirky Kovacs keeps it. Two years later he learns who ordered it: Kitty Genovese, the New York woman raped and tortured while her neighbors stood by. As Kovacs explains, "Some of them even watched. Do you understand? . . . I knew what people were, then, behind all the evasions, all the self-deception. Ashamed for humanity, I went home. I took the remains of her unwanted dress . . . and made a face that I could bear to look at in the mirror."

At night, the scrawny Kovacs dons his eerie mask and steps out as Rorschach, a brutal vigilante who maims both innocents and criminals in his self-appointed role as New York's administrator of street justice. Ultimately Kovacs must battle Jon Osterman, a radioactive mutant with superhuman power. Osterman's radioactive charge gives his lovers cancer, and his visions of a doomed future haunt him. He may be immortal and all-powerful, but he's also the most alienated creature in the universe.

The two characters' bleak worldviews appeal to Kevin because in some way each resembles a different side of the young hacker. Kevin shares Kovacs's physical inferiority, his history of abandonment, and his search for power through an alternate identity. Osterman, on the other hand, represents the superpower Kevin becomes through hacking, and the danger he poses to those closest to him—and to the world. So, it's not surprising that when Kevin has trouble paying his phone bill, he enlists the help of his superheroes. He starts phone service as the *Watchmen* vigilante Walter Kovacs, and when Kovacs is disconnected a few months later, John Osterman takes over.

There's an irony in Kevin's fascination with the Watchmen. His electronic powers give him the possibility of self-knowledge, but the cyberpunk with revolving identities never looks inward to search for the mother and father he's never met. Like Kovacs, Kevin is too busy fighting his war against the powers that be to consider himself.

———■———

By now, Kevin has a dozen different techniques to crack a System. One evening, he hacks a Pac Bell network in nearby Hayward and leapfrogs to a local area network at San Ramon, Pac Bell's massive administrative headquarters. Once inside the San Ramon net, he changes a variable, shifting the way the system interprets keystrokes to trick it into launching a simple editing program that enables him to slip into yet another network. From San Ramon, Kevin scans for files named "dial-up," and finds one that doesn't require a password since it's designed to go only from Pac Bell's most secure network to its less secure network. Kevin cleverly turns off the dial-up and reverses it, connecting himself to the Bell Application Network Control System. Within BANCS Kevin can run nearly every Pac Bell ordering or maintenance program—Premis, Lmos, Sword, Word. He can retrieve everything from customer names to telephone numbers, addresses, and billing and credit information.

It's as if Kevin is playing Dungeons & Dragons, pressing for combat, pushing harder to see if he can get Pac Bell's attention and goad them into a counterattack. A couple of weeks later, he gets the response he seems to want. While perusing for security memos, Kevin finds one headed "Break-in." On September 9, 1987, Robert Tracy, a Pac Bell local area network administrator, began learning about Kevin. After documenting the intruder's movements, Tracy shut down the system and changed passwords. He wrote a memo to Gerri Lyons, a Pac Bell security investigator, including an ongoing chronology of the attacks and his countermeasures. He also detailed the company-wide plan to move to a "Gordian key," a credit card–like ID with a chip that would be issued to dial in employees. The card would generate new random numbers every ten seconds or so, and theoretically seal the leaks. But Kevin knew the Gordian knot had yet to be tied.

———■———

Kevin borrows a briefcase for the job, packs his lock picks, and tosses in a phone book for dead weight. He drives his Mustang with the top down over the San Mateo Bridge and past the rolling brown hills to Pac Bell's sparkling new administrative headquarters in San Ramon. The week before, while cruising Pac Bell's network, Kevin intercepted an announcement of a power outage scheduled the following Sunday. That settled the date for Kevin. No power would mean no people and no questions.

He ambles into the lobby and places his badge on the security guard's desk. Kevin is about to discover another limitation of Pac Bell's security. The employee pass for one Pac Bell building can get him a pass for another. Kevin clips the temporary ID the guard gives him on his shirt and walks calmly past the lobby and down the hall into the huge, darkened offices. He spots a guard at the end of a hall, but he doesn't panic. He knows all he has to do is have the guts to walk straight toward the guard until he can make out his ID.

This is what makes Kevin unique. He's breaking the mold for a hacker, proving that a cyberpunk can straddle both electronic and physical worlds. Plenty of kids can hack on-line, but how many are willing to take the risk of looking down the barrel of a security guard's gun? Intellectually he knows the difference between his physical break-ins and on-line adventures, but Kevin's never been punished. He's been breaking into Pac Bell offices for a couple of years and he's never even had a close call. Why would his luck change now?

Kevin approaches the desk where network administrator Robert Tracy has been doing his damnedest to catch him. He opens his briefcase, deftly picks the locked desk drawer, and fishes out Tracy's logbook.

Sure enough, it holds the very secret Kevin seeks, proof that Pac Bell has traced his calls and snared a clue. Ron had naively let Kevin call through his home phone to mask his intrusions into Pac Bell's databases, and just as Kevin had suspected, Tracy had picked up Ron's number. Kevin is just about to Xerox the handwritten log when he remembers the power is off. He flips back a few months on Tracy's daily calendar, tears off a page, and transcribes the notes word for word.

———■———

Lesser hackers might consider the trace put on Ron's line a warning, a good reason to call it quits, but Kevin considers it a challenge. On September 19, 1987, Kevin pulls up a particularly interesting Cosmos record. To someone without Kevin's knowledge, it's technical gibberish, but midway down the eighteenth line he reads, "2790//GREEN/ SAN FRAN 94123." Kevin, it seems, has pulled up the Pacific Heights address of the San Francisco Soviet consulate.

A few weeks later, Gilligan sends Kevin e-mail about Masnet, an Arpanet Army network that caught his eye. The banner Gilligan e-mails to Kevin includes a warning that unauthorized access will be prosecuted under Title 18 Section 1030 of the Computer Fraud and Abuse Act, a veritable invitation to a hacker. Just what Kevin does with the Soviet consulate records or the Army network isn't clear, but the timing of his intrusions will one day be the source of much investigation. By a twist of fate in November of 1987 Kevin is sent to Austin, Texas, for a military exercise called Caber Dragon 88.

A plastic laminated security badge pinned to his T-shirt, Kevin marvels at the huge inflatable green tent. Giant fans keep it bulging, and Kevin guesses it's the size of a basketball court, maybe bigger. Inside the colossal tent, nearly a hundred Army officers and troops mill about, their voices drowned out by the hum of the fans. Kevin's job is to make sure SRI's computers are properly installed, and help with Unix if need be. But the systems are running fine, so Kevin passes the time drinking coffee and sneaking out to watch the lightning streak the sky.

One day he's asked to write a quick fix to a program that isn't working quite right. "There's a problem in our program," one of Kevin's SRI supervisors tells him. "It can't handle the Army's data." It seems the "real" data of the military exercise is giving their program fits. Kevin quickly writes an interim fix and thinks nothing more of it.

———■———

Back at SRI two project leaders pull chairs up around Kevin's cubicle and tell the hacker how they need some more extensive coding done on the program Kevin modified at Caber Dragon.

One of the men diagrams the program on a piece of paper, explaining their predicament. "Blue Flag is just a few weeks away," he continues, referring to an important Army exercise. "Could you write some shell scripts?"

"Sure," Kevin volunteers, always eager to program. On another piece of paper the men scribble down the specifications of the scripts. Once the men leave, Kevin quickly breaks the program into its parts. Since the problem began with using phony data, the project leaders have given Kevin real Air Force tasking orders with actual bombing coordinates for live foreign targets. Kevin tinkers on the scripts most of the day, and by 4:30 P.M. he's ready to put them to the test. The final specification requires Kevin to copy the highest numbered tasking order into his SRI workstation.

Kevin is pleased with himself as he watches the tasking order pop into his workstation's directory. He walks down to one of the project leaders' offices, informs him the test was a success, and lets him know where the scripts are stored. On his SRI time card for November 25, 1987, Kevin charges the day to Ron Lee, SRI project leader for the Army contract.

His luck is about to run out.

THE ANTI-HACKER

His name is Justin Tanner Petersen, but that's about to change. He knows how to do it, he's seen it on television. At the Martin Luther King Library in Washington, D.C., he searches for the right newspaper article, a fatal accident about twenty years ago in a state far from home. He mails the ten-dollar fee to the Bureau of Vital Statistics, and two weeks later, the death certificate arrives with the place of birth and the mother's maiden name. He phones the county recorder in Ventura, California, and sends away for the birth certificate, leaving the return address of an abandoned house. Then, with the birth certificate as his identification, he takes and passes the driver's license test.

As a young boy, Justin had always loved controlling his environment, monkeying with the lights, alarms, and public address system at school. Trouble was never far away. At fourteen, Justin ripped off a bank's drive-up window and the feds gave him probation. A few months later he wasn't so lucky. Caught stealing phone gear from Ma Bell service vans, he was sentenced to eight months in juvenile detention. Justin dropped out of Southeast High in Lincoln, Nebraska, in the fall of his senior year, and moved with his twice-divorced mother to Washington, D.C. Without a high school diploma or formal training, he was relegated to the blue-collar drudge work of the high-tech revolution. He repaired microfilm cameras, installed alarms, and plugged in computer circuit boards, disk drives, and power suppliers. He never lasted very long at a job. He knew he was smarter than his bosses.

At the late age of twenty-three, Justin began experimenting with computers and passing his free time on the hacker bulletin boards. Justin liked the idea of being a hacker. Depending on his mood, he was "Phucked Agent 004" or "Agent Steal," and if he lacked technical expertise, he made up for it with moxie. Agent Steal had attitude. He stole Sprint access codes and hinted at other crimes to an admiring gang of teen hackers.

Steal didn't know or care about the history and culture of phreaking and hacking. Ethics didn't matter to him. He remembered how his father had told him he regretted having a child, and how his stepdad split before he could get to know him. The only hackers Justin knew were the ones getting busted or about to be busted. He'd read of the government crackdowns, saw the headlines the teens were making for messing with the System. Hackers were changing and so was the meaning of the word. Justin was a new generation of hacker, not the third generation inspired by innocent wonder that Levy eulogized in *Hackers* but a disenfranchised fourth generation driven by anger.

———■———

Whatever Justin's latest crimes might be, in his mind they're enough to end his life. He charges up his credit cards, writes as many bad checks as he can, and says his goodbyes. He has no idea how hard the cops might look for him, so he cuts himself off from everyone and everything he's known, destroying anything with his old name on it. He rents a Ryder moving truck, packs up his computers and sound gear, and, dogged by five Montgomery County felony warrants, heads west to California. He has a new life to look forward to.

Within a year, Justin's Hollywood makeover is complete. Along with the new name, he's had his nose done to perfect his new identity.

He works as a soundman with a rock-and-roll band to skim off the groupies. Days are for sleeping and nights are for club hopping or an occasional gig with the band. Once in a while he squeezes in some hacking too.

On a cool spring night in 1985, well past the midnight hour, Justin phones up Lisa, a petite Jewish girl who enjoys his bondage games. Why not buzz over on the old bike?

Justin hits the freeway and cranks it way up, about a hundred miles an hour, before he sees flashing red lights in the rearview. No chance of passing any Breathalyzer tonight. Full throttle off the exit ramp, sweeping into the side streets, stop signs blurring at about eighty. He spots the dog out of the corner of his eye, a flash of brown. THUMP!

The bike slams into a curb, flinging Justin onto someone's neatly mowed front lawn. One roll and he's up and running like G.I. Joe. He leaps a wall, jumps a fence, stops a second to catch his breath.

Shit! Another dog.

Justin laughs, spotting a six-inch-high ankle biter. Five minutes later the loud hum drops out of the sky, an LAPD copter buzzing overhead, briefly circling the neighborhood, then flying in a straight line—away from Justin.

He makes a break for it, hurtling a fence into a front yard, hitting the street at a full run. Suddenly the headlights of a cop car barrel down. He sprints. Run, run, run! Back across another lawn, up and over another fence. And then—SPLASH!

"Hey! Get the fuck out of there!" a voice yells.

Like I really want to swim in your pool, asshole.

He can barely drag himself out of the water, his down parka suddenly feeling like a load of lead feathers. He dumps it and runs straight, sloshing through rosebushes that tear at his thighs. He jumps another fence and rips a long gash in his Levi's. Back out on the street, he slogs to the nearest gas station, phones a cab, and waits, shivering behind a trash dumpster.

A half hour later Lisa greets him at the door in her silk nightie.

"What the hell happened to you?"

---■---

Justin is keyed. This is the first time, not counting kid pranks, he's ever tried to tap someone's phone. Most people would look at him as a Peeping Tom, or worse. But to Justin his plan is proof of how much he really cares about Lisa. The tap is an expression of his commitment.

He spies the crawl space where the phone lines run to a terminal box on the side of her house. He buys a telephone coupling transformer and a voice-activated cassette tape recorder. On his next visit, while Lisa showers, Justin slips on his trousers and sneaks out the back door. He crawls under the house, attaches the transformer to her line, and plugs it into the auxiliary input on his tape recorder.

"What do you want?" Justin whispers to Lisa's dog, as the mutt watches him finish the wiretap.

The dog cocks its head knowingly. But Justin doesn't have a conscience.

OK. What are you going to do, tell her?

Back at his apartment, after crawling under the house again to retrieve his first tape, Justin settles in and presses play. He's proud of his first tap. This is what's so cool about hacking phones. Not the technology, but the power, the control.

"Hi . . . Tonight? . . . Sure, I'm free."

The bitch, Justin thinks. She's seeing two other guys, and lying to all three of us.

—■—

On the rebound, Justin is making his rounds. Tonight's menu features two leather-bound nasties visiting from the Big Apple. Rockers with shoe-polish black hair, black lipstick, and pierced noses who prefer kink to small talk. Justin and his pal squire them up to his friend's pad off Sunset Plaza in the Hollywood Hills. Justin doesn't invade her privacy by bothering with her name, but he has his fun with her until six in the morning, when he says his goodbyes, opens the throttle on his bike, and roars down into the smoggy haze of a Los Angeles dawn.

First, the sound of a revved V-6 engine. Then he sees it out of the corner of his eye, an early-model green Chevrolet Impala.

Justin leaps from his bike, barely clearing the Impala.

Curl up in a ball! Curl up in a ball!

His foot jams the asphalt, and the scene skids into slow motion: he's sliding on his back, his arms cradling his knees, head tucked, his body skidding through the intersection, his bike a few feet behind him, closer, closer . . .

It's going to hit me! It's going to hit me!

Everything stops. Justin is on the Strip, Sunset and La Cienega, but he isn't going anywhere. A few feet away his bike lies in a crumpled heap. He's slid about a hundred feet right before a group of startled commuters waiting for an early bus.

"Shit."

He struggles up and flops back like a fish out of water. Then he sees it, his leg bent backward, ninety degrees, just below the knee, his blood pouring onto the pavement.

"You OK? You OK? " someone frantically yells.

Justin thinks for a second and touches his forehead.

"Yeah . . . I'm OK. Where's my sunglasses at?"

Puzzled, a bystander retrieves Justin's scratched glasses. Justin puts them on and looks again.

The green Chevrolet Impala is gone.

"I'm a doctor!" shouts a man who wraps his belt around Justin's thigh.

Snow begins to fall. Like on a fuzzy TV set, the flakes getting bigger and bigger, while everything else fades. He's sure he's a goner. But then they stick the IV in his arm and pump him with blood or plasma, he doesn't know which, and it's like a switch going on. He's on a stretcher in the ambulance, a doctor next to him, his leg jammed in a wood splint.

"Put me out! Put me out!" Justin begs.

Finally, at Cedars-Sinai Hospital in Beverly Hills, they prepare the anesthesia. But the doctor has bad news.

PART III

THE STORAGE LOCKER

W hat could possibly be better than working for SRI?

What if Kevin could learn at the feet of the world's premier Unix experts? What if he could join the company bringing networking and powerful, inexpensive workstations to corporate America? And what if they'd pay him a lot more than he's been making at SRI, enough money to end his financial problems?

Gilligan doesn't need to resort to much persuasion to talk Kevin into following him over to Sun Microsystems in nearby Mountain View. It's not as if things are going well at SRI. Kevin's credit problems and late-night phone phreaking habit have limited his opportunities for advancement at the think tank and defense contractor. To Kevin it's a no-brainer. A job with Sun is a chance to ride the latest wave of technology and climb aboard one of the nation's fastest-growing companies.

As a system administrator, it's Kevin's job to support the thousands of users on Sun's internal network and upgrade systems as new capabilities come on-line. To a hacker, the job is akin to being paid to stay abreast of the latest advancements in networking. It's Kevin's responsibility to know the ins and outs of the network, to determine quickly if a user has made a routine error or been blindsided by a bug. Kevin, like other "sys admins," is given super-user powers, or root privileges—the power to access any Unix system without the user's password, knowledge, or permission. In short, Kevin's got a great job at one of the hottest companies in Silicon Valley. And there is another plus to working for Sun. When Kevin feels the central office urge, it's that much easier to schedule an evening adventure with Gilligan.

———■———

A file sits open on the desk of Larry Tyson, the owner of Menlo Atherton Storage: Locker number 219, John Anderson of 1267 Ravenswood, Menlo Park. A $42 second-story locker, plus the $10 a month for 24-hour access. The rent is overdue a hundred days with $162.50 delinquent. Two preliminary lien notices were sent to two addresses, but both were returned stamped "undeliverable."

Tyson, a straight-talking, balding ex-cop, decides the time has come to cut Anderson's lock and see if it's abandoned or there's something worth selling. He shuttles his brother and Scott Welsch, a cop who moonlights for him, down the row of identical sheds bordering Silicon Valley's bustling 101 corridor to Building I, storage locker 219.

Welsch snaps open the lock with bolt cutters and looks in at piles of phone gear. He pokes around and unearths a pay phone, old switching equipment, Pac Bell manuals, some nine-inch reels of computer tape, and what appear to be the tools of a burglar or forger: a full locksmith set, razor blades, and a laminator. When they see the papers on the Russian consulate and the Legion of Doom hacker gang articles they call Tyson down to take a look. But Tyson has an awful realization when he studies the file more closely. Anderson came in just a few days ago and paid seventy dollars toward his outstanding rent. Concerned about the possibility of a lawsuit, Tyson phones a judge he knows who directs him to the FBI.

"We just opened the locker of this guy," Tyson excitedly tells a San Francisco FBI agent over the phone. "He's got stuff on the Russian embassy, the U.S. military . . ."

"What's your name and phone number?" the FBI agent asks routinely.

"Well, are you guys coming down?" Tyson demands.

"That's another agent's territory. If he's interested he'll get in touch with you."

But Tyson isn't about to let this one slip away. He phones his Redwood City police buddies, knowing that even though it's Menlo Park's jurisdiction Redwood City won't blow it off.

As the Redwood City cops confess they don't know who to call at Pac Bell, Tyson picks up a stack of phone bills lying in the storage locker—hundreds of pages of calls made by Pac Bell security officers.

"Here's all their names," says Tyson.

———■———

Kurt Von Brauch, a barbell-armed Pac Bell security officer, shakes his head at the name on the cut lock that once secured Anderson's locker stash of phone gear: Pac Bell.

Wondering whether the guy could be a Pac Bell employee, Von Brauch wades inside the locker, surveying the mounds of papers and equipment.

"Damn! These are ours!" Von Brauch exclaims as he sees a box of phone bills that he realizes must have come from 140 New Montgomery. Von Brauch knows that Pac Bell requires its security agents to send their monthly phone bills to the San Francisco office: every phone call a security officer has made to other law enforcement agencies, to relatives, wives, or girlfriends.

"Damn," Von Brauch repeats, lifting a bill with his name. But it's not just the phone bills. Von Brauch's police training helps him see the big picture. The Soviet stuff troubles him, and the microfiche cable maps, too. One map shows a central office near the San Francisco International Airport. Maybe this guy's trying to find out where the radar circuits go from the airport. Could he be a terrorist? The nine-inch computer tapes raise another concern. Could they hold proprietary information? Later, James Neal, a polite, slender, mild-mannered Menlo Park police detective, meets Von Brauch and another Pac Bell investigator, Steve Dougherty, at the locker.

Neal is glad the two Pac Bell security guys have come along to help sort out the contents. He doesn't know the first thing about phones or computers. For the next two hours the three men prepare a detailed inventory, filling twenty boxes with well over a hundred items: monitors, phones, telecommunications equipment, Pac Bell manuals, maps, and a hacksaw. It isn't until Neal sees the two snapshots that he begins to understand. In the first, a young man with long brown hair and a bright white jumpsuit kneels in front of a telecommunications trailer door, intent on picking the lock. The next photo is proof of his success. The young man stands inside the trailer, surrounded by switching equipment, grinning at the camera.

Three days later, on February 12, 1988, John Anderson arrives in his 1974 convertible Fiat to pay the outstanding rent on his locker. Tyson greets him from behind the counter and then realizes who he is. "Hold on a second," he tells Anderson, then walks to the back room to make the phone call.

A couple of minutes later, Tyson returns. "You know we had some trouble with the address you gave us."

"Oh, I just moved. My new address is 4021 Jefferson."

Tyson resists smiling. Jefferson used to be his beat. There is no four thousand block.

Suddenly Anderson hears his real name called from behind him by a Menlo Park cop.

—■—

Kevin waits for Detective Neal in the suburban police station's temporary holding cell, just a few hundred yards from SRI's main entrance.

"Have a seat right there." Neal points to the blue metal bench equipped with leg manacles and handcuffs.

"I guess I'm in big trouble," Kevin says sheepishly.

The detective starts slow and easy, talking about the traffic warrants out for Kevin. Neal was the arresting officer on one of them, a driving without a license rap.

"Well, you got promoted," Kevin momentarily distracts Neal.

"Yeah," acknowledges the detective.

"Congratulations."

The detective thanks Kevin and continues. He'd like to know which of the addresses he has for Kevin is real.

"I'm at 1055 Pine Street," Kevin replies.

"And what's your phone number there?"

"My phone was just disconnected."

Kevin knows he's telling the truth. There's no phone he's paying for. None that Pac Bell ever bills anyone for.

"Your full name is?"

"Kevin Lee Poulsen."

"And what other names do you use? Kevin Alexander Locke?"

"That's right, that's what I drive with." Kevin has yet another alias.

"Are you on probation or parole?"

"I'd take a guess I'm on probation because of the driving on the suspended license conviction . . ."

Neal ambles along Columbo-style. He reads Kevin his rights, tells him he has the right to a lawyer, then asks him if he wishes to talk without one.

"OK," Kevin says calmly.

It's a game, and if Kevin wants to win he figures he needs to know what he's up against. Does the cop know he was almost caught at a nearby Pac Bell office a couple of weeks ago? Does he know it's Kevin who has been running wild through Pac Bell's computers? And besides, why in the world would he want a lawyer? Kevin doesn't need help. A lawyer would just get in the way.

Neal prods Kevin into revealing he used a phony birth certificate to get a driver's license and then asks why he used another name at the storage locker.

"This isn't easy to admit," Kevin confesses, sounding uneasy and sincere. "I used the name because . . . I'm very financially irresponsible. I felt at some point there might be a problem with me renting a storage area, and I didn't want it to affect my credit rating."

"What was stored there?"

"I had some electronic equipment, a lamination machine, some miscellaneous telephone stuff. I collect telephone equipment . . ."

"What about the laminating machine," Neals asks. "Ever used that machine to make ID cards?"

"Just to make joke IDs," Kevin says coolly. "To show my friends."

Neal tries something concrete. He asks Kevin if he's been in the nearby Palo Alto phone company office.

"I've been in that one on the tour ... two or three years ago."

Kevin figures he's telling the truth, except for a slight error of omission.

But Neal doesn't relent. "OK. Have you ever been in there under false pretenses or with a false ID?"

Ask the right question, get the right answer. "Under false pretenses, I have been in there more recently than the past three years," Kevin admits. "I had an expired Pacific Bell ID card that I found in the trash can."

"And did you take anything out of the building?"

"Nothing at all. In fact, I met somebody there and they showed me around the building."

True, true. Kevin did meet an employee at the Palo Alto office after breaking in, and miraculously talked him into giving him a guided tour.

"Who was that person?" Neal presses.

"I'm afraid I don't know his name," Kevin says, suddenly realizing Neal knows more than he thought. "Can you tell me offhand what I'm going to be charged with ... ?"

"Well, right now, possession of stolen property ... all the ID cards you have here, it sort of fits a trend ... and I'd like for you to be honest, because I'm aware of your past. I know that you were involved in that incident in Southern California with Ron Austin."

Minutes later, Kevin is on the jail phone, trying to rustle up $2,700 in bail. His friend doesn't sound too eager to help. "I'll definitely pay you back," Kevin promises, offering his paycheck. When that isn't enough, he swears he'll sell everything he owns. "The quicker you get started on this the better. 'Cause after a certain point ... I'll have to spend the whole weekend in Redwood City Jail."

———■———

Detective Neal continues asking about Kevin's involvement with Austin.

"I was never charged with anything," Kevin insists. "In fact, I was very young."

"My concern is that you're doing that again. That would be a logical conclusion."

"I'm not sure of the legality of going through trash cans, but I have been doing that, and I've been finding some equipment . . ."

"So you're saying . . . you have not been involved in that same type of activity that occurred back in '83, '84, when your friend Ron Austin was arrested . . ."

"I haven't been continuing *that* activity at all."

In Kevin's mind he's telling the truth. He hasn't bothered with "that" activity—harmless Internet hacking—for years. He's a serious phone hacker now, burglarizing Pac Bell and routinely cracking the company's computers.

"OK. So the computer equipment that you have [at home] now, would have no bearing on any of that activity . . . ?"

"No."

"To prove that, would you be willing to have me take a look at the equipment that you have at your home?"

THE BUST

◾

Kevin takes a gamble and opens the door to his Pine Street condo, letting in Neal, two other Menlo Park cops and Von Brauch and Dougherty of Pac Bell. He figures it's the lesser of two evils. Neal said he would post guards outside the condo until the warrant came through if Kevin withheld his permission. This way, maybe they'll give him a break.

"Wow!" exclaims Dougherty, grinning broadly. Smack in the middle of the living room sits the enormous Traffic Service Position System console festooned with bright buttons and switches and lamps that glow when the phone hooked up to it rings. "A TSPS console," Dougherty muses. "That's a pretty unusual piece of furniture."

"I'm kind of into the phone company," confesses Kevin.

The condo resembles a science fiction movie set, a curious amalgam of past and future. A pay phone hangs on the wall, and strewn around the room are telecommunications panels, terminals, monitors, parts of switches, boxes overflowing with cables, countless phones, and a trunk test set inscribed with a nearby Pac Bell office address. Upstairs an old wooden switch room sign hangs over a door. Antique phones clutter a desk, and tape recorders are plugged into phone jacks on either side of Kevin's computer. It's an eclectic mix, ranging from celebrity magazines and amateur photos of Molly Ringwald and Ally Sheedy to books on how to buy stocks, a yellow report book filled with handwritten notes titled "Burglar Alarm Procedures," and a thick copy of the *Watchmen* comic book.

Von Brauch flips on his tape recorder and begins dictating, while Kevin leans against his bedroom door, his look of disgust captured by the camera of one of the policemen. The Pac Bell security man methodically describes a military ID: "On the windowsill to the left is one Blue Flag controller ID badge 88–1 ('If found please return to 441 TTT-DUS Elgin Air Force Base, Florida')," then rattles off what seems to be evidence of phone phreaking. "We have a wire . . . organization chart for [Pac Bell] San Diego . . . several Cosmos direct link telephone numbers." Next to the bed, he finds a spiral notebook filled with Kevin's handwriting: "Tuesday, lunch with Allen A., install DI tap begin monitor, 853–5937." There's also a John Osterman Pac Bell calling card, a Best lock blank ground off on one side to make a master key, notepads marked United States Central Command, and a black bag with four hundred dollars cash.

"Are you Walter Kovacs and Osterman?" Von Brauch asks Kevin after momentarily shutting off the tape.

"Yes."

Von Brauch dumps a burlap bag onto the floor and out spills a secret document with an SRI control number. From Kevin's right-hand desk drawer Von Brauch pulls out a "Tactical Air Command" document, an "Air Force base telephone directory," and a warning not to discuss classified information on nonsecured telephones. From a bag and backpack the security man pulls vinyl gloves, a lock pick, a graphite lock burner, and a G. S. Holt Pacific Telesis ID. Dougherty finds a Pac Bell security memo to the Menlo Park office, asking them to build out a cross-connect, in other words, a wiretap.

Then he spots a Pac Bell printout of a special customer. He slips into another room and phones Pac Bell's director of technical network operations. He thinks the FBI should know Kevin Poulsen may be prying into the phone service of the San Francisco Soviet consulate.

—■—

"How'd your weekend go?" Kevin's boss asks him at Sun Microsystems.

"Not so good," Kevin replies in a major understatement. Just as he had feared, after the search, Kevin was "transported" to the grungy Redwood City Jail where he shared a cell with drug dealers, thieves, and foul-smelling drunks. Gilligan didn't come through with the cash to bail him out for several hours, and the time he spent behind bars made a strong impression. Kevin told Lottor being in jail was like being dead.

Two or three hours later, Kevin's boss asks him to meet with him and his supervisor about that weekend that didn't go so well. They tell him they're pleased with his work and they're sorry this had to come up. "What were you doing?" they ask.

"I collect a lot of old phone equipment," Kevin replies cautiously, assuring them that there's no reason to worry.

His bosses aren't so sure. "Our information is things are moving faster than you think."

———■———

On February 23, 1988, FBI special agent Phillip Crumm submits the search warrant affidavit for a second search of Kevin's condominium, quoting liberally from his technical expert, Von Brauch of Pac Bell. Just how Poulsen is breaking the law isn't clear, but he certainly seems dangerous. Von Brauch states that "all or most of" the property seized at the Menlo Atherton Storage locker had been stolen from Pac Bell, and that Poulsen had an "unauthorized clandestine telephone hook-up" whose sole purpose was to gain "access to telephone lines without authorization." Crumm concludes that "Von Brauch immediately seized some of the items because of their highly classified nature."

At 10 A.M. on February 24, agents from the Federal Bureau of Investigation arrive at 1055 Pine Street, presumably figuring that at such an hour the two inhabitants will be off at work. But Kevin is home sick and Lottor is sound asleep.

An agent knocks on Lottor's bedroom door.

"Go away, I'm still sleeping!" Lottor shouts.

"Open up or we'll break down the door," yells the FBI.

Reluctantly, Lottor opens the door, and immediately realizes he's made a terrible mistake. The FBI agents spot his SRI terminal, and to Lottor, it seems as if they've spotted a bomb.

"Is that connected to SRI?" asks one of the FBI agents.

"Yes," replies Lottor.

"Do you know when it was installed?" persists one of the agents.

"No," replies Lottor.

"Do you know who installed it?"

"No."

"Was it installed when you got here?"

"Yes."

"Is that real?" asks the G-man, pointing to something plastic. Lottor wonders if he's joking about his plastic squirt machine gun, but then sees to his disbelief that he's serious. Could this be the technical level of the nation's most talented cybercops? Lottor decides he doesn't want to find out, dresses, and leaves.

To the Federal Bureau of Investigation, nearly everything in the condominium is a potential instrument of crime or terrorism. " Check out that map!" orders one FBI agent when he sees the cluster of United States Geographical Survey maps of the San Francisco Peninsula plastered across one wall. "Look it over for pinholes."

The agents meticulously examine the dozen topographic maps for telltale clues of secret hacker targets. There aren't any, but suddenly in the "switch room" one of the G-men discovers Kevin Poulsen has an FBI badge.

"Look at this!" exclaims the agent, picking it up.

"That's mine," the other agent confesses, stuffing the badge back in his pocket.

But Kevin is hardly amused when he sees the FBI is taking every last piece of electronics or scrap of paper Pac Bell hasn't already seized. They take his six antique rotary dial phones, his two ordinary phones, his Osterman and Kovacs phone bills and disconnect notices, his *Health and Fitness Magazine* business cards for Kevin A. Locke, his Al's Lock 'n' Key business card for Kevin A. Locke.

When he sees what they're taking from his roommate, he cringes. It isn't just his prized radar guns. They take his grow lights, his supersoil potting mix, his "home-made drying device," his "dry leaves," and his blue glass water pipe. They take something else that also appears unrelated to computer hacking: a videotape of Lottor having sex.

---■---

Kurt Von Brauch of Pac Bell security briefs John O'Loughlin, Sun Microsystems' head of security, on Kevin's suspected crimes. Finally, after two to three weeks of regular updates, O'Loughlin meets with Kevin's supervisor at Sun, and recommends suspending Kevin with pay. Still the supervisor wants to give Kevin a second chance. Sun, like a lot of Silicon Valley companies, was practically launched by hackers. But when Pac Bell informs Sun that Kevin never returned a terminal and modem loaned to him by SRI, the hacker loses his last defender. "You've got five minutes to grab your things and go," his boss tells him on the phone, suspending him.

But what they do next insults Kevin. Immediately after escorting him out of the building, Sun Microsystems changes all of the dial-up numbers for its thousands of networked computers. To Kevin this is an insult not only to his principles but to his ingenuity. Do they really think that would stop him?

---■---

Von Brauch of Pac Bell pounds Sun with daily updates on past intrusions traced to Kevin Poulsen. Finally, Von Brauch and another Pac Bell official ask for a meeting with Sun. Attendees include O'Loughlin, Sun's general counsel, and its vice president of Corporate Resources. Von Brauch repeats his allegations. Poulsen has broken into Pac Bell offices all over the Bay Area, picking locks and assuming identities, even infiltrating the company's downtown headquarters. He's gained detailed knowledge of wiretaps, and appears to have been accessing Pac Bell computers at will.

The officials mention Pac Bell's plan to continue using Sun's advanced workstations to manage its vast networks. The officials are uneasy when they learn that Poulsen's job has potentially given him access to the inner workings of Sun's operating system software.

"What could he do to us?" a Pac Bell official wonders out loud.

Sun can't fire Poulsen because of unproven allegations, no matter how serious they might appear. There are questions of fairness, of due process, of basic worker's rights. But the Phone Company has come to deal. The Phone Company is conducting its own investigation and wants to exact its own speedy justice. It wants Kevin Poulsen terminated. If there is a price to pay, they will gladly foot the bill. Pac Bell offers and signs the contract, accepting potential liability for the termination of one Kevin Lee Poulsen.

———■———

Day by day Von Brauch has been pushing the case. He's tracked down stolen manuals, tried to trace the origin of the TSPS console, even made numerous attempts to contact Molly Ringwald after they found a tape recording of what sounded like her voice. The physical evidence he's amassed is impressive: printouts from Pac Bell databases, Best keys and lock cores for Pac Bell central offices, lock picking tools, and a test set and coin telephone that formerly resided in a Pac Bell office.

But not everything pans out. The reel-to-reel magnetic computer tapes Von Brauch took from Poulsen's locker turn out to be SRI's property after all, but he keeps the tapes anyway, until a Pac Bell technician admits he has no idea how to extract the data. After the tapes are sent back to Neal a few days later, the detective returns them to SRI, which determines the data is stored in an ordinary Unix format. Deeming the data personal and not proprietary to SRI, the company suggests they be returned to Poulsen.

Von Brauch keeps pounding the pavement. A trip to a Palo Alto central office museum reveals thefts from July of 1987 to January of 1988. Calls to Pac Bell's 140 New Montgomery headquarters confirm missing IDs of the type found in Poulsen's locker. While examining one of Poulsen's floppy disks, Von Brauch finds a program to create IDs and a date stamp that suggests February 1987. At 140 New Montgomery, the investigator checks hundreds of pages of logbook entries for the alias G. S. Holt and finds Poulsen's signature on that February night a year before.

Kevin Poulsen seems to have committed an amazing range of

crimes. Bob Tracy of Pac Bell at San Ramon confirms there was a network break-in the previous fall, and identifies the memo taken from his computer. But what about the notes made on calendar pages in Poulsen's handwriting? Tracy could swear that they detail a conversation between him and Gerri Lyons, a Pac Bell security investigator. Had Poulsen wiretapped Tracy's phone?

Lyons, in a memo, postulates an even more disturbing possibility. Poulsen had apparently taken Cosmos printouts with handwritten notes and a diagram detailing wiretaps run through the Menlo Park office. How could he possibly know about the taps? She retraces her steps. Just weeks before, on January 25, Lyons had phoned Bill Hewins, the Menlo Park office frame chief, and told him she needed three cross-connects, or wiretaps. She gave Hewins the cable pair numbers of the wiretaps. She put it in writing, of course, but Lyons and Hewins observed all the security measures required by federal law, making it virtually impossible for anyone to seize the paper describing the FBI wiretap.

Hewins, too, believes Poulsen must have known where to look. "I did not authorize anyone to listen in on either of the previously described telephone calls," writes Hewins in his statement for the investigators. "And to my knowledge no one other than the one party I was talking to on each call was listening to these conversations." Could Poulsen have wiretapped the wiretappers?

On March 16, Neal turns the reel-to-reel magnetic tape over to Von Brauch. Pac Bell has flown in three experts from Bellcore in New Jersey to investigate, and this time the Bellcore experts and a Pac Bell technician quickly access the ordinary Unix formatted tape. The following week, March 25, Von Brauch's progress report file notes excitedly, "... *They've dumped some Pac Bell & Possibly DOD stuff.*"

Three days later, Von Brauch receives the printouts. "*Dumps consist of files of our offices and what appears to be gov. logistical plans for military maneuvers. Showed the above to John Zent, FBI. Concerned!*"

BLINDFOLDED

———■———

I t begins with a seventy-five-cent accounting error.

Clifford Stoll, a quirky astronomer with a tangle of hair and a fondness for yo-yos, is asked to investigate the minor discrepancy at his new job as a systems manager at Berkeley's Livermore Labs. Stoll dives into the task, and when he discovers a hacker roaming about the labs' computers, he decides to play a game of cat and mouse. For the next ten months Stoll and half a dozen investigative agencies trail the hacker as he slips through military, industrial, and university networks around the world.

Finally, Stoll and the team of investigators dangle a morsel the hacker can't resist, a file of bogus Star Wars information titled "SDI Network Project." The trap works. In early 1988, authorities trace the call to a Hanover apartment and arrest a number of hackers. As the prosecution unfolds, authorities learn that the trail ultimately led to East Berlin and a delivery made to a KGB agent. The rogue hackers sold hacker techniques and printouts on U.S. high-tech research to the Russians.

The long feared hacker attack on the military has finally come true. The *WarGames* formula, where the young hacker rescues the System run amok, has been flipped on its head. Now, it's a scientist who is hip and powerful, a cybercop tracking down a corrupt hacker to foil the KGB. Hackers aren't heroes anymore.

———■———

Blindfolded and carefully led into Kevin's car, Ron tries to figure out where they are headed, but soon he realizes that Kevin is driving in circles, looping around in a maze of turns to disrupt his internal compass.

When the car stops at the secret destination, Kevin dumps Ron in front so they won't be seen together while he parks. Ron removes his blindfold and does as Kevin told him, looking down at the pavement, following the fence down the driveway like a blind man. Suddenly, he hears a car.

"What are you doing here?" booms a cop who happens upon the odd scene.

Ron mumbles vaguely.

"You staking out the place?" suggests the other cop.

Ron doesn't know what to say. He's having a tough enough time just focusing his eyes on the two cops.

"What's the last thing you were doing?"

It's a straightforward question. But when Ron says he was watching a movie in Century City, fifteen miles away, the cop asks him how he got there. Ron doesn't have a very good answer other than the truth he doesn't dare tell the police—that Kevin had demanded the elaborate Dungeons & Dragons routine to keep the location of his new apartment a secret, that once again Kevin was drawing him into his world.

———■———

The run-in with the cops gets Ron to thinking. Why did he agree to be blindfolded and driven to the sparsely furnished North Hollywood apartment Kevin had rented after moving out of Lottor's condo?

A few weeks ago Kevin had phoned Ron from a West Los Angeles 7-Eleven pay phone, and waited for his old hacker pal to arrive for a chat in the convenience store lot. The moment Ron pulled up, Kevin had asked him whether he thought the feds would try to press a case against him. They talked by their cars, Ron nervous about being seen with Kevin. At first, Ron didn't think the government had anything serious, but as Kevin filled him in on the evidence they'd seized, he caught himself. He hadn't thought the Los Angeles district attorney had anything serious in his case, either.

Ron knew very well that he shouldn't be talking or meeting with Kevin. He might even be violating his three-year probation, which is just about to end. Perhaps it was just boredom that drew Ron back or the allure of hanging out with Kevin now that his elite hacking had finally earned the attention of the FBI. At first, it seemed to Ron that they were just having fun. Kevin showed him how to access Pac Bell's Premis to link customer addresses to phone numbers magically. They perused maps of the Hollywood stars' homes, plugged in the addresses of Sylvester Stallone, Barbra Streisand, and other big names and instantly retrieved their unlisted phone numbers. Sometimes there was a twist, like Madonna's second line under another woman's name. When they felt the urge, they'd dial a star just to hear a famous voice. On one call, they managed to engage the pretty actress from *All the Right Moves* and *Space Camp* in conversation. And when Ron uttered his usual, "Hi, is Joe there?" to whoever picked up the phone at Michael Jackson's unlisted number, a voice that sounded like the real pop star squeaked back, "No, not yet."

It was as if they'd discovered a way to make those kids' X-ray glasses that used to be advertised on the back of cereal boxes really work. Kevin had tapped into a ubiquitous, invisible network that linked real people with trunks full of private information. Addresses yielded phone numbers and numbers generated whole profiles of individuals, from birthdates to social security numbers and jobs. Ron isn't sure where it will end, but he is no longer sure that he can stop.

———■———

The news Kevin has heard on the grapevine isn't good. The FBI searched Gilligan's place from top to bottom and dispatched an agent to question Sean about Kevin's wiretap. From the little bits and pieces

Kevin has gleaned from Gilligan and a friend of Sean's, it appears that the FBI believes he violated national security.

At first, Kevin is in shock, stunned by how quickly his career and life have taken a nosedive. But his dismay gradually turns to angry resignation. Kevin has no doubt that Pac Bell ordered Sun Microsystems to fire him, and he believes it's hopeless to try to find another position in the computer industry. He thinks Pac Bell would just track down his new employer and have him fired again.

As to the facts of his case, Kevin knows that the truth seldom matters with hacker busts. He knows that just a year ago the nation's papers were full of headlines about a gang of hackers who moved satellites with a few keystrokes. The truth didn't matter in the satellite case either. Even when the New Jersey D.A.'s office retracted its startling assertion after experts said the stunt never happened, "the satellite caper" remained real, as *Time* wrote, "a dramatic reminder that for a bright youngster steeped in the secret arts of the computer age, anything is possible."

Kevin knows that Pac Bell and the FBI believe he can bring the System to its knees. They've got the media's ear, and Kevin believes they can make whatever unfounded charges they want. How can he fight public opinion? How can he change the fate they've already chosen for him?

━ ■ ━

Freed from the daily grind of a regular job, Kevin has plenty of time on his hands, enough to get out regularly for the first time in his life and check out clubs, the music scene, and yes, girls. It's a remarkable transition for a hacker once known for his painful shyness, but then Kevin has developed a Midas touch.

He meets his first candidate at God Save the Queen, a Gothic heavy metal club in downtown Los Angeles. Kevin wears a black turtleneck, black leather jacket, and black rubber-soled shoes, his days of wearing white behind him. He's sipping a margarita, his first and only drink of the night. He never knows when he might need to drive.

"Gotta cigarette?"

She too is in black. Hair dyed jet black, skin pasty pale, pretty, though Kevin wishes she had black lipstick too.

"No, sorry, I don't," Kevin confesses.

"You suck," spits the girl.

She watches Kevin's stunned face, then cracks a smile.

The second time they meet she takes Kevin to her apartment in Hollywood, where they listen to the angry cries of Sisters of Mercy. He asks what she does, and, as if on cue, she inquires about his chosen profession.

"I'm a computer hacker," Kevin proudly explains. "Yeah, I'm kind of into some shady stuff."

When it doesn't seem to bother her, he takes it a little further, mentioning a few of his favorite Sisters of Mercy tunes. Just as he expected, she likes them too. From there it's a small step to introduce the subject of radio stations. "KROQ used to be really good. Now they're so commercial." Kevin makes his segue. "The only difference between them and KIIS is they don't give away twenty thousand dollars every week."

Kevin lets that sink in for a second, and then continues his setup. "You ever tried one of those contests? I can win anytime I want to. I just hate listening to the music."

"Really?"

Kevin laughs. "The problem is they probably wouldn't like it if the same guy won every week."

"Well," she said eagerly, "you could always help me win."

———■———

The ethical question is easier than Kevin expected. How could anyone look at his scheme as a crime? He isn't robbing a bank. Everybody will get what they want. Well, just about everybody. Kevin looks at it like a stockbroker acting on a really good tip. In his mind there's no victim. He's only thinking about winning something that's being given away, and maybe the rent that needs to be paid.

Kevin's decision to begin hacking for cash might seem brazen in light of the FBI's heightened interest in his activities. Wouldn't he be cleaning up his act instead of inviting danger? But within Kevin's virtual world, his actions are logical. Competition breeds excellence. Kevin wants to be a great hacker. What greater challenge than to hack in the face of an ongoing FBI investigation?

Kevin has singled out something so simple it's brilliant. He'll just dial a different number from the one the station advertises. Nearly every station has a series of incoming lines, but they only give out the first number. The other numbers are linked in sequence, what the phone company calls "in hunt." So when the first line is busy, the call hunts the second line and so on down the line.

Take the second line out of hunt and it's like breaking a chain. Only a person who knows the second or third numbers can call them, a person who can look up the numbers in Cosmos, a person like Kevin Poulsen. The odds depend on how many lines are in hunt and how many lines Kevin takes out of sequence. Take out the third line of a four-line contest and your odds are about fifty-fifty; the second of a three-line contest bumps you up to 66 percent. The trick isn't simply winning, but how to win the same contest over and over again without raising suspicions.

Every Thursday at 7 A.M. KRTH 101.1 radio in Los Angeles announces what hour that day it will award its weekly trip to Hawaii and thousand-dollar prize. Kevin only takes the last two of KRTH's four lines out of hunt, affording each of his handpicked contestants a 50 percent chance of victory. Timing is critical too. Taking lines out of hunt in Cosmos won't do. Since the database only processes orders at periodic times in the day, the station might notice the nonringing lines and report the problem to Pac Bell. So Kevin goes right into Mizar, a front end to the central office's switching computer. Seconds before the contest begins, he issues the command to disconnect the hunt sequence.

The sting doesn't even require him to see his accomplice. Kevin manipulates the station's lines remotely from his apartment, while his designated contestant waits by her phone to be three-wayed to the station for the winning call. She doesn't know his real name or where he lives. It's part of the game, part of the appeal. No one, not even a girl, can get that close.

Kevin takes satisfaction in knowing that there are few purer hacks. Hacking radio prizes is about beating the System, skimming the cream of society. The station gets the advertising it wants, the public doesn't know what it's missing. What's the harm in a little demonstration of the power of the individual, a few acts of divine hacker intervention?

Just as Kevin promised, the girl in black squeals with joy for tens of thousands to hear. Kim, his second lucky winner, likes her mysterious benefactor so much that she invites him along to Oahu. Kevin likes Kim too, but sun and sand just aren't his cup of tea. When he returns to Los Angeles, Kevin decides not to mix business with pleasure. He lets the girls keep the trips and, like a gentleman, just keeps half the cash prize. Each girl has a friend, and for a while, anytime a pale young woman in black walks into KRTH to collect her trip to Hawaii and thousand-dollar prize, there's a good chance she too is Kevin Poulsen's friend.

THE MEETING

—■—

At 8 P.M. on the evening of November 2, 1988, Robert Tappan Morris, the son of a world-famous NSA cryptographer, copies a program he's written to an account known to be frequented by hackers. After watching his creation for twenty minutes or so, the young computer science graduate student leaves Cornell's Upson Hall and walks home.

On the Internet, Morris's worm is awakening. One hour and twenty-four minutes after its East Coast release, the worm squirms across the country and into the computers of a Santa Monica defense contractor, the Rand Corporation. In two hours it hits the major network gateway at the University of California in Berkeley; the Lawrence Livermore Laboratories in Berkeley and Livermore; and the Los Alamos National Laboratory in New Mexico. Then the infection erupts. The worm cycles through its arsenal of attack methods, clones itself on victim computers, and then seeks out new targets. Emergency teams at Berkeley, MIT, and other computer centers work frantically to stop the invader. Shortly before midnight, one of the Berkeley scientists on the front line fires out an electronic SOS over the crashing Net: "We are under attack from an Internet virus."

By midnight, NASA's Ames Research Center, in Silicon Valley, shuts off all communications with outside researchers, stranding

52,000 computer users. At 12:21 computers at the University of Utah are running smoothly at 5 percent of capacity. Forty minutes later, the load reaches 16 percent, and incredibly, in just another five minutes, the system tops out at 100 percent, choking to a standstill.

It will be months before the final costs of the Internet worm are tallied. Roughly 10 percent of the Internet's 60,000 hosts are infected, denying computing power to tens of thousands of the nation's top military and university researchers. The tab for the wasted time and lost computer resources is initially estimated at a staggering $15 million.

Finally, the long predicted hacker-caused disaster has come true, a dangerous worm that reproduces so widely throughout the Internet that it all but shuts down the world's largest computer network. As the story hits the front page of the *New York Times*, the hacker's motivations become clear. Morris saw his worm as a bold experiment, a test to see if he could infect the world's computers without anyone ever finding out. Later, he will admit that his schoolboy adventure turned into an international incident because he naively set his worm's internal reproduction clock at a pace that crippled the Internet within hours. The world was left to wonder what might have happened if the young hacker had actually intended to wreak havoc.

———■———

As the world cleans up after the Internet worm, Kevin weighs a strange ad he's read in a local classified newspaper. The advertiser is "looking for Tel Co. BSPs," the Bell Systems Practices that hold the secrets to controlling the phone network. Kevin can't see how it could hurt to make just a single call from a 7-Eleven phone booth, a harmless inquiry to check out the person bold enough to place the ad.

"It can't be legitimate," Ron warns as they wind down past the nightclubs and giant billboards of Sunset Boulevard to their rendezvous. "Maybe he's working for the feds," Ron hypothesizes. "Maybe the ad is aimed at us."

Kevin smiles. "Maybe it's aimed at me."

The man has agreed to meet at ten that night at what seems a peculiar choice for a hacker encounter: the rock 'n' roll Denny's on the Strip.

Just a few blocks from some of the hottest clubs in Hollywood, the twenty-four-hour chain restaurant serves as an after-hours joint for the young and restless, a front-row seat on the neon Strip.

Kevin is prepared. Ron will be Dave, and Kevin will be John on the off chance that the man in the ad isn't an aspiring hacker. The caller waits in a red booth not far from the door. He says he's notorious in the computer underground. Long brown teased hair falls past his shoulders. High cheekbones, his nose a little too straight. He doesn't look anything like the typical hacker. Could he really have a little makeup, a touch of blush, a hint of mascara? And that David Copperfield attire—a vest, silk shirt, and a cane. He says his name is Eric, and everybody in Hollywood seems to know him. Kevin and Ron order pie and coffee and watch in amazement as a continuous parade of longhaired acquaintances cruise by, half of them beautiful women, each planting a kiss on Eric's lips.

"I've cracked a major Pac Bell system at corporate offices in San Ramon," Kevin offers, figuring the disclosure will grab Eric's attention. But Eric stares off blankly and says nothing for several seconds. "You know Denny's pissed me off once," Eric casually counters, gesturing around his favorite restaurant. "I climbed up onto the roof and shut off their gas," he smiles, savoring the memory of the night's havoc. "Denny's had to stop serving hot food that night."

Eric flaunts his crimes, bragging of how he stole $10,000 worth of business phones right from under a company's nose, and tapped Tymnet's lines in broad daylight by packing a loaded .45, entering their Sherman Oaks hub office, and sticking a tape recorder on the modem line. He waxes on the perfection of his lineman's disguise and Kevin is intrigued, inquiring where he stole his Pac Bell cap and lineman's tool set. Next, Eric runs down his criminal record. "I picked up some warrants," he says. "They nailed me as the middleman in a coke deal, and I skipped bail." The stories go on and on, and while they speak more to Eric's skills as a criminal than as a hacker, there's no doubt he has a certain hard-nosed appeal.

A few minutes later, after listening to how Kevin had cracked another Pac Bell computer, Eric makes an unusual disclosure. "I've informed on people before," Eric warns his new pals. "But never to help myself."

———■———

"I don't trust him," Ron warns Kevin later that night. " You heard him talk about informing on people."

Kevin shrugs it off. He thought that was just for show. "Yeah, but what's the story with this guy? I mean he's a rock 'n' roller and a hacker on top of everything else."

Ron is the wrong person to be warning Kevin about Eric. Ron won't even join Kevin on his late-night central office visits or take the smallest physical risk. How can he possibly let him know how odd the whole scenario strikes him?

"Do you think I'd be taking a chance if I hacked with him?" Kevin asks.

Ron nods, knowing it doesn't matter what he says. "Yes."

———■———

Eric's real name was Justin Tanner Petersen, though he wasn't quite the same person since his motorcycle accident. When he woke from the anesthesia at Cedars-Sinai in Beverly Hills, Eric looked like a cyborg, a huge gap in his calf with metal pins holding together the flesh.

Several months later they cut off the leg below the knee and Eric figured the world owed him. He and his buddy Grant Straus pulled an elaborate phone-hacking, check-kiting scam on a couple of L.A. check-cashing outlets. While Straus played the front man, cashing a phony check, Eric clipped into the lines at the outlet's phone closet, intercepted their calls, and impersonated Straus's bank and the business that supposedly wrote the check. It worked perfectly until Straus tried to hit the same place two days running. The none too pleased check-cashing outlet owners responded by sending several armed thugs over to see the young check kiters. Eric and Straus were kidnapped at gunpoint, and Eric was ordered to strip in the back of a Lincoln in Beverly Hills to make it tougher to escape. As Straus was forced into his bank to pay back the victims, Eric made a dash for it in his boxers and his prosthetic leg, running down a crowded Beverly Hills sidewalk, chased by a man swinging a baseball bat.

Straus was caught and pled guilty to a felony while Eric managed to go scot-free. The lesson Eric learned from his near death experience in Beverly Hills was simple: rip off victims who don't have guns. When he needed new wheels he simply made a $2,000 down payment and drove a blue 944 Porsche off a Sunset Boulevard dealer's lot. He didn't have to worry about someone coming after him one day with a baseball bat. He created a dummy name, phony job, fake bank account and mail drop, and never made another payment.

The Porsche was Eric's turning point. He saw nothing wrong with what authorities might call fraud and grand theft. Without even trying, Eric began picking up women at traffic lights and in parking lots. He had the car, the hair, the look, all the essentials in a town of first impressions.

Nearly every night after 10 P.M., Eric would pull up in his Porsche, step out with his steel-tipped cane, and toss his keys to the valet in the Rainbow Bar and Grill parking lot. He was a glam-rock king. Shag hair with the Farrah Fawcett highlights, a deft makeup job, long nails, cowboy boots, and depending on the evening, a linen suit or torn jeans. Eric would walk to the front of the dimly lit club and make his rounds with Straus among the red Naugahyde booths, pausing when they sensed a look, exchanging a high five with a male rocker friend.

Eric's sexual prowess—he claimed to be approaching a thousand conquests—was not solely attributable to his stolen Porsche, technological mastery, or physical makeover. He had a system. Just as he had methodically wiretapped to gain his hacker access, he had diligently sought the secret to easy sex with strippers, mud wrestlers, call girls, and porn stars. Eric picked up girls not only at the Rainbow and other Hollywood hangouts but on their working nights at strip clubs. He'd sit in the back in his torn jeans with a calculated look of disinterest. His technique was irresistible, Eric figured, because strippers weren't accustomed to such indifference. Sometimes Eric had to pinch himself to remember that it was real. Had he hacked his way into Paradise?

———■———

Kevin circles the windowless building a couple of times, dressed in his now customary black. Midnight has come and gone; the last Pac Bell tech has already left with the day's billing tapes. Kevin scans the lot for normal "civilian" cars, finds it empty, and tells Eric that means there's nothing to worry about. That is unless one of the many Pac Bell cars or trucks parked in the fenced lot happens to be from a Pac Bell Switching Control Center over for a few late-night tests. As to the ground rules for Eric's first central office break-in, Kevin has already laid down the law. No stealing big-ticket items until they get to know one another a little better.

They hop the fence and crouch behind the trash dumpster, Eric's heart racing as he watches Kevin slip up to pick the lock. With Eric close behind, Kevin tiptoes through the dark building, tiny red and white lights on the frames twinkling like stars in a dark sky. The warning signs only heighten Eric's excitement. He's been messing with phones since he was a kid, and now, finally, he's stepped into the labyrinth. But huddled over a Simplex lock at room 314, Kevin is oblivious to his epiphany. He chose the room because it's locked, because it's there. Kevin is good with Simplex locks because he practiced picking one at home hundreds of times. His fingers sense the feedback from the lock's buttons. He knows the lock's limits, knows each button can be invoked only once in the combination. It's only a matter of patience and time. Five minutes later the door swings open. Everything looks ordinary at first. The usual metal desks . . .

What are those odd-looking terminals in the corner?

They look like old IBM 3270 terminals. The monitor catches his eye, with its dated built-in streamer cartridge drive to the right of the screen and the nearby black controller the size of two refrigerators. Kevin's never seen anything like it, certainly not in a CO. He takes a seat, grabs the nearest manual, and begins leafing through it:

Kevin is interested because he knows NTTs are numbered test trunks—a way of getting control of a phone line. He reads on about how the system does decibel and electrical checks on circuits, hits the on button, and begins following directions. The manual says he needs to enter his commands onto a cartridge tape, so he rummages around the desk, finds one of the blank, hand-sized cartridges, and pops it in the slot. A target? The number pops into his head, the pay phone he's used at the gas station at Coldwater and Roscoe, near his folks' house.

One step at a time. He searches the manual's directory and finds something called a SAS unit in Lankershim, the central office nearest the target pay phone. He enters the number of the unit, the corresponding test trunk, and the phone number of the data line of the SAS unit.

Kevin types a long series of keystrokes and watches a graphic unfold on his screen, symbolizing his data line connecting to the Lankershim SAS unit. Next, he types in the number of the phone sitting by him, and like magic the phone rings, the system's callback security routine.

"Hello," Kevin answers cheerily to no one, pleased with himself.

Eric glances over briefly, then continues surveying the computer equipment he plans to steal on a future trip. "Do you think this is a VGA or a CGA monitor?" Eric thoughtfully inquires.

Kevin ignores him and enters the target pay phone number. And listens.

KERCHUNK.

The thick, scratching click means his phone just accessed the Lankershim test trunk. The silence lasts a few seconds, then there's a clear audible click followed by a fainter one.

It sounds alive.

Kevin's screen comes to life, drawing a graphic display of a terminal board connected by lines to a phone circuit.

Could it be? Could it be a wiretap?

Ten minutes. That's all it takes. Kevin performs one of the maintenance tests to check the resistance on the pay phone line. Satisfied, he replaces the cartridge with the one that was there before and sticks the new one in the middle of a stack. Kevin takes a long look at the large controller. This is the brains, the device that's communicating to the Lankershim SAS unit. Kevin knows the unit has dialback security to make certain the caller is a central office employee. But he doesn't see why he needs the cumbersome controller. Why can't he clone the machine's function? His mind is working through the problem.

I'll cut through the extraneous layers. Find the protocol. There are ways of getting around dialback security.

Meanwhile, Eric continues merrily pricing out equipment. Kevin joins him and points thoughtfully at the SAS controller and terminal. "I think that's a Remob."

Captain Crunch, the legendary phone phreak, mused years ago about a Remob, a phone phreak's dream. You'd be able to dial in, punch in any phone number, and have a covert, remote computerized wiretap. The Remote Observation Machine seemed the stuff of fantasy, a Wizard's wand or Lancelot's sword, the Holy Grail that made the whole journey of discovery worthwhile.

"If that's not a Remob," Kevin says reverently, "it's the closest thing to it I've ever seen."

THE WIRETAP MACHINE

—■—

Ex-COMPUTER WHIZ KID HELD

ON NEW FRAUD COUNTS

Kevin reads the December 17, 1988, *Los Angeles Times* article with interest, even if the story about a notorious hacker is about another Kevin. Like any other self-respecting Los Angeles–bred hacker, Kevin knows the legend of Kevin Mitnick. Rumored break-ins to NORAD, the North American Defense Command, tales of judges and probation officers who had their credit records scrambled and phones disconnected, and most colorful of all, credit for inspiring the movie *WarGames*.

Few of the more outrageous charges have ever been proven, but this time, the government seems to have something solid on Mitnick. The hacker has been charged with causing $4 million in damages to a Digital Equipment Corporation computer, and a magistrate has ordered him held without bail, ruling that "when armed with a keyboard he posed a danger to the community."

When armed with a keyboard? The phrase angers Kevin. Nothing irritates Kevin more than government hype, and to him the Mitnick case reeks. Who has Mitnick hurt? he wonders. When will the $4 million figure cooked up by the government be knocked down twentyfold? In the days following Mitnick's arrest, the media hype builds to a frenzy.

Claims of threats to national security, and a page one *L.A. Times* article headlined "COMPUTER AN UMBILICAL CORD TO HIS SOUL: 'DARK SIDE' HACKER SEEN AS 'ELECTRONIC TERRORIST'"

It all starts to click. The sensationalist stories, the trumped-up charges, holding Mitnick without bail. Kevin sees the same thing about to happen to him. That's why he thinks the feds are making all the noise about national security. If they can get him held without bail they can win before they've begun. The government doesn't have to convict him, he figures. He'll already be in jail.

—■—

Kevin is back in room 314 at the Sunset central office. He's alone tonight.

He repeats the sequence of his previous visit, powering up the computer terminal, inserting a blank cartridge, and setting up the connection. Then, he clips a butt set onto the lines behind the terminal, listens until he finds the right line, and replaces it with a tape recorder. He's got the goods.

Back at his apartment, Kevin prepares to play back the keystrokes and commands he recorded at Sunset. He boots his terminal and dials a test line that produces minimal noise. He attaches alligator clips from the output jack on his recorder to his phone line, hits the play button, and types the modem answer command. Characters flash across the screen, and then the security callback sequence begins. Kevin takes notes by hand, deciphering a conversation between the controller in the Sunset central office and the SAS unit in the Lankershim central office. There are five transactions necessary to take control of a SAS unit to wiretap, and Kevin captures them all the first time, rewinding the tape and repeating it once more, just to be sure.

—■—

Kevin believes true hackers are free from ordinary human failings and ethical shortcomings. His is a simple hypothesis developed from personal experience and bits and pieces he's read. True hackers, in Kevin's mind, are good by definition, refined by the noble quest for electronic information, kung fu masters who use their lethal skills sparingly and wisely.

Kevin believes this credo so strongly that he can rationalize nearly anything. He can't know how much Eric shares his principles, and whether he too will one day develop into a "responsible" hacker. But then, as he thinks over the challenge, he sees it as a manageable problem. Kevin is a Dungeon Master. There's no reason he can't keep SAS a secret. Kevin starts by giving Eric limited Cosmos access and is pleased to see that Eric seems satisfied, content to wait until his more experienced mentor feels he's ready to move up to the next level. When Eric wants something he can't find through Cosmos, he invites Kevin over to his apartment. There, Kevin taps into the Pac Bell databases and plucks out the desired information, carefully erasing his temporary files in case Eric might later try to retrieve any clues he might have inadvertently left behind.

———■———

"Check out this groovy view," Eric says with a laugh, inviting Kevin and Ron onto the balcony of his new "executive studio."

Across the street looms the windowless, textured brick wall of the Sunset central office, an imposing, three story-structure shrouded by palms. The balcony provides a clear view of the back door and the fenced lot crowded with Pac Bell vans and cars. Incredibly, Eric has rented an apartment one hundred feet from a Pac Bell central office, proving that if he can't learn it by computer, he'll learn it by breaking and entering. Even Kevin is impressed by his commitment. They meet a little after midnight at the studio, survey the central office parking lot through Eric's binoculars, and then head over. Kevin tells him not to worry about being caught. Improbable as it sounds, the alarms on the doors generally go to an unmanned center.

The new partners settle into a routine, breaking and entering several times a week without fear of capture, claiming the switching offices as their private stomping grounds. They bring candy bars and chips and even scrounge food left behind by employees in the office fridge. The routine seldom varies: read manuals, examine systems, and rifle employee desks for passwords. Pac Bell makes it easy. Company policy requires that passwords be random. That's why Kevin and Eric know just what to look for, something strange like !*12$FG#.

Having so far largely played the role of a spectator, Ron surprises himself by letting Kevin and Eric talk him into joining them on one of the trips. Barely inside, the deafening clatter sets him on edge. Everywhere he looks are bold signs warning "Doors Alarmed!"

"What do you think are our odds of getting caught?" he nervously asks a calm Eric. "Oh, about one in ten." The rocker chuckles.

Ron runs for the door and clambers over the fence, his mind flashing back to his few weeks in jail. But while Ron isn't willing to take the physical risks that Kevin and Eric delight in, he finds the nightly adventures irresistible. Nearly every time Kevin meets Eric, Ron does too. Sometimes Ron just hangs out with Eric at his studio, trying to make sense of the spare furniture, the Nagel posters of perfectly shaped women, the single poster of a red 911 Porsche, and the video camera on a tripod next to the sliding closet mirrors and the bed.

On one visit, Ron watches Eric disappear into the bathroom to fix his hair, a half-hour operation that entails a wide variety of sprays, mousses, and two salon-quality blow dryers. While Ron busies himself watching Eric's large-screen television, he notices an extensive video collection, a couple of documentaries on computers, and then something else. Forty tapes or more, with different girls' names. Alex, Barbara, Cynthia . . .

Hair freshly teased, Eric emerges from his salon.

"What's this?" Ron asks.

Eric smiles and pops one of the videos into the VCR, a short, action feature, starring Eric and a girl tied to his bed. As the last moans fade, Eric explains how his image was carefully planned. "I figured it out. This is the person I am, this is the life I want to fit into.

"I used to be almost preppy," Eric says, showing Ron a snapshot of himself with a beard and trimmed hair. The man in front of Ron might as well be another person. The long teased hair, the John Lennon glasses, the carefully selected rags from trendy Melrose district boutiques.

"Your nose was different," Ron remarks.

"Yeah, I had it done."

———■———

One evening at Sunset while walking through the frame room Kevin and Eric notice a small rectangular metal box on the floor.

"HIKAMIN," spell the letters on the box, Kevin immediately recognizing that it's a digital number recorder, or DNR. There's a business card taped to it with a reference to John Venn of Pac Bell security. Kevin writes it all down, notes the office equipment number the box is connected to, and walks over to a Cosmos terminal and pulls up the record. It's all there, the telephone number of the tap and the office equipment number it's connected to on the frame.

Huh? No cable pair?

Most phone lines are coded so the frameman can know which set of wires or pairs go over which cable. But the DNR tap isn't like a normal phone line. It's more like a parasite, just hooking into someone else's cable pair on the frame. Since the tap doesn't leave the office, it doesn't need to be assigned a cable pair.

Kevin returns to find Eric disconnecting a butt set from the line the tap is connected to. The target. The number being tapped.

Kevin smiles wryly, wondering how he'll ever control Eric. He never asked for Kevin's permission. He just clipped in and dialed Pac Bell's automatic number announcement service to identify the subject of the tap.

"You ANA'd it," Kevin says incredulously. "You *know.*"

"Yeah," Eric shrugs. "I just had to know who it was."

———■———

It's a question of hacker ethics. Kevin has no choice but to investigate the tap he found with Eric in Sunset, for if the subject of the wiretap is a hacker, Kevin knows that he has a moral obligation to warn him the Phone Company is listening. Thanks to Eric, Kevin has the target's phone number, which makes it trivial for Kevin to look up his phone service in Cosmos. Henry Spiegel is his name, and he's got several phone lines. Running Spiegel through a few on-line databases turns up a criminal record, though Kevin can't make out for certain whether he's a hacker. Still, the abundance of phone lines is more than enough to warrant Kevin's continued investigation.

A thick SAS directory Kevin swiped from room 314 lists every Pac Bell service area in Southern California. Kevin finds Spiegel's Sunset central office, scans for the "no," or numbered test trunk, associated with Spiegel's prefix, selects the designated data phone number, and dials it with his modem.

First, he has to beat the callback security. As the system prepares to call back Kevin to ensure he's at an authorized location, Kevin turns off his modem but stays on the line. The instant the SAS unit dials the authorized line, Kevin flips back on his modem. Hacker parking is what it's called. The SAS unit is duped into thinking it's connected to the authorized line.

Kevin dials Spiegel's "monitor" phone number. He's in control now—and not just of Spiegel's tap. He can wiretap anyone served by Spiegel's prefix. He can surf from line to line, tapping dozens of people in a matter of minutes. And with a little clever programming, Kevin automates the process. He enters the SAS and test trunk numbers for his favorite central offices into a simple program. Now all he has to do is type the number he wishes to tap.

It's not a perfect remote wiretapping system. There's an audible click on older, electromechanical switches, and he can't tap until a call is in progress. But Kevin is happy to discover that alternatives exist. Northern Telecom's new digital switches—the DMS, or Digital Multiplexing System—have no such limitations. Kevin can tap whenever he wants in total silence on a DMS switch—before or during a call.

And Kevin can put up lengthy taps on electromechanical switches too. Years ago, when he overheard a lineman asking a frameman to put up some SAS shoes on a line, he was listening to a phone company method to test a line. Now, Kevin can put up SAS shoes too—to wiretap. He just tells the frameman to shoe the line he wants tapped—replace the line's lightning protector with a shoe plug and connect the other end to the test trunk Kevin's dialed. Shoes stay up a few days, until a frameman notices them and bothers to take them down. And there's no click.

Half the pleasure of wiretapping by computer is simply knowing you've got the power. Kevin uses SAS as a third eye, a remote polygraph. When he sees an item that interests him in the classifieds, he phones the seller and asks a few questions. The man names a high price and claims he can't budge because he's selling it for a friend. That's when Kevin wiretaps his line. When the owner calls the seller, Kevin listens in and, just as Kevin suspected, the friend reveals he's providing the item for considerably less than the seller had represented. Kevin passes on the item, pleased he could wiretap the truth.

There are other things he could do with SAS, but Kevin has limits. SAS is the ultimate information tool. If Kevin wants to know how something secret works, he can simply listen to the subject's phones or data lines and pick up key words and phrases that might later prove invaluable. Someone with access to SAS could listen in on law enforcement lines and monitor how the officers call in to get information: names, badge numbers, IDs, and lingo. Armed with that inside information, how hard would it be to social engineer the details on a warrant or other secrets?

———■———

Kevin drops in on the tap at the Sunset office with SAS and waits. A few minutes later, he hears Henry Spiegel dial and start talking to a friend about the Hollywood rock scene. Kevin listens a little longer and then drops off the line. It's a question of ethics. He won't need to notify the subject of the surveillance after all. Henry Spiegel, as far as Kevin can tell, is not a hacker.

HOME SHOPPING

—■—

The three of them meet at about 10 P.M. at Eric's Sunset pad. Kevin arrives in his customary black in time to watch Eric pull on his Pac Bell jacket and cap. As Ron watches Eric strap on his heavy leather lineman's belt stuffed with tools, he wonders whether half the fun for Eric is in getting dressed.

"You want to come along?" Eric teases him.

"No thanks."

"Then keep Frecia company, OK?"

"Sure," Ron replies warily, glancing at the shapely, olive skinned girl curled up by the TV. Frecia is Eric's true love, a pretty, dark-haired girl from New Mexico with a nine-to-five job at a financial firm. Eric met her at the Rainbow, but she's different from the other women that taxi in and out of his bed. Eric believes they have a relationship based on trust.

From the balcony, Ron watches Kevin and Eric open the back door to Sunset with a key Kevin cut for the lock. Ron can't see what happens next, but he knows what's up. The two intruders simply walk up to the board and find the keys. Within a couple of minutes, Ron hears the Pac Bell van start up in the lot, and then watches it pull slowly through the gate.

Tonight Kevin will test the limits of his hacker code. The opportunities are just too tempting to resist any longer. Pac Bell maintains an on-line list of every single piece of equipment it owns. It's like the Home Shopping Network, only instead of dialing 1-800 all they have to do is back up a Pac Bell van and load in whatever they fancy. After watching Eric's apartment fill up with equipment pilfered from Pac Bell, Kevin has finally decided to relax his self-proclaimed prohibition against blatant theft. This evening, he's asked Eric to join him on a heist at a central office that holds a large Unix-based minicomputer that he fancies. Kevin has always wanted to own his very own minicomputer.

Frecia is reading *David Copperfield,* and though Ron is ostensibly watching TV they soon strike up a conversation. Ron wants to find out whether she knows Eric's real name and background. She claims to know nothing about his true identity or past, but she knows what night he goes to which club, and without the slightest hint of irony she lays out his weekly entertainment schedule. Ron notes that not too many nights are left open for Frecia.

"We have an open relationship," Frecia observes optimistically, adding that she knows all about Eric's kinky films. "I told him, 'I know you have this camera and I don't want to be in one of your movies.'"

Ron doesn't say anything.

"You want to see one?"

"No thanks," Ron replies, certain that Eric has asked her to set him up to see how far he might go.

Three hours later Eric and Kevin return in high spirits. Kevin's computer had turned out to be even bulkier and heavier than they expected, and they laugh about how they had barely been able to hoist the hulking machine onto Pac Bell's van. Eric's take was substantial too: a couple of loaded personal computers, a few printers, and two fax machines. So what if a sheriff was parked up the road. What could be suspicious about a couple of Pac Bell employees in a company van backed up to the central office door?

———————■———————

Soon after his evening with Frecia, Ron finally feels comfortable enough to volunteer his unlisted home phone number to Eric.

"That's OK." Eric grins. "I've already got it."

Ron shrugs it off, chalking it up to hacker curiosity. But Kevin is troubled by the revelation, especially since he never gave Eric access to phone systems he'd need to deploy to find Ron's unlisted number. And there are other inexplicable events. Kevin begins to notice messages missing from his voice mail. Friends call and ask whether he's received their messages.

Then, Kevin discovers that Pac Bell security is investigating unauthorized activity in an advanced Pac Bell system. It's the very same one he accessed at Eric's apartment when he performed one of his favors, the same one that he refused to grant him access to until he knew him better. The system is being accessed in strange ways at odd hours of the night—all the signs of an amateur on the loose. Kevin investigates the intrusions on-line for a couple of days but finds nothing.

"Did you tap your own data line when I came over?" Kevin asks Eric on the phone.

"Well, if I did do it, I had the best of intentions."

Like a good boy, Eric had willingly agreed to the restrictions on his access, invited Kevin and Ron over to do favors at his apartment, and then cleverly tape-recorded everything that went out over his data and phone lines: accounts and passwords for high-level Pac Bell systems, Kevin's voice mail passcode, Ron's phone number, and perhaps more.

"'Best of intentions.' What do you mean best of intentions?" Kevin demands to know.

"Well, you know we'd all get along better if I had the same access you do."

Doesn't Eric see? He hasn't given him access because he can't handle access. In Kevin's mind, Eric's screwing around on Pac Bell's computers will likely boil down to one of two equally disastrous results. One, Eric might actually crash a system, a catastrophe for which Kevin believes he would undoubtedly be blamed. Or, two, his foolish wanderings might get Kevin caught.

"Look, Eric, I told you I was not going to give you things until I knew you better," Kevin tries to reason with Eric. "Tapping us doesn't encourage me to share."

That's when Eric begins listing what he believes Kevin has been withholding from him, a long list of things discovered on their nightly excursions, including that lone secret Kevin had found in room 314 of the Sunset central office—SAS.

"I'll get them one way or another," Eric warns.

———■———

Kevin's stormy relationship with Eric creates what for anyone else would be a dilemma. On the one hand, he's increasingly convinced that he can't trust Eric with SAS or other powerful phone company systems. On the other hand, he believes he's too involved and responsible simply to walk away from the problem. But Kevin believes he has a solution to his predicament: continue breaking into central offices with Eric, keep an eye on him, and keep controlling his access.

Ron acts almost as Kevin's undercover agent, secretly reporting back to Kevin on his findings. He begins hanging out at Eric's apartment and meeting his friends, a motley collection of musicians, coke dealers, and small-time cons. One night, when Ron returns with Eric to his apartment, they're surprised by an elderly black homeless woman on the stairs. Eric whips out a gun. "Get the fuck out of here or I'll blow your head off!" he yells, pressing the barrel to her head. Guns are part of Eric's trip. He brags of being able to hire a hit man for $5,000, and proudly shows Ron the holster he keeps hidden by his bed, ready to draw if someone makes an unannounced visit. For kicks, Eric fires his gun at random buildings or industrial tanks. He isn't worried about getting caught. He has a theory that with all the city noise you can always pop off a single shot in Hollywood. Late one night, seconds after leaving Eric's apartment, Ron hears a shot and flinches. "He's trying to off you," Kevin jokes when he hears the story.

To pay the rent, Eric sells phony birth certificates to gypsies and other small-time cons. For entertainment he wiretaps. When two cute girls move in down the hall, Eric taps them for a few days until he concludes they're just a couple of "coke whores." He keeps a tap on the Denny's pay phone live on a butt set near the television, just loud enough to hear people dialing, so if a call sounds interesting he can pick it up and listen. One afternoon Ron is surprised to hear the faint sound of a familiar woman's voice on Eric's butt set.

"Oh that's Frecia," Eric explains dryly.

"Don't you think she'd be kind of upset if she knew you were tapping her phone?"

"She knows," responds Eric, grabbing the receiver to listen in. "She doesn't care."

———■———

The man in the Pac Bell uniform arrives one morning at the Mutual of Omaha building on the corner of Wilshire and La Brea, near the target's central office. In the basement he finds what he's looking for, a large, unlocked telephone room, and inside a scramble of wires that will hide his contraption.

The ultimate target is the dial-up commercial network Telenet, brimming with accounts and passwords of some of the most exclusive on-line systems in the nation. The goal: a virtually endless tap into the heart of the information superhighway. Part of the tap is a custom piece of hardware built by a friend of Eric's that will answer a call. Eric's job is to connect the device to the line and hide it in the telephone room amid the countless wires.

Between them, only Kevin knows how to place the order in Cosmos, how to build in the circuit for the Mutual of Omaha line and set up the bridge lifter. He's creating a virtual phone extension that juts off one of Telenet's main lines to the Mutual of Omaha line Eric tapped. From there Kevin electronically connects the tapped line to Eric's apartment. It's the same method Kevin used to tap Sean—plus an additional line to Eric's apartment for security.

Eric dedicates two PCs he stole from Pac Bell to the task. He dials the new number Kevin created, hears the initial "swoosh," the silence of the dead Mutual of Omaha line, the ringing of the second line, and then, once again, the "swoosh" that means Telenet is in his control. Within seconds, data streams down the parallel screens. The two PCs make it possible to listen to both sides of the digital conversation—the passwords and accounts typed in by users, as well as the system information logged by the host computer.

Several times a week, Kevin scrolls through the sea of data: passwords to Bank of America's home banking system, TRW Credit, Information America, Nexis and Lexis, and even the California Department of Motor Vehicles. It's up to Kevin to learn the numerous commands to transform the DMV system into a veritable cornucopia of information. Within a couple of days, Kevin returns to Eric's and shows him what he's learned. Kevin can search licenses for everything from motorcyles to government vehicles to find names, birthdates, weight, height, eye color, addresses, and warrants. Or he can enter a name and get similar information—and a license number. Not a bad investigative tool for a hacker who's often wondering if someone's following him.

One day, Eric finds what seem to be passwords and codes for electronic money transfers at major banks. Within days, Kevin quickly determines that three different people in three different departments have to issue approvals to transfer the money to a set list of payees. The odds are against Kevin ever picking up all three passwords, but then the odds didn't count on Kevin poring through the data stream night after night.

Sure enough, Kevin uncovers all three passwords and codes for three different people in three different departments in Security Pacific bank. A search on Nexis reveals no published reference to a successful major electronic money transfer fraud. Could there be an additional review once the transaction is completed? What might he have overlooked?

There are some basic preparations that need to be made, like setting up an offshore account. But there are other problems he has to solve that he's unlikely to learn about on-line. Kevin suspects there must be other checks in place that might make it difficult to withdraw a large sum from a bank once it's transferred. There are probably a dozen ways to fail he hasn't even anticipated. Still, Ron and Eric are impressed at how far he's gotten, and how he just keeps plugging away at the problem. Kevin just won't let it go.

RISKY BUSINESS

———■———

Eric's got a girl over at his apartment. Erica's her name. She's got the Hollywood look. Silicone breasts, cortisone lips, thigh-high patent leather boots with six-inch heels, and long black gloves that ride past the tracks on her arms. Eric cuffed and manacled her once and used his little electrical clamps and the other tools in his black bag. But they're friends now. Erica is a junkie and a hard drinker and not particularly choosy about her company.

Erica is listening to his Denny's tap when suddenly Eric points to a number on his computer screen. "See that?"

Eric has pulled up the Cosmos record of the target of the tap he found in Sunset with Kevin. "These guys are in trouble," he says.

Erica looks over at the number on the screen. She can't believe her eyes.

"Fuck, dude, I know that number!"

———■———

Erica pounds on the locked door of the unfinished house where she rooms just across the Strip, a half block down Martel Street and around the corner from the rock 'n' roll Denny's.

Inside, Henry Spiegel checks his watch. Midnight. She knows he doesn't have drugs. Could she want money? But when Spiegel opens the door he's surprised. The guy with Erica is cleaner than most of her boyfriends. Sure, he has long hair and torn jeans, but he doesn't look like a junkie. And as Spiegel pushes aside his papers and magazines to make space to sit in the front room, the only one where carpet covers the plywood floor, he senses the man is intelligent. Spiegel decides to hear him out.

The man tells him about the surveillance on his line and Spiegel nods and asks a few questions. But Erica's friend won't talk much about himself. Spiegel thanks him for the warning, walks them to the door, and then trudges back up the plywood stairs to the mattress in the attic cluttered with his albums and old junk. He'll worry about the wiretap tomorrow.

———■———

"I don't have to say SHIT!" screams Erica.

Spiegel is handcuffed in another room. Several Secret Service agents, a few Sprint agents, and a couple of LAPD vice officers rip through his file cabinets and piles of paper searching for evidence.

They want to know about Spiegel and the phones. Erica knows about the phones. She and Spiegel have been tight for a year, ever since he found her nodding out in a plate of chicken-fried steak at the rock 'n' roll Denny's. Erica is afraid if she doesn't talk they're going to beat Spiegel.

"I know my rights!" yells Erica. "I don't have to say shit!"

Spiegel knows that the Secret Service normally doesn't get involved in internal phone company matters. But as he soon learns, the lead agent's boss owes a friend at Sprint a favor. Nobody can quite figure out how Spiegel has been able to run up about $150,000 in unpaid long distance calls.

Spiegel has programmed several computers with Sprint and MCI calling card numbers. All told, he has about thirty lines running into his house, a boiler room operation for ten ex-cons and Erica to telemarket investments in his latest scam, Domestic Gold Fund II. His scam isn't high-tech—he's just figured out a system to keep getting new long distance charge cards without ever paying a single bill.

Listening to the Secret Service agents threaten to beat him up, Spiegel thinks how lucky he was to have received the warning and been prepared for the raid. He already senses he's not going to get busted. Without Eric's timely tip, he might actually be in trouble.

———■———

Henry Spiegel has the look of a Svengali. Six feet tall, he has strong, square features, a thick ponytail, and the muscles of a man a decade younger than his near fifty years. Spiegel lifts weights and often wears sandals, black sweats, and a gold chain around his neck. Once a promising athlete, Spiegel dropped out of UCLA and began hanging out at the Whiskey or the Roxie on the Strip to watch the girls, listen to the bands, and shoot dope with the musicians.

By the mid-seventies Spiegel kicked heroin and started an escort service. He hit the big time in 1984 after Los Angeles vice officers arrested thousands of prostitutes in town for the Olympics. Just as he had suspected, Spiegel found that many of the phone numbers of the big Yellow Pages escort ads had been disconnected. He called Pac Bell and said he wanted to get the numbers turned on. Often, there was a balance due of a few hundred dollars, but Spiegel gladly paid a few hundred in return for an ad that normally cost several thousand dollars.

Soon, Spiegel was paying for thirty escort phone numbers all call-forwarded to his house on Martel. Girls would call the Yellow Pages ads looking for work, and Spiegel quickly had nearly three dozen on call—blondes, brunettes, blacks, Hispanics, Asians. Spiegel charged $411.76 an hour for their services, the odd figure a total of $350 plus a hefty credit card service charge. He grew a handlebar mustache, sported velour sweatsuits and fat gold rings encrusted with diamonds. Spiegel acquired all the pimp trimmings. A big car, a big hat, a big money clip, a cellular phone he carried in an alligator pouch, and a ruby and diamond bracelet that spelled his name like a marquee. But nothing lasts forever in Hollywood. The legendary Madam Alex was busted, and as Heidi Fleiss would learn years later, Madam Alex liked to talk. It seemed

Spiegel's companion, Winter, also turned tricks for Madam Alex. One evening at the rock 'n' roll Denny's, Winter introduced Spiegel to her new friend, Megan McElroy, a blond, attractive girl looking for work. Detective Megan McElroy was hired, and Henry Spiegel, aspiring Los Angeles pimp, was busted and on his way to six months in Los Angeles County Jail.

■

It's a three-way phone conversation and Spiegel has no idea how the call has been placed. "We run the phone company," announces Eric, introducing himself and one John Smith—Kevin's latest alias—on the line. "Trust us and you won't get into any trouble."

Spiegel has a feeling that this John Smith has another name, but he knows it isn't his place to ask questions. Hadn't Eric saved his ass by tipping him off to the tap on his line and the impending Secret Service raid? Maybe these guys really are the phone company. Whoever they are, trust doesn't have much to do with their budding relationship. Soon after the introduction, John Smith starts phoning Spiegel on his own, casually dropping key phrases Spiegel remembers saying to other people on previous calls in the day. Spiegel figures Smith is wiretapping him, and he gets the message. Smith isn't the kind of guy you can easily bullshit.

Spiegel decides to play along with the game. Mr. Smith likes to listen, and so when he phones, Spiegel lets him eavesdrop on anyone else who happens to call. One of those callers is David Star.

■

David Star is an actor, a player of bit parts. Like thousands of other desperate Hollywood hopefuls, the short, overweight man vainly presses his airbrushed publicity photos upon anyone who will look. But the real-life role Star pursues is as a great hacker and phone phreak. He brags of phenomenal contacts with the National Security Agency, the supersecret U.S. spy agency. Star carries a security badge and drives an old, undercover detective's car. He claims to have worked for Paramount Studios, and if he meets a girl, he's Dave Star Productions, a rising Hollywood movie producer. Spiegel finds Star a source of amusement, and often shares with him little scraps of information he picks up. When he tells Star of his recent encounters with Mr. Smith, Star smells an opportunity. Maybe Smith could hack Pac Bell and turn on the dead Yellow Pages lines for free?

The next time Mr. Smith calls Spiegel mentions the scheme. Spiegel's Olympic Yellow Pages scam led to Pac Bell issuing passwords, making it impossible to activate a dead line by paying the outstanding bill.

"Can you get the passwords for the ads?" Spiegel asks.

"Yeah, I could do that," Kevin says, thinking through the problem. "But I could do it another way."

"What do you mean?"

"We could turn it into a business for ourselves."

Kevin's mind races through the possibilities. He's thinking through the problem all the way to the working girls. To him it's the perfect hack, creating an electronic opportunity without any real victims. But when Kevin tells Ron about his scheme a few days later, his old friend reacts angrily. How could he conspire with a pimp he's never even seen? Is he crazy? Does he want to get arrested?

There's a disconnect taking place in Kevin's mind and he doesn't see it happening. This time his rationalizations can't possibly squeeze his conduct between the margins of his hacker code. Kevin is not just talking about fixing contests. He's planning to go into business with a pimp. But Kevin doesn't think about the sleazy side of prostitution. He convinces himself that the girls are escorts who are freely choosing to sell their favors, and that since he's only providing electronic services he's not really involved.

Kevin listens to his friend's concerns and then tells him why there's no danger in running an outcall escort service. Kevin will orchestrate every move. Spiegel thinks he's wiretapping him, thinks he knows his every word and thought. Spiegel doesn't even know his name. Smith hasn't even trusted him with a voice mail number, nor will he ever see him in person. He's nothing more than a voice on the phone, an ear always listening, the anonymous Watchman.

The man isn't listed in the phone book, and Eric thinks that's a good sign. He drives his Porsche to the elegant Beverly Hills address, and is impressed by the spacious office and sexy blond girl Friday. The Investigator greets him with a warm handshake. He has a round, sturdy face, tanned Mediterranean skin, hair cropped close like a golf green, and an infectious smile. His clothes convey the same ease: stonewashed designer jeans, cowboy boots, and a $150 cotton sport shirt that reeks of Beverly Hills. He has the gift of manners, and he quickly dispatches his girl Friday to pour Eric a drink.

Eric made the connection through a woman he picked up at the Rainbow who after hearing about his skills as a hacker and wiretapper said she knew just the person he should meet. She couldn't have been more right. The Investigator immediately takes to his intelligence, wit, and humor, even his savoir faire with the ladies. In Eric, the Investigator sees the ideal undercover man, someone capable of a sit-down dinner with the most prominent people or a wild night on the Strip with the rockers. Surveillance would be second nature. Eric is an unbelievable driver and he knows the streets of Hollywood better than any cab driver. That's the cover story anyway, the one the Investigator rehearses, the one for the cops or the feds if that day ever comes. The truth is the Investigator wants Eric for his access to Pac Bell and DMV databases. And his willingness to break the law.

———■———

"Where are you? Wake up, you fucking longhair!" booms the Investigator's voice on Eric's voice mail.

It's a little after two in the afternoon, too early for Eric. The Investigator has a job for Eric that requires his hardware skills: one of Heidi Fleiss's most frequently requested hookers, a blond, leggy bombshell featured in *Playboy*'s Girls of Summer. Her rich, coke-snorting sugar daddy boyfriend wants to know what she's up to.

Eric opens the bridging box outside the blonde's apartment, scans the pairs, and places the transmitter on her phone line. A few feet away, he parks a car with a receiver and a twelve-hour voice-activated tape recorder. Two grand is his take for the wiretap. Not much, considering he knows the Investigator charges $10,000 for the service, but then again the Investigator is discreet and has some heavy clients. Eric only listens to a little of the tape as he transfers it to regular cassettes for the client's easy listening. He's not the least bit surprised by what he hears. She's sleeping with some other guy.

Almost daily, the Investigator pages Eric with a new job, leaving him names, addresses, social security numbers, whatever leads the client has provided. Sometimes it's just a license plate number. Eric runs DMV records, pulls credit reports, searches for unlisted numbers and phone records. With swiped access codes and passwords it's all free. Eric organizes the database hits, types a few notes, and then faxes a nicely formatted report to his employer. That leaves time for errands, perhaps half an hour at Sunset Tanning, a short nap, and a little TV before he grooms for his evening on the Strip.

———■———

Kevin is intrigued by his venture into Hollywood prostitution. Who would ever imagine that a computer geek, obsessed with electronics and bits and bytes, could control a world of sex? But Kevin doesn't see call girls. He sees phone numbers and wasted Yellow Pages ads. An opportunity to use his mastery of the phone system to create a fully automated sex service.

Kevin juices the fifty Yellow Pages ad numbers that Henry Spiegel has told him are disconnected, but accessing the $200,000 worth of advertisements is just the start. Next, Kevin creates a system for Speigel's escorts to respond to johns' phone requests. Voice mail is ideal for the job, so Kevin wiretaps a data line at a branch office of American Voice Retrieval to snare the password and log-in commands. Quickly mastering the menu-driven system, Kevin creates a dozen voice mail boxes. Simply forwarding the incoming calls to his voice mail boxes won't do. Toll records would be generated by the longer calls, and Pac Bell might wonder why disconnected numbers are generating bills. But what about a series of short call forwards, splitting one toll call into two or more local calls? Kevin creates new digital DMS phone numbers, dials each new number with SAS, and punches the 72# command, forwarding the lines to a North Hollywood choke point before the mass of incoming calls feeds into his voice mail. There are no bills, no records, no sign of existence.

The system is seamless. A john calls the ad and hears a recorded message. "Thank you for calling College Girl Escorts. Please leave a message and one of our girls will call back immediately."

"I'm at the Beverly Hilton," one might say. "My number is . . ."

"I'd like a tall blond," a more discriminating client might inquire.

Whoever picks up the message first has first dibs. "This is Julie. I called back Jim. I'm going to take the call. It's at the Beverly Hilton, room number 304."

Kevin's system automatically broadcasts the "taken" message to the other escorts. And if they discover a john has checked in under an alias or don't like the sound of his voice, they'll alert their coworkers. "This is Sarah. I just talked to George. He sounds like a sick one. I'm not taking it."

Best of all, from Kevin's perspective, his elaborate system costs nobody and simply utilizes the excess capacity of Pac Bell and American Voice Retrieval. If the authorities catch on to the operation, Kevin can take control of his choke point with SAS and forward the ads to another voice mail company in minutes. And he's careful not to leave a trail. Kevin always randomly dials someone else's voice mail box before entering his number to step neatly over to his box. If anyone puts a trap on Kevin's box, all they'll trace is a call to another random box.

Once an escort reaches the designated hotel, she leaves a message on Spiegel's voice mail. Her call back to announce she's done also serves as an accounting check; perhaps an even better one than Spiegel suspects. Whether Spiegel knows it or not, Kevin listens to his messages to be sure he gets his twenty dollars per "date." Kevin never speaks to the escorts, and though Spiegel describes each escort to him over the phone, Kevin still thinks it odd that Spiegel requires them to supply nude snapshots for his book.

Kevin is fascinated by the barrage of Friday and Saturday night calls, interrupting his hacking frequently to make sure everything is running smoothly. He becomes so engrossed with the process of voice mail prostitution that he lets far more lucrative opportunities slide by. Radio contests with $10,000 prizes come and go, as Kevin follows the details of every "date," from a john's initial call to the escort's check-in message and occasional description of the trick.

Perhaps as a precaution to guard his own prized privacy, Kevin is careful to maintain his physical distance from Spiegel and the girls. But Ron suspects it's more than that. He sees the whole strange affair as a weirdly appropriate facsimile of a social life for a cyberpunk to whom technology is reality. Kevin watches, content with his one-way window glass.

"Is this a great country or what?" Kevin jokes to Ron. "Girls are going out and sleeping with guys, and I'm making money on it."

CONTROLLED DETONATION

I n late spring of 1989, a group calling itself the nuPrometheus League commits the ultimate computer hack. Like the mythical Greek hero Prometheus, the mysterious group of software artists steals fire from one of the gods of high tech, Apple Computer. Anonymous Apple employees mail the Macintosh's proprietary code to industry observers with a manifesto. "The nuPrometheus League has no ambition beyond seeing the genius of a few Apple employees benefit the entire world, not just dissipated by Apple through litigation and ill will."

In a sense it's logical that the nuPrometheus League would rebel at Apple. Though the maverick company first made its fortune by promoting the Individual over the System, its critics fear that by refusing to license its highly touted interface, Apple is crippling its own growth and denying the public the power of its intuitive computing. But there are consequences for stealing fire from the gods. When Zeus discovered Prometheus had given fire to mankind, he bound him to a rock and sent an eagle to peck him again and again for thousands of years. When Apple discovers the nuPrometheus rebels have copied its software, the corporation declares it piracy and a crime. Though the pirates appear to have a goal of free exchange of information, the age when Apple or the authorities might have listened to their idealistic philosophy is long past. Computers are a multibillion-dollar business, firmly entrenched in the establishment. Apple calls in the FBI to investigate.

———■———

Agent Steal is making waves on-line.

> *I'm here! Big deal right? Well some day I'll get busted and you will all hear about all the innovative, bold and crazy things I've done and can't talk about because most phreaks are narrow minded bull-shitting, immature, fuck heads that would narc on their girlfriend if the shit came down!*

Eric is finding himself on the hacker bulletin boards, stretching his electronic wings, creating his identity and entertaining his public. When Kevin comes over to Eric's pad for their evening central office outing, Eric is dishing off an e-mail post, asking Kevin to check whether he's gotten his techno facts straight. When Kevin spies a postscript he realizes he's been right all along not to trust Eric. Over the Net, for every hacker or government informant to see, Eric is hinting at their latest joint efforts.

> *Agent Steal*
>
> *I wish I was at liberty to explain to everyone the correct way to "monitor" dialups. However, doing so could draw attention to my current projects.*

Kevin is disgusted by Eric's arrogance. Why doesn't he just announce to the whole world that they have a tap on Telenet in the basement of the Mutual of Omaha building? Why not just hand over the number to the FBI? But then, Kevin doesn't understand Eric. Kevin has no need of an audience other than Ron and perhaps Eric. He can't fathom why Eric needs this outlet, why it's necessary to his sense of well-being, why he needs it just as badly as he needs to cruise the clubs nearly every night.

On-line, caught up in the moment, Eric imagines a utopian hacker's bulletin board.

> *I would like to announce the creation of a new sub . . . This sub will be exclusively for hack/phreaks that have been active for at least 3 years. Having been around for 10+ years and three handles I feel I have the justification in being the sponsor. I hope this can be a sub where we can talk with a little openness about some of the things we don't usually talk about on other subs. I plan on personally inviting the members and I hope some of you won't be insulted when you're not invited. . . .*

> *Agent Steal*

But Eric's on-line euphoria evaporates faster than a screen refresh. He may impress teens with hints of his crimes, but the hard-core hackers he boasts of inviting mock him for his technical blunders. Phiber Optik, a skilled hacker and phreak from the original and most famous gang of digital desperadoes, the Legion of Doom, slams one of Eric's posts. Suddenly it's an all-out attack. Acid Phreak, a talented and arrogant young New York member of the feared Masters of Deception gang, writes,

> *You should excuse your ignorance Mr. Steal . . . this is becoming one big joke . . . pardon my "abusive" and "embellishing" attitude. . . . Duh.*

But the insults don't dampen Eric's enthusiasm. He charges ahead, in search of celebrity status.

It makes no sense to Kevin. Why in the world would Eric spend days writing a twenty-page file for LOD's on-line technical journal? Why would he bother retyping detailed descriptions from stolen Pac Bell manuals, loosely disguising the lifted material with his own hacker commentary? Does he really believe this will provide him an entrée to the notorious gang?

Eric asks Kevin to offer critical suggestions on his opus, a detailed, behind-the-scenes look at how a central office and the local phone net work work. While Kevin does offer a few corrections, he isn't sure it's in his best interest to turn Eric into a public figure that might gain the attention of the authorities.

———■———

THE LOD/H TECHNICAL JOURNAL, ISSUE #4: FILE 04 OF 10

```
$$$$$$$$$$$$$$$$$$$$$$$$$$$$$$$$$$$$$$$$$$$$$$$$$$$$$
$                                                 $
$              Central Office Operations          $
$            Western Electric 1ESS,1AESS,          $
$          The end office network environment     $
$                                                 $
$              Written by Agent Steal 1989        $
$                                                 $
$$$$$$$$$$$$$$$$$$$$$$$$$$$$$$$$$$$$$$$$$$$$$$$$$$$$$
```

Topics covered in this article will be:

Call tracing
RCMAC
Input/output messages
SCC and SCCS
COSMOS and LMOS
BLV, (REMOB) and "No test trunks"

Did I get your attention? Good, everyone should read this. With the time, effort, and balls it has taken me to compile this knowledge it is certainly worth your time.

The article begins by describing the fundamentals of the Bell phone network, but there's no doubt that Agent Steal is trying to live up to his handle and advise his audience on how to commit crimes. He recommends calling through several different phone companies to avoid a trace and adds a postscript:

> *Special thanks to all the stupid people, for without them some of us wouldn't be so smart and might have to work for a living. Also all the usual Bell Labs, AT&T bla bla bla etc. etc.*

> *Agent Steal Inner (C)ircle 1989*

> *!!!!!*

> *!!!!! FREE KEVIN MITNICK !!!!!*

Kevin's carefully constructed plan of limited access for Eric hasn't quite worked out the way he hoped. He could point to a dozen violations, but for Kevin, Eric's detective work is the unforgivable crime. Kevin sees hacking as the ultimate expression of the individual in the age of high technology. To hack is to challenge corporate and governmental control over knowledge and information. But instead of placing that power in the hands of individuals, Eric is selling his access to a detective, who in turn is selling it to businesses and corporations. To Kevin's way of thinking, that transgression is far worse than his own small role in the world's oldest profession.

There's a practical matter too. Eric is jeopardizing their information stream by selling its bounty to the highest bidder. Suppose, Kevin argues, that Eric keeps selling DMV printouts to the detective and somebody blows the whistle. The private eye could get caught, and then it would only be a matter of time before Eric would get caught, and Kevin would be at risk too.

An all-out attack is being made on the Sunset CO. Windows are broken, doors are left ajar, alarms are tampered with, computers are unplugged, and smoke bombs blast warning plumes up into the sky. Kevin always figured that if Pac Bell ever suspected that anyone was breaking into its central offices the buildings would become more secure than an Air Force base. But try as Kevin might to draw attention to the break-ins, Pac Bell remains disinterested. He just can't seem to get them to do anything about their security problem.

The new guard is a start, but since none of the building's other security breaches have been remedied, the guard's hour break in the middle of the night provides an ample window of opportunity. If Pac Bell refuses to take responsibility for the powerful and dangerous secrets it holds within its walls, then someone or something more responsible is going to have to take on the task. If Pac Bell won't keep Eric out, then somebody will have to do the next best thing.

———■———

Kevin's warrior mentality is simple. His bold measures at Sunset have failed. Eric is getting too close to SAS, and Kevin fears that if he spends much more time in room 314 in Sunset, Eric will not only ruin the opportunity for Kevin but become a danger to society. Ultimately, Kevin sees it as a question of being faithful to his code. His hacker ethics require that he control whatever access Eric might have stumbled upon through their association.

"It's like a bomb being detonated in a field," Kevin says matter-of-factly to Ron one afternoon. "You detonate it under controlled circumstances. Eric is going to go off sooner or later, and who knows what's going to happen then."

Ron is stunned. Kevin has broken into dozens of central offices with Eric at his side. How could Kevin justify doing this to Eric?

"But if you get him caught he's going to tell about everything you've been doing!" Ron protests.

Kevin shrugs. "That's going to happen anyway."

In Kevin's mind Eric's arrest is a foregone conclusion. The controlled detonation is the most direct way to go about it. He knows, given the chance, Eric would do the same to him. This way he can get rid of

Eric cleanly without having to worry about being caught up in one of his stupid mistakes.

"I'd rather die," Kevin tells Ron in all seriousness, "than let Eric get SAS."

———■———

"You want to go?" Eric teases.

About a week has passed since Kevin's controlled detonation declaration. Ron is hanging out at Eric's apartment late one evening. Eric knows that despite Ron's reluctance, he still finds the idea of the nightly excursions appealing, something romantic and forbidden.

"No, I'll just stay here," Ron says, waving him on.

A couple of minutes later Eric's phone rings. It's the Watchman. He's surprised. What could Ron be doing at Eric's?

"Nothing," explains Ron. "I just dropped by to see Eric."

"Where's Eric?"

"Across the street."

"That's all I need to know," Kevin says, hanging up.

Ron's mind races. There still might be time. He could phone the Sunset public address system. If Eric's lucky, he might just hear him before it's too late.

Kevin calls a Pac Bell switching control center from a pay phone around the corner from Eric's. "I'm going into your Sunset CO," Kevin says simply. "There's nothing you can do to stop me."

He waits a block away, in the parking lot of Ralph's supermarket. Finally, after about ten minutes, a single LAPD squad car slowly cruises by.

Shit, not much of a response.

It seems almost impossible to get Pac Bell to acknowledge its security problem. Kevin drives to the corner mini-mall near Eric's, across the street from Sunset, and waits.

———■———

Kevin with his
first electronic test board

Kevin sitting on his TSPS
operator's console

Kevin's LAPD mug shot, the night
he narrowly escaped arrest

Kevin shortly after his
release following 5 years in jail

Justin Petersen, aka Agent Steal

Ron Austin with his father

Henry Spiegel

Ali Sheedy,
star of *WarGames*

Courtesy Nancy Ellison, SYGMA

Molly Ringwald,
star of *The Breakfast Club*

Courtesy SYGMA

Sean Randol,
Kevin's first crush

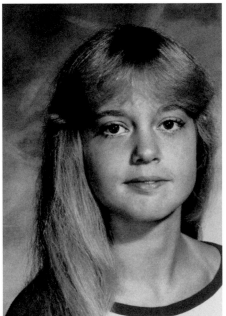

Courtesy Annette Randol

THE INVESTIGATORS

Bill Spradley,
LAPD vice detective

Terry Atchley,
Pacific Bell security investigator

Courtesy Terry Atchley

Courtesy Bill Spradley

Courtesy Jim Neal

Courtesy Kurt Von Brauch

Jim Neal,
Menlo Park police detective

Kurt Von Brauch,
Pac Bell security investigator

FBI WIRETAPS HACKED BY KEVIN

Kevin discovered the FBI was wiretapping foreign consulates and Ferdinand Marcos. He aso discovered the site in the Los Angeles FBI headquarters building where many governments taps are monitored. The FBI was concerned about Kevin's discovery of taps in Concord, home of the Naval Weapons Station.

Los Angeles FBI headquarters

Israeli consulate

Chinese consulate

South African consulate

Concord Naval Weapons Station

Pac Bell office where Kevin discovered
Ferdinand Marcos wiretap

Interior of a Palo Alto Pac Bell central office
Kevin broke into

Courtesy Unsolved Mysteries

SRI International, Kevin's employer

Pac Bell San Franscisco headquarters,
where Kevin broke in and investigated
Pac Bell's own investigators

Eric hears the Sunset phone ring and then the sound of a door opening, but he doesn't panic. He knows the layout better than the engineer who designed the place. He doesn't need a light to find his way through the vast frames and switches. So what if the cops are already in the building. Before they can take more than a few tentative steps, Eric is out the other door.

He hears the grinding copter blades overhead in the darkness and the roar of the squad cars racing toward him. He's tempted to run, but he relaxes. What kind of burglar or phone hacker would have teased blond hair below his shoulders and be dressed for a night on the Strip?

Cop cars screech in from every direction, choking the street. A copter shines its spotlight on Kevin's car for a moment, and then onto the dark, windowless building. Kevin calmly gets out of his car and sits on the curb. He chats with a couple of homeless men, counting the dozen or so LAPD squad cars and returning the glance of a suspicious cop. That's one of the Watchman's favorite parts. Watching the scene he's orchestrated play itself out.

———■———

Ron thinks about picking up the phone and making the call. Then, he thinks about what Kevin had said about controlled detonation. What might Kevin do if he messes with the fuse?

Five minutes slowly tick by. Eric's caught, Ron thinks to himself, as the first cop car arrives and the building lights up like a Christmas tree. He doesn't have a chance.

And then, Eric, a quirky smile on his face, strides into the apartment. He's excited. He's never seen anything quite like it. They lie on their stomachs in his living room, peering through the balcony rails, close enough to make out faces in the dark, watching Sunset crowd with squad cars and police dogs. The helicopter hovers above, its searchlight tracing the building.

"Do you think Kevin did this?"

When Kevin first mentioned his controlled detonation plan, Ron had always figured he would expose Eric's other criminal schemes, like supplying birth certificates to gypsies or wiretapping for the detective. Ron can see no logic in alerting the cops to the very place where they too committed their crimes. It's like leaving a trail for the authorities, like dropping crumbs that lead back to his own lair.

But lying there, next to Eric on the floor, Ron realizes that whether by plan or accident, he has been used. If Kevin has indeed set up Eric, it doesn't look good that Ron happened by that very night, waiting in the apartment to coordinate the critical timing of Kevin's threatening call to Pac Bell.

There's no way out. If Ron tells Eric the truth, Eric will likely see him as a rat since he pretended to be Eric's friend. But that's only the first of Ron's fears. To him, Kevin's idea of a controlled detonation is crazy. If Eric is caught or even just seriously challenged, he will certainly turn against Kevin, and quite probably Ron, too. It will be all out war.

"No," Ron reassures Eric, as they lie on their bellies looking out at the searchlights illuminating the building. "I really don't think he would do anything like this to you."

———■———

Kevin knows that Ron has completely misunderstood him. He only meant to spook Eric. Ron's job was to keep Eric from going inside. If Kevin had wanted Eric busted he would have called in the address of Eric's apartment to the Switch and Control Center. There was plenty of evidence of crimes in Eric's pad. By controlled detonation, Kevin meant detonating Sunset and Eric's hopes of getting SAS.

That's why Kevin used the word controlled. That's why one night after Eric goes out on the town, the Watchman enters his apartment building, picks the cheap lock on the telephone closet, and yanks on the secret cable to make it appear someone has been messing with it. Back at his apartment, he implements the electronic side of his plan.

The following evening, Ron is hanging out at Eric's pad when it happens. Eric keeps his phone line attached to his stereo speakers just in case someone is foolish enough to tamper with his line. That way, he figures, he'll hear the slightest modulation in sound.

"What the hell?" wonders Eric. Somebody or something has put tone on his line. Eric runs down to the street and looks around the B box. Nothing. He pries open the box and counts down the terminal posts to his line. Nothing unusual. Back at his apartment he checks the basement telephone closet. Ron watches Eric pale when he sees that his line has been tugged at.

In the morning Eric finds an authentic Best phone company lock on his B box. Then, Eric's apartment manager gets a phone call from Pac Bell, a few questions about how long Eric Peters (his alias) has lived in the building. That same day all of Eric Peters's free custom calling card features are removed from the system by someone called G. S. Security.

Kevin, of course, has ostensibly been out of town during the attacks, up north to attend to some business. On Friday afternoon, after everybody leaves for the day from Pac Bell's Southern California loop assignment centers, the Watchman changes the Cosmos password for the weekend, the same password that Eric has been using to provide the Investigator with services and enjoy free custom calling features. Eric immediately notices he can't get into Cosmos, but he's not sure what to make of it. He doubts even Kevin has the power to change the password that thousands of Pac Bell employees use.

That same Saturday night, Eric returns home drunk with Frecia, excited about the prospect of sex. But before he's even opened his door he knows there's trouble.

"Beep, beep, beep!" chimes the computer Eric keeps on-line with the Sunset switch. He stumbles in and stares at the flashing control "G"s on his screen. Call traces have been issued on his line.

Drunk as he is, Eric knows it's time to go into "secure mode." Eric calls Grant Straus and unplugs every piece of electronic gear he owns. He grabs his manuals and drags everything down the stairs into his Porsche and over to his friend's apartment. It's a lot of stuff to move in a drunken blur. Two computers, three terminals, five modems, and six boxes of manuals and gizmos.

Frecia will have to wait.

CLASSIFIED

———■———

Stamped "Secret" and filled with bombing coordinates and references to CBX Caber Dragon military exercises, the air tasking orders found on Kevin Poulsen's computer tape propel Pac Bell's Von Brauch into action. Fearing the worst, the investigator immediately notifies a local FBI foreign counterintelligence agent. But the FBI agent tells him the Pentagon says the documents are unclassified, and the evidence Von Brauch has passed along about Poulsen's possible compromising of federal wiretaps doesn't interest the Bureau.

So Von Brauch returns to his modest state case. He sees plenty of prosecutable crimes. Dozens of counts of illegal entry into a computer system and fraudulent wire communications. Half a dozen counts of wiretapping or interception of communications. Plus the old-fashioned crimes of burglary, possession of stolen property, and theft.

But then the feds decide to give Poulsen another look. Joe Burton, head of the San Jose U.S. attorney's office, calls Poulsen associate Mark Lottor before a grand jury. But the hacker with the silent grin takes the Fifth, and so goes Burton's interest. The prosecutor assigns the case to another assistant U.S. attorney in the office and, after the case languishes for a few months, Von Brauch is told that no one can find more than two misdemeanor charges, hardly sufficient to bring a federal indictment.

By March of 1989, Von Brauch begins to worry. How long can he count on finding enthusiastic district attorneys when the feds keep jerking the case away from him every few months and then leaving it in limbo? But Von Brauch never considers quitting. He knows something about adversity. He'd done a tour in Vietnam, and walked a beat for the rough-and-tumble Oakland Police Department. The bull-necked, tough-talking Von Brauch has earned the dubious distinction of being fired twice by the Oakland Police Department. He's knocked a man unconscious with a beaver tail sap, and kicked out a window at the Hell's Angels Oakland clubhouse. The first time Von Brauch appealed and won back his job with back pay. The second time, when the department fired him for violating numerous police department codes, including those regarding "use of physical force" and "truthfulness," Von Brauch decided to take a job at Pac Bell, later appealing his case and winning back wages and legal fees.

A determined Von Brauch writes the U.S. attorney and asks whether the feds are going to fish or cut bait.

Dear Mr. Russoniello:

On February 9, 1988, Pacific Bell Security and the Menlo Park Police Department opened an investigative case on Kevin Poulsen and Mark Lottor. As a result of information obtained in two searches, the FBI was notified of evidence indicating interception of communication and national defense violations by the suspects. . . . Due to the Federal charges and Assistant U.S. Attorney Burton's insistence on Federal prosecution, local authorities have been reluctant to proceed. . . .

This case has caused great effort and expenditure of funds by Pacific Bell. As a corporation, we are very interested in seeing this case prosecuted to the fullest as soon as possible. I respectfully request clarification of the U.S. Government's position on prosecution. If Federal prosecution is not forthcoming, the release of this case to local authorities for prosecution would be greatly appreciated.

K. J. Von Brauch
Security Investigator

Rob Crowe can read between the lines.

"Crowe, this is going to be like recreation. It's going to be a really fun case, and it's also going to be like a law school exam," Joe Burton says in February of 1989, soon after Crowe begins working at the San Jose U.S. attorney's office. "The mission is to find federal charges here."

Crowe knows that as the new kid on the block he's being handed the office dregs. Short and stocky with a boyish face, Crowe had worked in the Brooklyn D.A.'s office for four years, prosecuting robberies, murders, and drug deals. A native Chicagoan, Crowe appreciates directness. That's what he likes about Von Brauch's letter. The man sounds earnest. He writes back and promises that the federal merry-go-round will stop.

Dear Mr. Von Brauch:

I am writing in response to your letter of March 6, 1989, to Mr. Joseph P. Russoniello, United States Attorney for the Northern District of California, regarding the referenced matter. I have been assigned to this case. Our Office regards this as a most serious matter deserving rigorous prosecution of all possible federal offenses. Please call me at your earliest convenience during the week of March 27, 1989, so that we may arrange a meeting to discuss the facts, any further investigative steps that may be necessary and the specific federal offenses for which we can prosecute these individuals.

Very truly yours,
Joseph P. Russoniello
United States Attorney

Robert K. Crowe
Assistant United States Attorney

Von Brauch is impressed by Crowe's reply and his phone call the very same day. Finally, somebody in the U.S. attorney's office is interested.

Crowe pens Von Brauch in for a meeting at his office on the thirty-first of March, but when the day arrives, the assistant U.S. attorney cancels. Nor does he make the next three meetings they schedule. This time Von Brauch is pushed aside by a 20,000-pound marijuana smuggling case and a $56 million fraud case. Crowe is working over sixty hours a week, and the truth is that he, like the two attorneys before him, can't find time for Poulsen.

———■———

On April 28, 1989, Von Brauch finally finds himself face-to-face with Rob Crowe and Special Agent Jim Monte in a conference room at the San Jose U.S. attorney's office. The chemistry surprises both men. Crowe had expected some techie dweeb, not a 250-pound streetsmart former cop busting out of his suit like the Terminator. Both men pump iron, and there's a sense of mutual respect. Von Brauch respects Crowe's experience as a D.A. in Brooklyn, while Crowe looks to Von Brauch for guidance because he doesn't know anything about computers or phones.

They open up the federal code and start analyzing the charges. This is what Von Brauch likes best about working a case. He's always considered himself creative, skilled at turning up obscure laws. "Bail stacking," he calls it. Take literally every possible charge and then "whack" the defendant. Let Poulsen prove his innocence.

Crowe believes Poulsen's crimes are morally reprehensible, but he isn't sure whether statutes have been enacted to cover his electronic violations. He's flipping through his paperback copy of the *Federal Criminal Code and Rules* when Von Brauch makes an unusual suggestion. "How about the charge of using a false social security number?"

"I've never heard of that," a puzzled Crowe replies.

The Pac Bell man smiles. "It's Title Forty-two."

The minor social security charge, almost never brought in a federal case, symbolizes the new attitude the Pac Bell man and the prosecutor bring to the case. Possibilities, that's what they're developing, and neither man wants to limit himself to traditional ideas of crime and punishment. By the end of the day they've mustered thirty-five possible felony counts against the hacker. Crowe is rolling. In early July he begins calling witnesses and convening grand juries. He's laid out the felony charges on paper. Now, he's got to persuade a jury that they merit a federal indictment.

———■———

Molly Ringwald places her hand on the Bible and takes the oath. She had not wanted to appear before the grand jury, declining to cooperate with the investigation until the subpoena forced her from Hollywood to the San Jose courtroom three hundred miles north. Dressed plainly and without makeup, she looks entirely ordinary, not at all the rosy-cheeked star of *The Breakfast Club*.

Crowe and the grand jurors await Ringwald's arrival with anticipation, for what greater proof of the all-encompassing power of a dangerous computer hacker could there be than his victimization of a rising young starlet? Last week Ringwald's sister and brother had testified under oath before the grand jury. Kevin Poulsen, the government charged, had tapped the phone of a movie star.

———■———

"I am going to play a tape for you at this time, Ms. Ringwald," Crowe begins after swearing her in. "Will you please see if you can listen to the voice and identify the voice on the tape."

Crowe plays the tape confiscated from Poulsen, a strange message left on the unlisted phone at Ringwald's parents' North Hollywood home. The grand jury hears words they never expected.

"Does it sound like your voice?" asks the prosecutor.

"Not to me," replies Ringwald.

Crowe asks her to read the transcript out loud so they can compare it to the tape.

"Excuse me. Can you hold on for a second?" Ringwald interrupts the prosecutor. "I need to call for a recess."

To Crowe, Ringwald appears pale, almost as if she's about to be physically ill.

A few minutes later, an ashen Molly Ringwald returns to the stand.

"Ms. Ringwald, have you had an adequate opportunity to consult with your attorney?"

"Yes."

"Do you wish to continue at this time?"

"Yes."

Crowe tests the microphone and shows Ringwald which button to press to play the recording.

"Ready?" she asks.

"Yeah," replies Crowe.

"This is 509-0338. If you're calling and looking for Scott, he's not here and you should have figured that out by now. If you call again, I swear I am going to call the police because there's nobody here by that name. It's driving me up a fucking wall. . . ."

Still shaken, Ringwald ended her gut-wrenching testimony, uncertain if Poulsen's intrusions into her life were over. Crowe wasn't happy about having to put her through the ordeal, but if Poulsen were to be stopped, he'd have to prove his crimes. That was why he was proud of his interrogation. For despite Ringwald's vague denials, the voice on the tape seemed to be hers.

But what exactly had the prosecutor proved? If he'd just listened to the tape closely he would have seen that Ringwald's testimony couldn't prove a wiretap. The government had merely established that Kevin Poulsen had phoned the unlisted number of a Hollywood star and tape-recorded her outgoing answering machine message.

The Ringwald fiasco doesn't bother Crowe. He's got an ace in the hole, the military orders found in Kevin's locker. Crowe makes an appointment with Special Agent Monte, one of the G-men working on the Poulsen case. Monte walks to the evidence room and carries the file to his office. The assistant U.S. attorney can't copy anything or take it from the FBI agent's office. To do so would be a federal crime.

The first air tasking order Crowe reviews is stamped "Secret" and dated November 25, 1987. He can barely make out that it's from Bergstrom Air Force Base to an Army base at Fort Bragg, North Carolina. The heading reads, "EXER/CABE DRAGON."

The rest is gibberish to Crowe. He starts asking Monte concrete questions. Was the exercise real? Were there planes flying? What was happening on the ground? But Monte doesn't know. He phones somebody in the Air Force Office of Special Investigations, and then the AFOSI guy phones somebody in the Pentagon. The game of telephone requires three or four people for Crowe to get a reply, and the answers aren't consistent.

At first Crowe is told there's one air tasking order, then, two: a 1987 exercise with real bombing coordinates for Nicaragua and a 1986 exercise targeting Iraq. Crowe is told the Iraq exercise had planes in Georgia simulating the dropping of bombs over a geographical overlay of Iraq. He struggles to sort through the muddle of previous inquiries. Back in March of 1988 an FBI memo reported there was no classified information on Poulsen's computer tapes. In April of 1988 an FBI agent was told by a major in the Pentagon that the 1986 ATO, at least, had been declassified.

None of these setbacks slow Crowe. The records on the first inquiries are so shoddy that he's not sure what they prove. Perhaps the military wrongly assumed the 1986 ATO had been declassified because it mistakenly believed the Georgia targets were fictional? But Crowe sees no such confusion on the 1987 ATO. The document is stamped "Secret" and has real bombing targets. SRI supplied the computers and technicians to run the computer simulations on the ground. And Nicaragua? That makes Crowe stop and think. Wasn't Reagan rattling his saber against the Sandinistas and General Ortega about then?

"This thing has to be classified," Crowe insists to Monte. "I want someone to review this again."

So Monte picks up the telephone once more. A colonel who was contacted before is sent the 1987 ATO. He checks the document's classification codes and again concludes the document was declassified after the exercise. Crowe requests and receives the classification code, and after studying it decides the colonel must be mistaken. As he sees it, the code suggests the document should never have been declassified.

In early August, Crowe abandons trying to change the colonel's mind and finds a Major Lecklieder who flew in the exercise. Monte sends Major Lecklieder the ATO and receives a telegram from the Air Force's Office of Special Investigations on August 9, 1989. "Major Lecklieder looked at the information and advised the information was and still remains classified...." The following week, on August 17, 1989, an FBI teletype reads, "San Francisco is re-opening this matter due to 8/10 determination of Air Force OSI that information stolen by subject was classified...."

Maybe they're classified, maybe they're not. Either way Crowe knows the ATOs have national security implications, and Poulsen's got no business having copies of them. Crowe doesn't have the slightest idea whether Poulsen took them while working for SRI on the exercises or hacked the military's computers, but he knows the hacker was given a second chance and a security clearance and abused the trust SRI and the government put in him. The arrogance of Poulsen's Pac Bell break-ins, his invasions of privacy, his inquiries about the Soviet consulate and federal wiretaps, his lies to Detective Neil—all these facts weigh on Crowe.

Crowe makes his request to the Justice Department in Washington, D.C., unaware that he's asking the federal government to make history. No computer hacker has ever before been charged with espionage.

TAP DANCING

—■—

Kevin sees what others don't.

When Eric spots the thin metal DNR tap lying on the floor of the Sunset CO, he only sees a hunk of steel connected to the frame. But Kevin looks beyond the physical discovery. He's interested in general principles, the greater framework. If he can understand how a single tap is placed perhaps he can understand others. Perhaps he can anticipate the taps he fears Pac Bell might place on the lines of his parents and friends.

So Kevin checks Cosmos and finds a clue. The on-line record does not—like a normal telephone number—include a cable pair assignment. From his apartment, Kevin dials Cosmos and begins searching for more of these unusual phone numbers. The first pass turns up over a hundred records, far too many taps for a single central office, and Kevin chastises himself for not anticipating the problem. Foreign exchanges, numbers that ring in one office and then run over a carrier to another office, don't show a cable pair, nor do remotely call forwarded numbers.

Kevin begins a crude search for every Pac Bell DNR tap in the state of California. When the sheer volume of the search bogs down in Cosmos, Kevin writes a program to streamline the process. Pac Bell's computers do his grunt work. His program runs on twenty Cosmos machines, half of them located in San Diego, the other half in Hayward, searching millions of telephone lines.

In just ninety minutes, Kevin Poulsen turns up roughly seven Pac Bell wiretaps spread around the state. He could visit the central office where each tap is located, to listen in, but he doesn't need to—he's got SAS. Kevin checks the first line. He hears a high-pitched tone, a signal to the phone company's tape recorders that the phone is on the hook and there's nothing to record. Then, the curtain of sound suddenly lifts, and he hears modem breath. Kevin watches someone upload a program to a bulletin board, then skips to a couple of other lines—a conversation, and more data transmission. He types a one-line description of what he finds on each tap.

Only Kevin knows exactly why he eavesdrops. The illicit taps have an obvious attraction for a hacker, but for Kevin maybe it's a question of survival, of checking the taps in case they lead back to him. Or perhaps something simpler, the allure of playing Jimmy Stewart in Hitchcock's *Rear Window.* Could Kevin have a higher goal? Might he be looking out for phone phreaks or others he believes are being unfairly targeted by the Phone Company? Whatever his motivations, that evening Kevin doesn't find anyone who merits his protection.

Each afternoon, Kevin searches the offices that switch Eric's, Ron's, his parents', and his own calls, canvassing every phone line in North Hollywood, Glendale, Sunset, Beverly Hills, and Van Nuys. He can begin hacking before his search is complete, because he knows how the system works. The records are entered into Cosmos a day or so before the technician physically hooks up the tap to the frame. It's a remarkable insight. The Watchman has developed the power to anticipate every Pac Bell wiretap in the state of California.

———■———

Kevin finds it in a B box on the street one night, a thin metal device with phone wires going in one end and out the other, and a big red sticker that warns, "Do not remove this device! Please call security at . . ."

Something tells Kevin this is different from the DNR tap he found on Spiegel's line. At his apartment, he runs the circuit number listed on the device through Word, a Pac Bell system that tracks private circuits. "Please contact Mark Yelchak in security," says the file, giving an address of 180 New Montgomery. That's funny, Kevin thinks, remembering his late-night visit to Pac Bell's New Montgomery headquarters.

He pulls up the building in various Pac Bell systems, checking floor by floor. Something doesn't look right. Suddenly it hits him. The building he burglarized was 140 New Montgomery—not 180. Kevin zeros in on a single floor dedicated to security, a department called Electronic Operations, and finds fifty phone lines all grouped together. Electronic Operations—what could it mean? The files on each line contain a reference to the Pac Bell Computer Security System, and reveal the equipment on each line. Tape recorders. Fifty of them.

Kevin isn't totally surprised by his discovery. He knows that Pac Bell and other phone companies are required by law to carry out federal, state, and local court-ordered wiretaps. It's a carefully monitored legal process. The federal criminal code orders the assistant attorney general to "reveal the identity of the ... law enforcement officer making the application ... [and] make a ... statement as to whether or not other investigative procedures have been tried and failed." Only specific crimes such as murder, espionage, kidnapping, racketeering, drug dealing, bribery, and fraud can justify taps. Even U.S. intelligence agencies have to apply to the Foreign Intelligence Surveillance Act court for national security wiretaps.

The Pac Bell taps Kevin has discovered appear to be DNRs which can double as wiretaps. That's what troubles Kevin. He knows there's nothing stopping Pac Bell from tapping dozens of lines on a moment's notice. Phone companies are the only entities in America that can wiretap with impunity, the only entities granted more power than the CIA, the NSA, or the FBI. The federal statute states that it is "not unlawful" for "an operator of a switchboard, or an officer, employee, or agent of a provider of wire or electronic communication service" to use that same service to "intercept ... that communication" in the "protection of the rights or property of the provider of that service...."

Somehow this doesn't make sense to Kevin. Other companies can't invade their customers' private conversations. Why shouldn't Pac Bell and other phone companies turn their fraud cases over to the proper law enforcement agencies, and let justice take its course, like other corporations?

But Kevin knows that the taps are only the tip of the iceberg. The statute is silent on the right of phone companies to perform traps and traces and detailed analyses of a suspect's calling patterns. If Pac Bell wished to hide an investigation from the FBI or Secret Service, no court could force it to reveal the nature or target of its inquiry. Even the annual number of taps is secret. Does Pac Bell wiretap ten people a year, fifty, or a thousand?

Kevin decides to find out. First he dials the fifty phone numbers at 180 New Montgomery and discovers that no matter what the hour they ring endlessly or are forever busy. Then he wiretaps all fifty lines with SAS. If he hears anything—conversation, modem tones—he writes a one-line summary. He comes up with seven working taps.

Kevin repeats his statewide Cosmos Pac Bell wiretap search, and ninety minutes later he can't believe what he's found. Seven numbers, the same figure he found in 180 New Montgomery. He drops in on the Cosmos taps scattered around the state and hears the same voices and sees the same data. It's as if he's stumbled onto a parallel universe. Every Pac Bell tap has two different monitor lines, one in the local central office attached to the suspect's line and another at 180 New Montgomery attached to a tape recorder and the Pac Bell Computer Security System. Security investigators can dial any of those fifty numbers and enter a remarkably easy one- to eight-digit security code. And Kevin knows that if the monitor line happens to be down the tap will be sitting there waiting to be exploited. Kevin won't even need SAS. Just dial the number plus the security code and wiretap the wiretapped.

———■———

Kevin hasn't forgotten about Mark Yelchak at 180 New Montgomery. He begins perusing random circuits on-line, and after a little checking, finds another record that suggests he contact Yelchak. Kevin compares it to the first circuit he found in the B box. Both are identified by two random numbers, then the letters AFLA, followed by a string of random digits. That isn't all the two circuits have in common. Both originate in ordinary B boxes and terminate at 11000 Wilshire, the federal building, Los Angeles headquarters for the FBI. After further study, Kevin finds a couple of alarm pairs that don't run to the Federal building but share the AFLA designation. Kevin can't explain the false positives, but then he doesn't really need to: over 90 percent of the AFLA circuits he finds are federal wiretaps.

What surprises Kevin is how easy the federal government makes it to crack their vaunted veil of security. Since the early days of Hoover, wiretaps have been the secret weapon of the FBI, powerful enough to ensnare gangsters and keep political enemies and presidents in check. Indeed, traditionally wiretaps have been what separates the government from the crooks. The idea that an ambitious hacker with a PC could expose federal taps is absurd. If that's all it takes, then how well could the FBI be expected to investigate mobsters, corrupt politicians, and spies?

But as Kevin learns more about how the government and Pac Bell track federal wiretaps, he discovers that it's even worse than he thought. The Bureau is not the only federal agency that permits Pac Bell to track its taps on-line. Kevin soon finds taps running to two occupants of the Los Angeles World Trade Center, the DEA and the Secret Service—the primary federal agency entrusted with investigating hackers. And when Kevin enters "AFLA" circuits into another Pac Bell system to find out who ordered them, he finds that federal agents may actually have a sense of humor. "Acme" and the "Busy Bee" answering service order lots of federal wiretaps.

Being curious, Kevin sometimes wants to know who's being tapped. He could find the actual B box on the street, pry it open, and trace the wires from the metal federal tap to the binding post and the specific cable and pair numbers. Then, with Cosmos, he could turn the cable and pair into a phone number that could be entered into other systems to reveal the person's name, social security number, birthdate, driver's license, and finally the street address.

But Kevin checks few taps this way. Why rely on physical crutches if he can hack the answer? Many of the federal taps are in the San Fernando Valley, and Kevin sets out to learn why. Since Pac Bell's computers volunteer the B box of the tap, Kevin systematically checks the lines of the businesses within the building or block. Most appear ordinary: insurance companies, accountants, and lawyers. But then there's a red flag, the company name for what seems to be a publisher or producer of pornography. It makes sense. Los Angeles, and specifically the San Fernando Valley, produces much of the world's pornography.

Kevin can definitively locate the porn tap without ever leaving his apartment. He can remotely tap the tapped line in the B box with SAS shoes, then dial the suspected porn business or call every number within the target building. The proof? The sound of his own phone ringing on the federally tapped line—through his own tap. He'd have the phone number of the target of a federal investigation, and could, if he wished to, listen in.

Why should the government hold all the cards? If they're going to pursue him, why shouldn't he be able to track their moves? That's why Kevin has to take it further and write the program that will blast a massive hole in whatever false sense of security the federal government holds in its ability to play Big Brother. And really, why not? The founding fathers didn't promote spying in the Constitution. Far from it, they instead wrote the Fourth Amendment, prohibiting warrantless searches and seizures, and emphasized the right to bear arms to counter any government that might one day prove unrepresentative or corrupt.

Once a day, Kevin's computer polls the Southern California systems, checking dozens of central offices at a time. Each day, in a little over half an hour, the computer accomplishes a task for which the mob or foreign agents would gladly pay thousands of dollars. Kevin knows every FBI wiretap in Southern California, more than half of the largest state in the Union, boasting the sixth largest economy in the world, and some of the most advanced, classified technology in the nation. Kevin doesn't simply know the existing wiretaps. Pac Bell enters the circuit identifier and subscriber information, such as "Acme," into its computers the very day it receives a federal court order. But it's often days or even weeks before the taps are installed, days or weeks in which Kevin holds the power to compromise the moves of the FBI, the DEA, or even the Secret Service.

Who could possibly be wiretapping thirteen lines?

Kevin has found a building with thirteen taps, far more taps than he's ever found clustered in one location. Publicly, the FBI claimed that it wiretapped less than 250 people the previous year. How then could there be thirteen wiretaps focused within a single building in Beverly Hills?

Few federal judges would authorize thirteen wiretaps on a single individual or business. Even the biggest mob investigations seldom reach that size. No, Kevin has hit on something larger. Excited, he learns that the thirteen lines are being monitored from the federal building. He traces the tap back to its target, a process that is now second nature. At first, the Beverly Hills address means nothing to him. What could be so interesting across the street from the Beverly Center, the posh shopping mall for movie stars, celebrities, and the rich?

Not more than a few hundred feet from the shopping center stands the South African consulate. Could it really be true?

———■———

Ron punches up South Africa in Nexis, and watches the stream of stories mentioning nuclear power leap from the screen. The two hackers are dumbfounded. They've stumbled onto real life, honest-to-God spy taps, the stuff of espionage and national security. Kevin and Ron can't possibly know whether the taps are authorized under the Foreign Intelligence Surveillance Act by the Washington, D.C., court that grants taps to the CIA and other spy agencies. Unlike common FBI and state and local wiretaps, the court authorizations for spy taps have, according to the Justice Department, never been made public. But what the hackers have uncovered stuns them. Pac Bell's own on-line, Net accessible records provide irrefutable evidence the spy taps have been in place for several years.

It's just the beginning. Kevin finds ten more wiretaps that run back to the federal building, ten wiretaps in the Los Angeles consulate of our friendly ally Israel. And there's more. Incredibly, Kevin uncovers fourteen taps near an office of the American Civil Liberties Union around Wilshire and Sixth Street. Could one of the biggest FBI counterintelligence operations in Los Angeles be targeting the American Civil Liberties Union? Kevin checks all the businesses within the ACLU's building and finds one with five lines and another with two. There's no match, so his hunch about the ACLU must be wrong. But the Chinese consulate, on Shatto Street, off Wilshire, three doors down the street from the ACLU, has fourteen lines. And something else is unusual. Instead of running back to the federal building like the other foreign taps, the Chinese taps loop, jumping up to another floor, and then dropping downstairs. Could the feds be listening to the Chinese from an upstairs office?

The game of hacking has suddenly drawn Kevin into a dangerous world of international espionage. He can systematically ferret out spy taps anywhere in Southern California, and he knows that it's a small step to extend that capability to the rest of the nation, and even, potentially, overseas. Kevin could send evidence of the taps to the South Africans, the Israelis, the Chinese, or even the *Los Angeles Times*. What might the Israelis think about the ten wiretaps? And what might the FBI think about its secret taps being featured on the evening news? What might it think about a couple of hackers delving into national secrets?

Ron phones the number Kevin has dug up for the FBI's counterintelligence front operation at the Chinese consulate building and pretends to be looking for a job. The spies at J. W. Collins & Associates can't seem to get their story straight. One day they're in the publishing business, the next they're in the information business. What side of the information business J. W. Collins & Associates pursues is not something the company cares to discuss. Ron decides to pay a visit to the consulate, a large, white office building. As he gets out of his car he notices some dilapidated apartments across the way, and has the uneasy sensation he's being watched. He strolls through the marble lobby, past the cheap chandelier and half-dozing security guard, and takes the elevator to the second floor. A laminated plaque next to the tall brown doors tells him he's in the right place, J. W. Collins & Associates.

The office is larger than he imagined, covering nearly half the floor of the consulate's building, and resembling a law firm. Magazines are neatly arranged around the chairs and table in the waiting room, and Ron can see numerous Macintosh computers and desks beyond. The only crack in the FBI's counterintelligence facade is the absence of people during normal business hours. Nobody seems to be home. The woman comes out after quite some time, a little old lady right out of the pages of a John le Carré novel.

"Can I help you?"

KEVIN'S COURT

——■——

Malibu?

Kevin's found his first wiretap in the coastal home to Hollywood's stars. As he investigates further, he notices that the Malibu tap runs to a regional FBI office in Van Nuys. Why, Kevin wonders, is this tap running to a small office, situated farther from the tap than the federal building?

This time Kevin sees no easy method to divine the subject of the federal eavesdropping. SAS doesn't work with GTE, which handles service in Malibu. So how can he do it? The easiest method would be to drive out to the actual B box in Malibu and physically trace the lines, but Kevin keeps his actions secret. All Ron knows is that Kevin discovers that along with the FBI field office, a nearby Malibu residence has been set up as a listening post, and to add to the mystery, the subject of the wiretap appears to be a tony restaurant on the edge of the Pacific.

Why would the feds take such elaborate security measures for a restaurant? Ron searches the restaurant's name in Nexis and a story begins to unfold. An October 1988 *L.A. Times* article describes a Prudential Bache executive who "accepted a $2 million post-dated check from ZZZZ Best carpet-cleaning kingpin Barry Minkow after he flew her to Los Angeles" and "took her out for an intimate seaside dinner . . . at Malibu's Splash restaurant."

Kevin and Ron, like just about everybody in Los Angeles, remember the ZZZZ Best scandal. The story became a parable for the greedy eighties, an improbable tale of a kid who seduced Wall Street and bilked thousands of investors with a carpet-cleaning pyramid scheme. But how does Splash fit in? And why would the feds still be tapping the joint long after Minkow had been exposed? Another article describes Splash's manager as Ronnie Lorenzo, "a member of the New York–based Bonnano crime family" and then names prominent New York mafiosos who frequented Splash and muscled in on the ZZZZ Best scam.

Kevin has hacked his way into one of the most publicized scams of the last two years, a national front-page story that led to congressional hearings. The federal attention and media circus only highlights Kevin's phenomenal find. Advance knowledge of federal wiretaps is indeed a powerful tool, and the more Kevin thinks about it, the more he realizes how fortunate it is that he's continued his vigilance against Eric. Eric already works for a detective who has no scruples about illegal wiretaps. What would stop Eric from offering his services to the mob to uncover federal wiretaps? Kevin knows it's not a hypothetical question. Although Minkow's in jail, the Splash tap is still live. Very live. Incredibly, within weeks of Kevin's discovery, Ronald Lorenzo, the owner of the trendy Malibu nightspot, begins having a series of phone chats with one Robert Franchi, an undercover FBI agent, over the very same line Kevin knows is being tapped by the FBI.

——■——

Kevin makes the seven-hour drive to Northern California to visit Lottor and Gilligan, but it's a little too long for his oil-leaking clunker. Just short of the Menlo Park exit, the engine seizes and the car dies on the freeway. Lottor isn't at his condo when he straggles in, and without a car Kevin wonders how he'll pass the afternoon. Then he remembers. There's a tap in the neighborhood he could check.

Kevin doesn't have long to wait before a white van pulls up to the B box. The driver, wearing a suit and a tie, doesn't look like a Pac Bell technician. Kevin sits on the wall near the 7-Eleven and sips the Coke he just bought. The man looks at Kevin and Kevin looks back. Even from a distance, Kevin sees him carry the six-inch-long metal tap from the van. He can't quite make out the rest, but he can guess the routine. The man will connect the eavesdropped line to one end and the federal line to the other, lock the box, and be on his way. Kevin knows it's almost certain the box holds a federal tap: the FBI is about the only entity that bothers to lock B boxes.

Finally, after all his years as a hacker, Kevin has witnessed the placing of a federal tap. But far from being impressed, he's amused at what seems an amateur process. By its own count, the Bureau taps fewer than a few hundred people a year. So if the FBI considers the subject of the tap important enough to merit surveillance, why does it execute the final physical connection with all the subtlety and secrecy of Maxwell Smart?

———■———

Tucked away behind the hills east of Oakland, Concord draws Bay Area professionals for its warm weather, open space, and outdoor concerts. Kevin's heard of Concord, but it's always seemed sleepy. That's why he's surprised to find that the suburban community is home to a hotbed of FBI wiretaps.

A Nexis search would open his eyes to another side of the East Bay community. Concord is also home to the Concord Naval Weapons Station, the major West Coast supply center for military weapons and ammunition. Numerous reports, never confirmed by the military, say the station houses nuclear weapons. During the 1980s, the station became a trigger point for demonstrations about arms shipments to Central America. Antiwar demonstrators believed an elite FBI counterterrorist unit at the Concord office was specifically tracking one of the leading protesters. Brian Wilson, a former Vietnam Air Force Intelligence officer, had learned that the station shipped deadly white phosphorus explosives to El Salvador.

Then, in September of 1987, a terrible "accident" at the weapons station raised an international stir. Wilson lost both legs trying to block a train carrying munitions for the Contras and was declared a "courageous peace fighter" by Soviet newspapers. A fired FBI agent told the

L.A. Times that the Bureau considered Wilson a terrorist, engaged in a "violent conspiracy" against the government. Congresswoman Barbara Boxer demanded to know why the Navy train didn't stop. Was it an unavoidable accident? Or was the fired FBI agent correct that the Bureau considered Wilson a terrorist? And could the FBI have tapped the phones of Wilson and other protesters?

———■———

Kevin is more secretive about the Concord taps than he's ever been before, this time mentioning nothing to Ron and encrypting his files several times. Whether Kevin is alerting any of the targets of federal surveillance is hard to know. He has the tools and the knowledge, but it's not simply a technical question. Kevin weighs who he believes is deserving. If he encounters a hacker he deems worthy Kevin feels he has no choice but to warn him of the surveillance.

One evening, Kevin discovers a tap at 180 New Montgomery and listens to Shadow Warrior and a friend, a couple of young hackers toying with internal phone company test numbers and computers that respond in synthesized voices. Kevin takes to them immediately and decides they must be warned, but he can't just break in and say Dark Dante is coming to the rescue. Kevin prizes his ability to find taps for his own protection. How can he warn the hackers without clueing Pac Bell into his knowledge?

Just then, Shadow Warrior's friend three-ways off to listen to the synthesized voice of a credit card approval system.

"APPROVED FOR FIFTY DOLLARS," booms the staccato voice, and then mechanically reads off a phone number. The credit card system performed an ANA, an automatic number announcement check, and spat back the kid's phone number.

This is my opportunity.

Kevin punches the number on his test set.

"Oh shit," says the friend as his call waiting beeps. "Should I answer it?"

"Yeah! Answer it! Answer it!" shouts Shadow Warrior.

But his friend chickens out. "Oh shit, now I'll never know."

Don't worry, you'll get a second chance.

Kevin waits a minute, then punches redial. This time the friend picks up the call. "Yeah right!" Kevin swaggers, trying to sound like a cop. "We know all about you and your buddy Shadow Warrior, and you'll be hearing from us soon."

Kevin is surprised by his emotions. His voice shook a little as he alerted the kid to the tap. He hangs up and cavesdrops on Shadow Warrior's monitor line.

"Oh shit, what was that?" the friend frantically asks Shadow Warrior.

"What happened?" asks Shadow Warrior.

"This guy!" exclaims the friend. "Man, he was serious business!" And then the conversation slips into what sounds like code. They seem to have gotten the point. They start talking about meeting somewhere. Kevin doesn't need to listen anymore.

The Watchman has done his part.

———■———

But Kevin's duty is not only to warn those being targeted by the phone company. When necessary, he taps his own enemies.

"I don't want to talk to you anymore, I don't want to hear from you anymore!" Eric declares in an unusually stiff, angry voice mail to Kevin not long after Kevin spooked him from Sunset. "We're finished because you tried to mislead me from valuable access! You should forget that I exist! Any attempts to locate my whereabouts will not be tolerated!"

Kevin has a quick retort: "I'll be happy to forget you existed provided that no evidence of your existence is forced upon me." But a few weeks later, while combing Pac Bell's on-line security memos, Kevin finds what he believes to be damning evidence of Eric's existence. Months before, not long after the three met, an anonymous tipster asked for Steve in the security department, and said an L.A. hacker had cracked the BANCS network at Pac Bell's San Ramon offices. "I also am a hacker in Los Angeles," the memo quoted the tipster, and then noted, "the caller sounded young."

Kevin calls Ron for an emergency meeting. Ron is his court, his magistrate, and Kevin rarely taps without his approval. Kevin formally presents his evidence, an official computer printout of Pac Bell's security memo, and makes his argument that Eric must be the rat. "See how it mentions both the intruder and the tipster are from L.A."

Ron considers this for a moment. He recognizes his role as magistrate is to consider the suspect's rights fairly. "Yeah, but it says he's young," he notes. "Eric doesn't sound young on the phone."

Kevin reluctantly agrees that Eric doesn't sound young—for a hacker. But he has another, more compelling argument. "OK, but how many hackers who have access to BANCS are going to be snitched on, and are going to ask specifically for Steve in the security department?" Kevin seems to have a point. He had told Eric about Steve Dougherty, one of the Pac Bell investigators who searched his condo in Menlo Park.

"All right, you win," Ron declares. "You've got probable cause."

Kevin is pleased at having won his wiretap order through a fair, judicious proceeding. He knows he had to fight for the tap just like an assistant U.S. attorney, and he knows that Ron gave it a lot more consideration than the countless federal judges who routinely rubber stamp applications for wiretaps.

A straight SAS tap is out of the question because Eric's phone service is through an old electromechanical switch and he would likely notice the click. But Kevin's got just the thing. He takes one of the clunky metal federal taps he swiped from a B box and installs it in the phone closet of a random business on Cahuenga in Hollywood. He connects the side that normally would run to the federal building to a phone line that he juices. Next, he bridge lifts the Cahuenga line to Eric's Sunset central office, where he cleverly wires it to Eric's line on a place on the frame where he'll never find it. Finally, Kevin dials the new line he's created at the Cahuenga phone closet with SAS.

There's no click on Eric's end, and if someone happened to dial the number he just created all they would get would be a disconnect recording. It's not just ingenious. It's a good example of the level of sophistication the feds might employ if they wanted to make their taps harder to detect.

Two days after putting up the tap, Kevin has listened to several of Eric's calls to Frecia, when he hears him phone a friend and announce,

"You know me. I'm a live-and-let-live type of guy." The phrase sounds crafted for Kevin's ears, though there's virtually no technological clue Eric might have uncovered to prove he's being tapped. But there's one problem even Kevin can't avoid. Eric, being a wiretapper himself, has every reason to assume that Kevin can't resist the temptation to put him under electronic surveillance.

———■———

Kevin phones Eric and suggests a face-to-face meeting. They meet a couple of blocks from Eric's old Sunset apartment, in the crowded parking lot of Ralph's Supermarket.

Kevin starts by confronting Eric with the evidence he's found in Pac Bell's security files that suggest Eric's informed on him, but Eric wants to talk about something else.

"There's something I can't tell you, something about my past," Eric begins mysteriously.

Kevin doesn't see what Eric's past can possibly have to do with his betrayal. "What, you mean that you informed on your friends?"

"No, what I mean is there is a reason I'm here in L.A., a reason underlying everything I'm doing here, and I can't tell you anything more about it."

"OK, Eric. Great. So why'd you rat on me?"

"I wouldn't snitch on you."

"Really. Then what about this tip?"

Eric laughs, a quick, short, humorless laugh.

"I'd just have you killed."

GRAND JURY

———■———

Detective Bill Spradley is an old-fashioned cop fighting an old-fashioned war. He joined the LAPD in the early seventies and worked Hollywood vice, battling the tide of hookers working Sunset and the streets beyond. Work began with roll call at three-thirty in the afternoon. Dinner was something bought at McDonald's or Pioneer Chicken and eaten out of Styrofoam on the hood of a car. Spradley would start by picking up a rental car or an old junker from Bundy's Rent A Wreck, and despite his slim build, mild demeanor, and meticulous grooming, he always managed to look the part of a man on the make.

Spradley had a job that might drive some men crazy. Every night it was his duty to pick out a prostitute, invite her into his car, get her to solicit him, and then, if he was lucky, maneuver the car and his companion back to the designated arrest post before she caught on. On a good night he'd arrest several girls before his shift ended at 3 A.M. He'd get home and to sleep by about four-thirty and then rise about a quarter past seven to be ready to testify in court.

Over the years he'd had a number of close calls. Sometimes when a prostitute realized he was a cop, she would try to leap from his moving car. Other times they'd jam their high heels on the accelerator or reach for the keys. The desperate ones would lunge at Spradley and grope for

180

his gun, a particularly vain effort since early on he'd learned to sit on his revolver.

Until he heard the story in September of 1989, Spradley thought he'd seen it all. He gathered it in bits and pieces, never getting the whole story from any one prostitute. On street corners, between tricks, they told him what they knew. One said the Yellow Pages ad bill wasn't paid. Another said she knew how to get a free phone number. Still another said she knew how to get a phone number that would be billed to somebody else.

When Spradley pieced it all together he began to see a pattern. Someone in Hollywood could get free Yellow Pages outcall ads. Everybody knew somebody who told them it could be done, but try as he might, he couldn't get to that somebody to solve the mystery.

——— ■ ———

"Please state your name and your occupation," Robert Crowe calmly asks.

"Last name is Von Brauch, first name, Kurt," the bull-necked former cop introduces himself. "Occupation, security investigator for Pacific Bell."

"The telephone company?"

Crowe drives home the point. The telephone company itself is on the stand. The date is September 6, 1989, and once again Crowe stands before a secret grand jury. Under Crowe's direction Von Brauch provides an overview of the evidence taken from Poulsen's locker and condo, everything from pay phones to Pac Bell printouts on the San Francisco Soviet consulate, even a 660 communications panel with a sticker that states that it contains confidential material that will "bring the person into trouble with the federal government."

It's not as dangerous as Von Brauch claims. The 660 is simply a routine multiline central office phone, and the stickers are World War II memorabilia Kevin bought at a surplus store. But while the government is exaggerating, there's no doubt that Kevin is playing with fire. On what appears to be a page from Kevin's calendar, Von Brauch found what he believes to be a transcription of a private conversation of a Pac

Bell investigator who works in the department that wiretaps for the federal government.

"Is it correct to say that when the federal government, usually the FBI, obtains a court order for a wiretap, that Pacific Bell, pursuant to a contract with the government, actually conducts the wiretap?" Crowe asks.

"Yes, sir."

"Does Pacific Bell take certain security precautions to make sure the information is not disclosed to the public?"

"Our lab that performs that type of operation . . . [is] in a locked and alarmed facility. They have all papers and court orders maintained per government specifications in an approved safe. . . ."

"Did you discover in Kevin Poulsen's bedroom papers indicating that he had gained access to some of those federal court order wiretaps from Pacific Bell offices?"

"Yes, sir. We found three pieces of paper that . . . call the telephone number, the line equipment and cable and pair of the targeted telephone number."

"In this case, do we know what these were involved in?"

"Yes. The three wiretaps that Mr. Poulsen had intercepted and interfered with involved the tapping of the telephone of Ferdinand Marcos and associates."

But there's an even more startling fact that Von Brauch doesn't tell the grand jury. The Marcos tap was run by the foreign counterintelligence arm of the FBI.

———■———

"At some point, did Pacific Bell internal security people draw up a memorandum regarding Kevin Poulsen's access to Pacific Bell internal documents?"

"Yes, sir, they did."

"Did you have occasion to find this memorandum during your searches of the storage locker or of Poulsen's apartment?"

"Yes, sir, I did."

"Did you conduct an inquiry as to how Kevin Poulsen could have entered these internal Pacific Bell documents?"

Crowe's careful phrasing has a purpose. He wants to conjure up the image of old-fashioned criminal "breaking and entering," an act not yet equated with mere unauthorized computer "access."

"Yes, sir. That document involved the entry into a computer in San Ramon.... I believe the man's name was Robert Tracy at our San Ramon facility, and the contents of the memo indicated that Tracy had discovered an illegal entry."

"Did you have any conversation with Mr. Tracy or Ms. [Gerri] Lyons regarding an unusual phone call they received, an inquiry concerning this particular memo?"

"Yes, sir . . . there was an attempt to obtain that particular memo, with the person who was calling claiming to be someone else."

"Who did that person claim to be?"

"He claimed to be a high-ranking management official at Pacific Bell."

"Did they also give the correct callback number?"

"Yes, sir, they did."

Von Brauch first explains how he discovered the executive's phone had been surreptitiously call-forwarded to a pay phone, and then Crowe suggests a likely culprit. "Did you find in Poulsen's apartment, or in the storage room, Pacific Bell directories indicating the names of the top-ranking Pacific Bell officers, security personnel, and their telephone numbers?"

"Yes, sir."

———■———

Von Brauch mistakes some of Kevin's junk for wiretapping and military equipment. The antique three-hundred-pound TSPS console suddenly "allows an operator to break into calls...." A sixteen-button phone used for routine testing is represented as a "military communications system." A mechanized lube testing trunk test set and a direct access testing unit, or DATU, enables the hacker to tap "any telephone literally within the country."

Unfamiliar with Poulsen's electronic world, the grand jury needs a simple, physical sense of the hacker's powers, and Von Brauch's colorful descriptions seem to do the trick. "Agent Von Brauch, you have talked about a room and called it the switching room. What does the name switch room come from?"

"'Switch room' is the term given to telephone switching rooms because that is basically what they are. They are in a room and they contain a telephone switch."

"Why did you refer to the room depicted in the photo as the switch room?"

"The sign 'switch room' here that you see in the left margin of this photograph was attached over the door of the third bedroom of the apartment at 1055 Pine Street in Menlo Park."

"So, in other words, Poulsen and Lottor . . . had placed a sign up there saying 'the switch room'?"

■

Crowe impresses upon the grand jury that the most relevant statute for their deliberation will be Section 1029 of Title 18 of the United States Code, Fraud and Related Activity in Connection with Access Devices. "Access" is the key word, and Crowe asserts that access has been obtained.

"Did your investigation come up with evidence whether Poulsen, Lottor, and Gilligan had access to various government equipment?" Crowe asks Von Brauch.

"Yes, sir."

"Let me show you this document. . . . Describe it," Crowe requests.

"That is a piece of electronic mail transmission we obtained from one of the data tapes that was recovered from Kevin Poulsen . . . mailed from Robert Gilligan. . . ."

Von Brauch continues, stating that the mail is evidence Gilligan accessed a military network called Masnet. The printout of the network's opening screen, Von Brauch asserts, proves he broke the law. "Underneath that Masnet label is a warning that states, and I will quote it: 'Unauthorized access to the use of this computer system is in violation of Title 18, U.S. Code, Section 1030. Violation will be prosecuted.'

"It then goes on to list a menu of ways to enter the system."

"Access codes?" Crowe leads his witness.

"Those are access codes," agrees Von Brauch, adding, "There is also a comment from Mr. Gilligan to Mr. Poulsen that says, 'Check this out!'"

The evidence appears solid. Robert Gilligan had allegedly "accessed" a government computer and Poulsen allegedly had in his possession the valuable access codes. The system banner itself warned that trespassers would be charged with a felony.

"During the course of the investigation did you obtain information from Kevin Poulsen as to whether he had accessed any classified military records?" questions Crowe.

"Yes, sir, I did."

"What did you pull off the computer that indicated that?"

"Are we at liberty to discuss that?"

"Yes."

"I found a detailed air attack task order that involved a military exercise of the Eighty-second Airborne Division, which involved all aircraft, air transporters plus fighter intercept and attack orders. The targets on the fighter interception and attack orders are current targets and are currently classified."

The allegations are all beginning to tie together. Kevin Poulsen has hacked access codes to military computers and obtained something that might be of real value to the Soviet consulate on Green Street in San Francisco.

"Did this particular document indicate it was classified at the secret level?" Crowe continues.

"Yes, sir, every page listed that classification."

"Did Poulsen, Lottor, and Gilligan have appropriate clearance to have access to those documents?"

"None of them have ever obtained any level of security clearance," Von Brauch states.

But Von Brauch is at least partly mistaken. Both Poulsen and Gilligan had government security clearances.

The grand jurors have a few questions for Von Brauch about the motivations of the hackers' eavesdropping. "Did you find a specific reason why they were doing it? Was it just a prank?"

"The one that was done on the college we believe was an experimental type of tap," Von Brauch begins. ". . . The taps of the family . . . down in the North Hollywood area, the one young lady was an ex-girlfriend of Kevin's. . . . The third one, which I don't believe we included here, was Molly Ringwald. Apparently he had a fixation with a certain number of stars, Janis Quey, Molly Ringwald, and I believe there was a third one."

"The equipment that they had," probes the persistent juror, "is there evidence of their using it for their own benefit . . . were [they] selling any kind of service with the equipment that they had?"

It's a good question, but neither Von Brauch nor any other federal witness called before the grand jury has an answer. And some basic questions need answering. Ignorant of Poulsen's mastery of SAS, the government can only guess at how he's wiretapping. And there are other mysteries. Why had this young man stuffed his apartment with swiped and scavenged telephone equipment? Why had he walked straight into the phone company's downtown San Francisco headquarters to have the run of its security offices? How did he know about the federal Marcos spy taps and possess phone records of the Soviet consulate and what appeared to be classified military documents? And, most of all, what did he plan to do with all of his secrets and access?

HAPPY BIRTHDAY

———■———

Ron rubs his sleepy eyes and squints at the alarm clock through his usual early-morning fog. It's 8:02 A.M., and he's only half awake when the caller's voice on the radio begins to penetrate his consciousness. No, it can't be, he thinks, remembering he set the alarm for seven. But the clock now says 8:03 A.M., and the voice continues on the air, the voice of an ecstatic winner of a Maserati TC convertible.

Ron swats his alarm clock to the floor and leaps out of bed to stomp on it. How could he be so stupid? If only his alarm had gone off on time! He crushes the clock again and feels a stab of pain. He's limping and swearing, and there's not a chance in hell he's going to be driving a Maserati anytime soon.

For the last five days, Ron has been in a holding pattern, dropping everything to stay within a minute or two of his phone and computer from seven in the morning till seven at night. Each day he's waited for KLSX to play the song, and each day it didn't happen. This was the last day of the contest, and Ron knew the station had announced to its listeners that it would give away the Maserati between seven and eight, a magic opportunity he's just kissed goodbye.

———■———

Eric listens patiently to Ron's elaborate explanation of how he was going to fix the Maserati contest. But the technique Ron is describing sounds too complicated to be practical, and Eric senses his friend isn't telling him the whole story. That's OK, Eric thinks. If they don't want to share, he can hatch his own hacking scams.

The throbbing in Ron's foot only heightens his dilemma. He knows Kevin would be furious with him for letting it slip that they'd devised a scheme to win contests, but he's tired of what he views as Kevin's double standard. Over and over Ron has listened to Kevin complain about Eric's lack of responsibility, his sellout to the Investigator, his coke dealer friends and petty scams. The way Kevin explains it, it all makes sense. Eric does seem to lack a conscience and have a natural inclination toward crime. Eric probably can't be trusted with SAS or some of the other advanced Pac Bell systems Kevin has discovered. But Ron also remembers the games Kevin played with him as a young phreak, the traps he has laid to deny him access. Does Kevin really believe he can still play Dungeon Master? How much of Kevin's righteous hacker's ethos is just a mask for his desire for control?

Ron isn't happy that Kevin has ignored his advice. He'd warned him against getting involved with Eric and Spiegel and Kevin hadn't listened. Then, just as Ron predicted, Kevin's escort operation had sparked trouble. A competitor bribed a phone company employee to steal some of the lines Kevin had activated. Outraged, Kevin countered, dialing into Cosmos on Friday nights to forward the swiped lines to Spiegel's escorts and steal back the brisk weekend business. Come Monday morning, Kevin let them have the lines back. He figured by just doing it over the weekend, he'd intercept their calls without them ever knowing.

But Kevin had opened Pandora's box. Competing outfits threatened one another and began warning Pac Bell that somebody was secretly turning on disconnected ad numbers. One day a Cadillac pulled up at Spiegel's place off Sunset, and a well-spoken black man, shimmering with gold and diamonds, chatted with Spiegel about business. They came to a mutual understanding. Spiegel wouldn't mess with his ads.

But Kevin was enjoying the fun. Even when Pac Bell finally took the protests seriously and started to issue on-line warnings to Cosmos system administrators, Kevin reacted with glee. In his mind, the chaos he'd spawned brought order. The new security measures would help keep Eric and the rest of the riffraff out. Best of all, he told Ron, Pac Bell would likely be lulled into a false sense of security.

Kevin knew he could always find a new route in. So what if the infighting he'd sparked might lead to a serious Pac Bell investigation? How could they possibly come looking for him? Kevin was wired so deep into Cosmos that he'd pick up their trail before they could take their first step.

———■———

Kevin and Ron decide to pool forces to increase their odds. Each will use SAS to commandeer two of KPWR Power 106 radio's station phone lines during its $10,000 birthday giveaway, and each will be responsible for lining up a stand-in to pick up their prize should they win. Ron doesn't hesitate in selecting his partner. If anything, Kevin's controlled detonation efforts have pushed him closer to Eric. At least Eric lets Ron know where he lives. The only way Ron can meet Kevin is to leave a voice mail suggesting a rendezvous at one of seven code-numbered coffee shops and fast food joints around Los Angeles. And as far as the fight over SAS goes, hadn't Kevin found the wiretapping system that first night with Eric? Why shouldn't Eric share in the bounty?

Eric, for his part, feels vindicated when Ron decides to deceive Kevin and share SAS. Over and over again Eric has told Kevin how he wished they could all be honest and work together. He's tried to be straight with Kevin, but Ron would tell him how it wouldn't work. "Kevin will never go for it," he would say. "He's always going to deny things to protect his access." To Eric, Kevin's efforts to keep him out of Sunset are simply proof of his inability to share.

When Ron begins to tell Eric how SAS can be used to win radio contests and wiretap, it just confirms what he's always told Kevin. If he would just share his phone company access they'd all get along better. SAS will be an incredible boon to Eric's detective work, enabling him to wiretap from the comfort of his apartment, and win an occasional radio contest when the fancy strikes him.

On September 28, 1989, at Eric's Sunset apartment, everything is ready to go. Frecia comes over to wish them luck and Eric borrows a neighbor's phone line to give them the four they'll need for the contest. Everything goes as scheduled. At the appointed moment, they take over two of KPWR Power 106's lines, and Ron makes the winning call, shouting out, "It's my birthday!" on cue. Kevin, oblivious to Eric's role in the scam, leaves Ron a voice mail, "Congratulations."

Ron and Eric drive over to KPWR radio in Universal City in Eric's Porsche, and Eric presents a phony ID he made with the winning birth date. They split the $10,000 prize fifty-fifty, and Eric, a magnanimous sort, donates his share of the windfall to pay for breast implants for Frecia. He feels it's only right since she fed him and shared her bed with him when he was in need. Eric knows that if you share you too will receive.

—■—

Spiegel listens carefully and follows John Smith's instructions, leaving a couple of passport photographs of himself in the P.O. box left slightly ajar at 8333 Sunset Boulevard. A few days later Spiegel retrieves a laminated IBM employee identification card with a new name and his photo.

"Tomorrow's the contest," John Smith reminds Spiegel. "Be by your phone."

Smith coolly explains that he will seize KPWR Power 106's lines to ensure that Spiegel will be the winning caller. The prize? Ten to twenty grand, split down the middle. The money sounds good to Spiegel, and besides, he figures it's an offer he can't refuse. The horror stories he's heard about hackers might come true. Smith already can wiretap him whenever he wants. How hard would it be for him to turn off his phones, repossess his car, or shut off his gas and water?

Kevin knows it's going to be a little trickier since Spiegel is at a remote location. He has to seize two of the station's lines at the precise moment and then bridge Spiegel to both of them. To do the job he's set up a PC with a split screen, two communication ports, and a couple of modems. If Kevin's lucky, one of the two lines will be answered by the DJ on the air. But Kevin has got to be quick. The instant he hears the DJ pick up, he's got to drop the modem on his other line. If he hesitates, the station might simultaneously hear the winner's voice on the air—and a losing line.

On October 12, 1989, the prize stands at an impressive $20,000. Spiegel waits at his Sunset digs, while Smith, several miles away at his Van Nuys office, juggles the lines. When the contest begins, Smith phones Spiegel and tells him to stand by. And then, before Smith knows what is happening, the station's disk jockey is talking to him.

"It's my birthday!" Spiegel shouts to Los Angeles with all the trumped-up excitement he can muster. Today, October 12, is the birth date for Corey Phillip Reuben, the name Smith picked for his front man, his voice on the phone, his persona to claim the check.

———■———

Spiegel drives to KPWR and proudly presents his new temporary California driver's license and his IBM identification card. A couple of days later, the station hands him a $20,000 check made out to Corey Phillip Reuben. Spiegel promptly cashes the check with his false IDs and places $10,000 in hundred-dollar bills inside the P.O. box.

It seems to be just the beginning of their criminal joint ventures. Smith tells Spiegel he's looking for another contest for him to win. Impressed with how smooth Spiegel had been on the phone, how quickly and easily he had been able to cash such a large check with a false ID, Smith hints at a new venture on the telephone. Something to do with a million-dollar wire transfer. "Do you think you could open a bank account in the Cayman Islands?"

THE INDICTMENT

Ⓘn the fall of 1989 Kevin receives an intriguing voice mail message from the FBI. Special Agent James Monte takes Kevin's return call and gets right to the point. "We're working on an indictment against you."

The day the hacker has dreaded for over a year and a half has suddenly struck. Kevin knew grand jury hearings were being conducted and witnesses were being interviewed, but the investigation had dragged on for so long a part of him believed it would eventually just stall out and die. Still, he has been careful. He's never given the FBI a phone number or current address. They have no idea where he's living, and can only reach him through voice mail.

The San Jose FBI agent promises to leave Kevin a message when his indictment is imminent to give him time to hire an attorney. He tells Kevin all he has to do is show up, go before a magistrate, get his bond, and he'll be on his way. "All right," Kevin cautiously replies. "Just let me know when and I'll be there. I'll get a lawyer."

At least, Kevin thinks, he'll be able to walk into the courtroom in street clothes and present a better image for the judge and, hopefully, win bail. At least they won't drag him in shackles and prison togs before the judge like a criminal.

Kevin is in denial.

He exchanges glances with the Secret Service agent fifteen feet away. Kevin's making a statement about his intentions, and he's not afraid to make it publicly, right in the face of his enemy. So what if the FBI has warned him that any day now he may be indicted on federal computer hacking charges. Kevin isn't going to let a little thing like that slow him down.

Kevin sees no reason to rein in his passion or interrupt his continuing education. Why not cruise down the 405 freeway to the giant Anaheim Convention Center, near Disneyland, and join thousands of professionals attending a major telecommunications conference? Kevin grabs a front-row seat for one promising seminar. Security professionals and management from Sprint, MCI, and GTE crowd the conference room, "suits" who work for phone companies of one sort or another, all hoping to learn how to protect against phone fraud.

The distinguished gray-haired head of the Secret Service's computer crime division encourages the security professionals to work with law enforcement to combat telephone fraud, warning that it isn't enough to beef up internal security, that there will always be one hacker talented enough to crack the weak link. The agent's goal is to frighten the audience into cooperating with the feds, to dramatize the threat that sits attentively in the front row, watching and listening to his every word. To rally his audience against the enemy, the Secret Service man reads "The Hacker Manifesto," the cyber underworld's Declaration of Independence, posted on-line years before by The Mentor.

The Mentor's Last Words . . .

Another one got caught today, it's all over the papers. "Teenager Arrested in Computer Crime Scandal," "Hacker Arrested after Bank Tampering" . . . Damn kids. They're all alike. But did you, in your three-piece psychology and 1950s technobrain, ever take a look behind the eyes of the hacker? Did you ever wonder what made him tick, what forces shaped him, what may have molded him?

I am a hacker, enter my world.... I'm smarter than most of the other kids, this crap they teach us bores me.... I made a discovery today. I found a computer.... It does what I want it to. If it makes a mistake, it's because I screwed it up. Not because it doesn't like me. ... Or feels threatened by me.... And then it happened... a door opened to a world... rushing through the phone line like heroin through an addict's veins, an electronic pulse is sent out, a refuge from the day-to-day incompetencies is sought... a board is found.

... This is our world now... the world of the electron and the switch, the beauty of the baud. We make use of a service already existing without paying for what could be dirt-cheap if it wasn't run by profiteering gluttons, and you call us criminals.... We seek after knowledge... and you call us criminals.... You build atomic bombs, you wage wars, you murder, cheat, and lie to us and try to make us believe it's for our own good, yet we're the criminals.

Yes, I am a criminal. My crime is that of curiosity.... My crime is that of outsmarting you, something that you will never forgive me for. I am a hacker, and this is my manifesto. You may stop this individual, but you can't stop us all... after all, we're all alike.

+++The Mentor+++

The Secret Service man pauses and scans the concerned faces of the telecommunications professionals and one very bemused hacker sitting in the front row.

"Pretty scary, huh?"

The show has only just begun. The seminar's other main speaker is John Venn, head of corporate security for Pac Bell in San Francisco. Kevin knows Venn's name from on-line Pac Bell security memos and some of the papers he lifted from 140 New Montgomery, everything from wiretap orders to hacker investigations. And he knows Venn is Steve Dougherty's boss, the Pac Bell security man who helped search his Menlo Park locker and condo. Venn has never previously met the hacker in person, but he's seen his photograph and knows plenty about his intrusions. Each man, for professional reasons, has made a point of learning about the other, a backdrop that makes the Anaheim encounter only more ironic. For Venn has no choice but to deliver his talk, no choice but to reveal how Pac Bell protects its vast multibillion-dollar phone network against the hacker a few feet away.

Kevin listens as Venn advises the Sprints, the MCIs, and the GTEs of the world to delay bringing in law enforcement when investigating phone fraud. Did Kevin hear him right? The Secret Service's computer crime man had just encouraged the audience to engage and cooperate with the law. But then Venn explains why it makes sense to keep investigations unofficial as long as possible. Before the law gets involved phone companies can legally do their own "voice monitoring" without warrants. Kevin, of course, has seen evidence of the taps on-line and even listened to a few. But the prospect of warrantless wiretaps visibly stuns the professional audience.

"Can a phone company really do that legally?" asks one attendee.

"It's right in the statute, Title 18 Section 2511," Venn cites from memory.

———■———

Agent Monte phones Kevin's voice mail within a few days, and though Kevin figures there must be a connection, the FBI man mentions nothing of Kevin's front-row seat at the phone fraud seminar. Nor is this the promised warning of his upcoming federal indictment. The G-man simply instructs Kevin to call Charley Price of the Los Angeles FBI office. Monte is so casual that Kevin would think nothing of it if not for the odd call his parents had gotten a couple of days before. An old high school acquaintance had phoned and asked for Kevin's number. It sounded like a social engineering job to Kevin, what the feds call a pretext call. He figures it was either Eric or the feds.

But Kevin has been preparing for this day, perfecting the art of making virtually untraceable calls. By his workstation, a trunk test set wired into his phone hangs at head level from a mechanical arm. Coal black with matching keys, the metal laptop-sized box speaks dual tone multifrequency, or DTMF: the voice that directs phone calls through the network, the sounds that command trunks and tandems.

Kevin hits the start button on the test set, hits pause twice, and dials the number he actually wants to reach. The whole sequence is stored in the test trunk's memory. He's set up a number in Cosmos so that when he picks up his line, instead of getting dial tone, he drops on a random Van Nuys trunk. Normally, something called a route index channels calls through a limited path of trunks and tandems. But Kevin has learned to build his own custom route indexes.

Kevin toggles the test set's on button and his line begins executing his new route index. Kevin blindfolds the route index—holding back the number he's calling—batting his call back and forth between random Van Nuys and Sherman Oaks trunks, until the test set drops in the number he's calling and the call finally connects.

The technique buys Kevin time. Pac Bell could trace his call to the Sherman Oaks office. The switch would reveal a Van Nuys trunk number, and a technician would then query Van Nuys for the phone number. But instead the technician would only find another Sherman Oaks trunk, and another Van Nuys trunk, and on and on.

■

To phone the Los Angeles office of the FBI Kevin uses his magic route index and a new trick. First, he picks a large federal agency in Los Angeles, and creates a secret number at its local central office. Then, he programs that number to dial automatically an incoming trunk at the federal agency's private branch exchange. Once on the local PBX, Kevin's new route index sends it a 9. Kevin has an outside line.

Now he can call Charley Price at the FBI from the ordinary pay phone, disguising his call to appear as if it originated from within the federal agency itself. But Kevin's hack isn't just about technology, it's about style and gamesmanship. If the government is messing with him, he wants to send it a message, just like Robert Redford did in *Three Days of the Condor*, the classic phone phreak movie. In the movie, the CIA says it is trying to protect Redford. But when Redford goes out to grab lunch one day, he returns to find everyone at his CIA front office murdered. Then, people start trying to kill him. Redford wires together dozens of lines in a central office to call his CIA control. The agency's trace locks in and for a moment Redford's duplicitous spymasters think they have him, only to discover the call has been wired to look like dozens of people simultaneously phoning the CIA.

———■———

On November 1, 1989, a secret indictment is filed under court seal against Kevin L. Poulsen and a warrant is issued for his arrest. So secret is the filing that even its target, Kevin Poulsen, a master of countersurveillance, is unaware that he is under indictment. Unsuccessful in learning Poulsen's whereabouts, the FBI is hoping that the secret arrest warrant and electronic surveillance might ensnare the hacker. U.S. District Judge William Ingram, responding to a series of applications by Assistant U.S. Attorney Rob Crowe, orders the first of a web of traps and traces:

> It is hereby ordered, pursuant to Title 28, United States Code, Section 1651, that the Pacific Bell Telephone Company shall provide the Federal Bureau of Investigation with the necessary services, equipment and technical assistance to install a dial number recorder and trap and trace on phone number 818–765–4205, commencing as soon as practical and continuing through January 1990, or terminating upon the arrest of . . . the fugitive Kevin L. Poulsen.

Kevin Poulsen is officially wanted by the FBI. The sealed court order demands that Pac Bell put virtually every form of electronic surveillance possible on Poulsen's parents' home line, providing the FBI a twenty-four-hour watch on who calls in and who calls out. Additional court orders are issued for surveillance on a number where Kevin tells the FBI he can be reached, as well as his voice mail box. Crowe seems especially hopeful the voice mail trap might lead to a tip:

> His mother, Lee Poulsen, contacts Kevin L. Poulsen through this service and told Special Agents of the FBI that they also could reach

Judge Ingram orders that Pac Bell and General Telephone "make no disclosure of the existence of this Application, the Supporting Verification and order for the installation of Dial Number Recorder and Trap and Trace" and further instructs the clerk of the court to seal both the U.S. attorney's applications and the orders.

———■———

In late November of 1989, Detective Spradley's persistence results in a possible break in the mystifying Yellow Pages case. Spradley gets a felony warrant for a madam who has fled California, and her attorney calls and says she has valuable information to trade for her continued freedom. Spradley plays it cool, not letting her know he isn't planning to chase her cross-country. Then the madam reveals her secret. She knows the guy who can turn on phones without generating bills.

The madam lists the numbers that had been turned on for her, and Spradley serves warrants on the phone company for the corresponding phone bills. A few days later Spradley is informed that the numbers are not in service. The detective thinks this strange, and decides to try a test. He dials the number listed in the big Yellow Pages ad for Final Touch Escorts, and is greeted by a sexy drawl.

"Hellooo, may I help you?"

After getting similar results from the Cover Girls Yellow Pages number, the lieutenant makes an appointment with Terry Atchley of Pac Bell Security at 1010 Wilshire Boulevard.

———■———

A quarter century on the job had taught the slim, chain-smoking Atchley plenty about telephones and the criminal mind. Atchley had joined Pacific Telephone in 1964 as a frame man, working out of the Van Nuys CO, but within a year he enlisted in the Navy, serving tours of duty on the USS *Wiltsie* in the Gulf of Tonkin and the Saigon River. A sonar technician, Atchley sat in a cramped compartment high atop the destroyer, searching for signs of torpedoes from enemy PT boats.

Four years later Atchley returned to the Van Nuys office and maintained crossbar and stepper switches. His career spanned the phone network's evolution from a hodgepodge of wires, mechanical switches, and relays to a streamlined national system dominated by computers. In 1979, a year after he became supervisor of the North Hollywood central office—the same office that served Kevin Poulsen's parents—Atchley was asked if he wanted to be an electronic fraud investigator, and he welcomed the challenge. Blue boxes, much like the sort Jobs and Wozniak had made a few years before, were the main target. Atchley deployed secret telco equipment and programs that would pick up the boxes' telltale 2,600 hertz tone, learned to write search warrants and affidavits, and became adept at surveillance. Many of the suspects were drug dealers. He found them in homes, on the street, even in a bank, and once tracked the 2,600 hertz tone to a Beverly Hills movie director who worried that it might slip out that he, of all people, was a phone phreak.

Before the term had been invented, Atchley was well on his way to becoming one of the nation's first cybercops. When hackers and phreaks burst upon the Los Angeles scene in the early 1980s, it was Atchley, behind the scenes, writing the searches, laying traps and traces, and chasing down the new enemies of Ma Bell. Atchley worked the first major computer hacker cases against the legendary Kevin Mitnick, Susan Thunder, and Lewis Depayne. He was there in North Hollywood when Kevin Poulsen was raided in 1983. If there was a phone phreak or hacker bust in Los Angeles in those years, the odds were that Atchley was in on it.

———■———

Atchley and Spradley sit down and begin flipping through the hundreds of pages of escort ads in the nine greater Los Angeles phone books. Spradley reads the phone numbers and Atchley punches them into his computer. One by one, they find advertised escort numbers with no billing records, no statement, no credit application, no history of anything at all, except the unmistakable fact that the ghost numbers ring and women pick up the lines offering sex.

Once they find a ghost escort number, Atchley traps the line to determine where it's ringing, and they're both surprised at the scope of the scam: Beverly Hills, Santa Monica, West L.A., the L.A. airport, West Valley, East Valley. There's no set pattern, and within a few hours they've discovered over fifty phantom lines ringing all over Los Angeles. And as Atchley continues his investigation, he discovers another twist. Legitimately owned Yellow Pages escort numbers are being diverted to other outcall businesses for an hour or so at a time so that calls from johns can be intercepted and prostitutes dispatched, all without the duped owner of the number ever being the wiser.

But what about the larger question of legitimacy? There's an irony to the investigation that neither man pays much attention to. They've found escort numbers not being paid for, but then in a broader sense, none of the numbers are legal—even the paid ones. Prostitution is a crime in California, and virtually all of the "escort" ads are fronts for outcall call girls. But in practice the establishment permits the escort ads until the police can prove an ad is a front for prostitution. Thus, Spradley's paradox. Facing a sea of pimps and madams criminally abusing the Yellow Pages, the vice cop isn't looking for outcall operators but someone clever enough to bring dead outcall ads back to life.

The madam says it's an inside job, masterminded by a Pac Bell employee. The other possibility they consider—a hacker—seems unlikely. Atchley knows that hackers hack for access, fame, or revenge, but seldom for profit. The dozens of ghost lines call to mind a different psychological profile, one that Atchley knows more commonly fits that of a dishonest employee. And there's another, practical reason the suspect must be a Pac Bell employee. Who else could have seemingly unlimited access to Pac Bell's computers?

——■——

Special Agent Charley Price sounds friendlier to Kevin than his Northern California counterpart. Agent Monte, it seems, has sent down some two hundred pages of documents seized from Kevin's storage locker pertaining to something called "Masnet." The Defense Department, for purposes of what Price calls "damage control," wants Kevin to clue them in. "Defense is putting pressure on Monte," explains Agent Price over the phone. "So he's offering you limited immunity from prosecution for anything you tell them about the Masnet documents."

"Have I been indicted?" Kevin asks. "I have an agreement with Monte that I'm going to self-surrender in court."

"No, you haven't been indicted," the Los Angeles FBI agent insists. "Absolutely not. We just want to talk to you about these documents."

That's what Kevin finds odd. As far as he can recall, he's never heard of Masnet. Kevin may have forgotten, but Price is talking about the Army network log-in banner Gilligan e-mailed to Kevin. Replete with warnings about the penalties for illegal trespassing, the Masnet screen appears quite serious. But in reality it's simply the equivalent of an electronic door. It's not a crime to look at it, it's not even a crime to copy it, and despite the talk of hundreds of pages, the government has no evidence that Kevin ventured inside.

"OK, I'll be happy to come in," Kevin tells the agent after thinking over the proposal. "I was just worried you guys might be trying to set me up. That you decided it would make better press, and look better for the judge, if you brought me in a jail uniform and handcuffs."

Agent Price laughs off the suggestion. He says he doesn't really care whether Kevin looks at the documents. He explains he's just a "lead" agent, making the call for Monte since his office is closer to Kevin. "Monte is pissed off that he has to give you immunity because of the Defense Department," Price explains. "He'd rather just prosecute you for Masnet and everything else.

"Look," backtracks Price. "If you don't want to come in and look at them, I'll just send them back up to Monte."

"That's OK, I'll come in," Kevin volunteers.

Masnet, Kevin puzzles, as he hangs up. Not only does he have no idea what the government is talking about, he's certain he never had two hundred pages on the subject. He hits the phone, polling his friends. Few are optimistic. When he tells Gilligan that he's decided to drop by the FBI to look at the documents, his old boss chuckles. "OK. Well, I guess you'll be arrested tomorrow. Bye."

The next morning, Kevin phones Price and surprises him with a change of heart, telling him he doesn't think he's going to be able to come in. Kevin doesn't tell the agent why, but his reasons are simple. The line about Price offering him immunity while Monte wants to play hardball just doesn't wash. Kevin doesn't trust the FBI, and he suspects he's been listening to a variation on the good cop, bad cop routine designed to lure him into a trap.

Kevin needs time to think before he acts. He needs a chance to learn the full extent of the charges against him. He needs to know how to counter the government's propaganda. So Kevin tells the FBI to get lost. "I think as a matter of policy," he informs Price, "I'm probably better off just not cooperating with the FBI in any way."

"Listen," Price argues, "Monte's just going to give you a grand jury subpoena, for you to come up there."

"If you give me a grand jury subpoena, I'll just take the Fifth," Kevin replies, noting Price has suddenly taken an interest in his case. "There's no point."

"He's going to do it anyway. Why don't you just come down and pick up your grand jury subpoena tomorrow?"

Kevin has been on the phone longer than he feels comfortable. He thinks over the proposal. First Price wanted him to look at the Defense Department documents. Now he just wants him to pick up his grand jury subpoena.

"If you get a grand jury subpoena, contact me," Kevin says, quickly hanging up the pay phone.

The Bureau's trace fails.

———■———

"Where's Kevin?" an FBI agent questions Mrs. Poulsen the following day at her North Hollywood home when the hacker fails to pick up his grand jury subpoena. Mrs. Poulsen has no idea, but that doesn't stop the

FBI from returning frequently to the Teasedale residence and Kevin's father's workplace to inquire about Kevin's whereabouts. Agent Richard Beasely, a veteran who specializes in capturing fugitives, pulls Mrs. Poulsen over one day as she's driving from her house, and pleads with her to do the right thing and turn in her son. Kevin doesn't appreciate the feds harassing his parents, but the real irritant is when someone messes with his voice mail. He can't believe it's happening to him, of all people. "You have entered an invalid passcode," repeats the female voice when he tries to pick up his messages. "You have entered an invalid passcode."

At first he wonders whether Eric might have changed his password, but when he discovers the line he routinely hijacks to control the system is dead, he knows he's up against something more serious. He crams his voice mail with so many dummy messages that it can't take any new messages from his friends for the FBI to read. Then he phones his friends and gives them a new voice mail number.

And just in case the FBI discovers his new voice mail box, Kevin makes certain the Bureau respects his skills. Kevin's new outgoing message is a computerized recording of a memorable movie line that reflects his predicament, the dramatic moment in *2001: A Space Odyssey* when Hal 9000, the spaceship's distraught computer, warns the astronauts who plan to disconnect him, "Dave, I know that you and Frank were planning on disconnecting me, and that is something I just cannot allow to happen."

PART IV

BLONDS HAVE MORE FUN

———■———

At 2:25 P.M., eastern time, January 15, 1990, the first AT&T long distance switch fails.

The program is built for just such a scenario. One switch fails and another takes over. No single failure can possibly incapacitate the network. The crashed New York switch fires a distress message to another switch. But the second switch crashes too, and a third and a fourth. Overload alarms flood the network, mowing down switches like summer grass. Is it a virus or a worm? Could it be a computer hacker?

All over America people are getting busy signals, and as the minutes tick by there's no sign of relief. Dozens of AT&T switching stations are paralyzed and half the network's 150 million daily calls fail, costing businesses millions of dollars in lost revenue. An AT&T spokesman tells the *New York Times* in a front-page article that the company can't rule out the possibility of a virus or worm planted by a computer hacker. Far-fetched as it sounds, it's hardly an improbable scenario. On trial this very week in Syracuse, New York, is one Robert Tappan Morris, who a little over a year ago launched the destructive Internet worm.

But it's Kevin Poulsen who makes the front page of the *New York Times* on January 17, 1990, and the pages of *Newsweek* the following week. "The federal government today charged three men in California with engaging in a widespread pattern of breaking into government and telephone company computers and obtaining classified information from a military computer," reads the *Times* article, which portrays the nation's phones and computers at great risk from a hacker with Poulsen's skill. "Poulsen could do whatever he wanted to do with the telephone system," says Rob Crowe, the prosecutor, "as well as with government computers."

There's only one problem. The government can't find Kevin Poulsen. The hacker had recently contacted the authorities, but according to the government, which sealed its indictment until this week in the hopes that secrecy would help it apprehend Poulsen, the hacker manipulated his call to evade a phone trace.

The day after the story breaks, the *New York Times* questions whether Poulsen had hacked classified military computers. Quoting experts who say that classified government networks are "isolated from the outside world," the *Times* sources suggest Poulsen probably obtained the air tasking orders by ordinary means, and infer that the information is probably inconsequential. Meanwhile, "Mr. Crowe," reports the *Times*, "said he could not discuss the evidence that led officials to believe the crime was computer related."

———■———

Robert Crowe is proud of his nineteen-count federal indictment. Being on the cutting edge is how Crowe sees it. Like his charges of unauthorized use of access devices—18 USC, section 1029. Crowe knows the statute applies to someone swiping an ATM or credit card and running up charges, but it's less clear that it applies to fraudulently using a Pac Bell calling card to make free phone calls. Something of value has to be obtained. None of the examples cited in the statute fit Poulsen's case, but then the phrase "any other thing of value" seems to leave a door open.

Phone calls are "things of value," Crowe figures. Why not charge it and make them "beat me, rather than not do anything." So he includes numerous counts for running up over a thousand dollars in charges on Pac Bell cards under *Watchmen* aliases, and asserts that the swiped calls affected interstate commerce. Another creative count describes everything from Poulsen's Pac Bell keys to his ID-making equipment as access device–making tools.

Poulsen, Gilligan, and Lottor are charged with conspiracy "to obtain unlawful access to electronically stored confidential information from United States Government and Pacific Bell Telephone Company computers." Citing three of Poulsen's break-ins and his illegal obtaining of the Soviet consulate's unlisted phone number, the indictment portrays the hacker as a master burglar who victimized Pac Bell offices to obtain access codes. Six of the eighteen counts charge Poulsen and Gilligan with minor offenses such as using fictitious names and social security card numbers to obtain Pac Bell calling cards and receive mail. Crowe later explained, "To sort of cover myself, I charged a very minor felony, like a fraudulent use of a social security number."

But there are serious felonies too. Two counts for access or "attempts" to access the Army Masnet Network, and to transfer "access codes" to the Army network; one count for obtaining classified air tasking orders with "intent to convert same to his use or gain"; three counts for wiretapping Sean and Annette Randol, and for intercepting "conversations between Pacific Bell security employees Gerri Lyons and Bob Tracy." All told, Gilligan and Lottor could each be sentenced to twenty years in prison, and Poulsen could face thirty-seven years.

———■———

Kevin feels the bleach sting his scalp as he stares up at the ceiling of Carlton's Hair Salon in the Valley. Kevin has been doing a lot of thinking since the news of his federal indictment hit the papers. He doesn't have the indictment, but judging from the articles he figures he doesn't need it. He never cracked government computers, and still has no idea what this "classified" Army Masnet network is all about. He sees the feds pressing all the hot buttons—the Soviet consulate, air tasking orders, government computers, and FBI wiretaps. Even the timing seems uncanny, calculated to inspire fear in the public. Could it really just be coincidence that the government unsealed his indictment the week AT&T's long distance network crashed and the Internet worm hacker went on trial?

It seems that everything Kevin predicted about the feds is coming true: just as he feared, the FBI attempted to trace his calls, double-crossed him on its offer to allow him to self-surrender, and brought trumped-up national security charges. He sees little consolation that some in the media aren't accepting all of the government's case. They aren't prosecutors or judges, and no amount of fine print is going to help Kevin. His trouble is the headlines. And that's what Kevin is now—a headline, a piece of news, a carefully packaged factoid alongside the AT&T meltdown and the Internet worm.

The phone crash spawns a flood of stories bemoaning a society dangerously dependent on computers. "It was caused by a new societal hazard of the '90s: the mysterious failure of a complicated computer-software program," writes *Newsweek.* "And the next time it happens, the result may be death rather than merely loss of dial tone." The unsealing of Kevin's indictment the day after the phone crash puts a face on the fear that is sweeping America. Software may not be bugproof, computers may not be error free, but at least one of the culprits of an age of electronic disasters can be put safely behind bars.

To Kevin, the feds and the media have made his choice inevitable. Publicly declared a fugitive in every major newspaper in America, Kevin figures the hype alone makes it impossible for him to turn himself in. He isn't interested in becoming a scapegoat. But the truth is there's more involved in Kevin's decision to remain a fugitive. If the feds are looking for him in Los Angeles, as the *Los Angeles Times* suggests, one solution would be to move. But Kevin likes Los Angeles, its anonymity, its endless streets, its sprawling size. Los Angeles is the closest Kevin has to a home. He isn't going to move. Besides, he wants to make the chase a challenge.

———■———

Kevin parks in the rock 'n' roll Denny's lot, while Ron hides from view in the back of the white Army van Kevin bought at a government auction and souped up for surveillance. Kevin tore out the old metal benches used for transporting soldiers, built panels and shelves, bought a couple of folding chairs, and installed a drape with Velcro to seal off the back. Finally, he had the back windows tinted.

Despite the federal indictment, Kevin feels he has more than the FBI to worry about. Obsessed with the idea that Eric betrayed him to the authorities, Kevin has been looking for the hacker. When Eric finally moved from Sunset, Kevin hacked out an ingenious program on Pac Bell's computers to find him. After sorting through thousands of normal Cosmos orders in the Hollywood area, his program turned up a dozen or so orders that weren't placed in the normal fashion. It wasn't hard to figure out who was Eric Heinz. He'd transformed his new building's elevator phone into a flat rate residential line—a dead giveaway for a hacker. Elevator phones are usually direct lines. Within minutes, Kevin had the address on Sierra Bonita, the phone number and his new alias. He paged Eric to a pay phone and enjoyed every second of the tantalizing call.

But Kevin was too clever for his own good. This time Eric was more careful when he moved, and Kevin's on-line method failed to pick up his new address. Frustrated, Kevin tried attaching a transmitter to Eric's Porsche while it was parked at the Rainbow. But when the device didn't work as planned, he decided to simply scour Eric's favorite haunts.

———■———

Kevin is just about to go into Denny's when he spies Eric drive up in his Porsche. He hops back in the van and whispers to Ron to stay put, but unfortunately he's already popped the back door open. To shut it Ron would have to slam it, and if he slams it Eric might hear. He's already seen Kevin, though he may not have recognized him because of his hair. "He's trying to look at you," Ron whispers from the back, watching through the tinted windows.

Kevin looks off to the side, trying to make it harder for Eric to get a good look.

"He's pulling into a parking place on your right," Ron tells Kevin.

Kevin looks off to the left to hide his face.

"He's still trying to get a look at you."

Finally, Eric turns off his car. Kevin waits a few seconds and then starts his engine and guns it. Kevin isn't likely to lose Eric in his Porsche, but he's willing to give it a shot. He straddles both lanes to make it tough for Eric to get a good look. He cuts quickly off Sunset and then zigzags on side streets. A couple of minutes later, he swings back on Sunset, takes another left onto a side street, and sees Eric right behind him. He hears a deep growl, and the Porsche shoots by and spins in front, cutting him off.

Kevin slams on the brakes, barely stopping in time. Eric and Grant Straus jump out and run up to Kevin's van, shouting, "What the fuck are you following us around for?"

Ron is still holding the back door. He can't let Eric know he's in the back because he's still been playing double agent, continuing his friendship with both men. Why, he even knows where Eric lives. Then, suddenly Ron feels a jolt against the van, like a body being slammed against the steel. Has Eric finally done it? he wonders. Has he finally shot Kevin?

"Oh I was just driving around," Kevin finally replies to Eric's question, and Ron sighs with relief.

"So why were you at Denny's?" Eric presses

"I was going to use the john," Kevin replies.

"What's with the blond hair?" Straus asks.

Eric, who knows something about personal grooming, waves his friend off. "It looks good on you."

———■———

After the high-speed chase, the three hackers call a truce and meet at a restaurant on Sunset Boulevard. Kevin is still furious at Eric because he thinks he tried to rat him out to Pac Bell, but considering all that's passed between them, they get along. Eric even tells Kevin where he lives on Sunset, though Kevin correctly deduces Eric is only willing to reveal his address because he's stopped paying rent and plans to move in a few months.

To an outsider the meeting is perplexing. Kevin is under federal indictment, a fugitive from the FBI. Why would he be entangling himself again with the very man he believes may be the greatest threat to his freedom? But in Kevin's mind the calculated risk makes perfect sense. Kevin likes to keep a close watch on his enemies.

Bored with L.A.'s central offices, Kevin and Eric set off to break into new ones outside the city's limits. Kevin drives his surveillance van and Eric navigates, reading out addresses from a Pac Bell directory that lists every CO and switching center in the state. They get a scare inside a Ventura CO when Kevin spies an employee. But Kevin is like a moth drawn to the light. The close calls just seem to inspire him to take greater risks, to see how close he can push to the edge. One night in Van Nuys Eric holds the flashlight while Kevin picks the lock of a Pac Bell building he suspects houses a good supply of the company's new 1990 IDs. But the second Kevin opens the door an alarm bell rings. As they screech away in Eric's Porsche, he jokes to his fugitive partner. "Kevin, do you think the building was alarmed?"

Minutes later the police radio crackles with the address of the Van Nuys office, but Kevin and Eric aren't the least bit worried. They're already miles away.

———■———

The timing of Kevin's decision to dive back into hacking couldn't have been worse. That spring, the pressure that had been building for nearly a decade finally burst in a huge series of raids. In early May 150 law enforcement agents in over a dozen cities swept down on the computer underground with twenty-seven search warrants. Led by the Secret Service and federal and state authorities in Phoenix, Operation Sundevil netted dozens of seized computers and thousands of floppy disks, stemming criminal bulletin boards estimated to be costing telephone companies millions of dollars a year. Gary M. Jenkins, the assistant director of the Secret Service, warned that the Service was sending a "clear message" to computer hackers who mistakenly believed they could hide behind their computer terminals.

The Hacker Crackdown of 1990 had begun.

THE GIVEAWAY

——■——

Triple play is what KIIS-FM 102 calls it. Every Monday morning at 7:10 A.M., in April and May of 1990, Dees plays three songs in sequence. The next time listeners hear the triple play—and Dees promises to play them again by the end of the day Friday—the countdown begins. "Win a Porsche by Friday," KIIS-FM dubs it, hyping the massive promotion as the biggest giveaway in radio history. Eight $50,000 Porsches given away once a week over two months, nearly half a million dollars.

Kevin and Ron have scored some pretty big radio prizes, but the Porsche contest is a public challenge. Wherever they go, the hackers can't miss the images of the candy red Porsche 944 convertibles. They're literally bombarded by Los Angeles's metaphor of wealth, freedom, and sex appeal. And if that isn't enough, the fantasy lives on the air, playing on radios in burger joints, malls, and cars passing in traffic. Nearly everyone is helpless before this dream, stuck playing a contest in which the odds of winning are minuscule. Nearly everyone, that is, except for a hacker.

——■——

Thanks to the contest's lengthy three-song sequence, Ron lounges by his apartment's swimming pool and even briefly walks or drives a few blocks away while listening to his portable radio without fear of blowing his opportunity.

Ron decides to power up when he hears the first beat of Janet Jackson's "Escapade." By the time he hears the familiar "Love Shack" riff, he's already called up the SAS unit and is sitting on it, waiting, knowing that the odds are that this, too, will just be a false alarm. But at the sound of the Prince tune, he drops onto the first of the station's eight lines. A couple more minutes now. The lines are off-hook at the station, preventing the auto dialers from jamming the lines, but Ron's got line number one under his total control. Finally, Prince's voice fades, and a voice declares, "That's it, we played the three songs."

Ron rings line number one at KIIS. The station makes it easy. Monkeys could be dialing, for all they know. Since they never listen whether somebody is on the line, they never know that the caller is always the same person. Just seconds elapse between each time Ron hears the countdown, and he wonders whether Kevin has seized one or two lines, whether their combined chances are roughly one in four or three in eight.

Suddenly, there's a man saying hello in his ear, the same man he's been listening to on the radio all day. "Who's this?" asks the DJ.

"Rick," Ron says.

"Rick, can I go for a ride in your brand-new 1990 red convertible Porsche 944 S2 Cabriolet?"

"Yeah, you're kidding!" Ron exclaims.

"You won it!"

"Yeah!" Ron shouts, his voice drowned out by a tape of a cheering audience.

"Rick. Rick, this car is red hot."

"Oh yeah!" Ron cries, getting into character.

"Wooo," the DJ croons. "It's not hot. We paid for it."

Probably not much, Ron thinks as the laugh track roars. Porsche probably considers this free advertising.

"Oh, man, you're going to look so hot cruising around this summer. Do you know the babe factor when you're in that car, man?"

"I don't know. What's the babe factor?"

"I took it out for a ride," says the DJ. "Even I got three phone numbers!"

"Whoa, that must be pretty high then."

Even the DJ laughs at the snappy comeback. "Hey, Rick, what radio station has the biggest Porsche giveaway in the history of mankind?"

"KIIS-FM, " Ron answers on cue.

"Rick, what's your last name?"

"Heacock."

The name too is part of the hacker's panache. If you're going to win, why not do it outrageously, why not choose a name that, spelled slowly, calls KIIS's acerbic disk jockey a name.

Rick, he a cock.

■

"Congratulations" is all Kevin says in his voice mail message, left seconds after the contest. Ron can't believe his good luck. All it had taken was two tries to win his very own, brand-new Porsche. The next day, he drives down to the station, presents his fake identification, and fills out the requisite form. No one thinks twice about his phony ID or his crude name. Down at Ogner Motors, the dealership supplying the Porsches for the contest, the salesman doesn't notice the name either, but he does wonder why the lanky towhead seems so nonchalant about winning a Porsche.

For Kevin, meanwhile, the car fantasy must wait. On May 4, Shelly Evers of Riverside wins, and on May 10, Deborah Court of Orange County. That's four Porsches down, leaving only four up for grabs. It's about that time that Kevin starts calling. As the Porsches disappear, what begins as a subtle suggestion becomes a demand. If by some chance, Kevin fails to win a Porsche, Ron will of course sell his car and split his winnings with his friend. It's the right thing to do, Kevin reminds him. Without Kevin's technical know-how Ron wouldn't have won a wheel, let alone a sports car. And Kevin still needs the money. He hasn't been able to pull off the Cayman Islands wire transfer scam.

———■———

Kevin parks next to the occult bookstore, surveys the seedy block, and likes what he sees. Tattered blue awnings hang over the red "International Newsstand" sign, the piles of newspapers and magazines giving the block the look of a bazaar. He crosses the street and notices an adult bookstore, a gay night club, and an unmarked door. He checks the address he tore out of the newspaper once more and buzzes. He's already checked on-line to make sure there are plenty of spare phone lines in the building.

Kevin isn't willing to take any more chances. This is week seven of the eight-week KIIS Porsche contest, and he has to prepare for the possibility that he'll lose and have just one more chance to win. The building manager has just what he's looking for. An office in back, a ten-by-twelve-foot patch of stained blue carpet with a view of the alley and a barbed wire fence. Kevin likes the two-hundred-dollar rent and the fact that he can move in immediately. Located just a few blocks from KIIS-FM, the office meets Kevin's other requirement, proximity.

Kevin tells Ron he needs his help, asking him to buy nine telephones from a nearby Radio Shack with a liberal return policy. Kevin furnishes the office with a couple of metal chairs and two tables to divide the phones between them. First, Kevin dials Cosmos to establish phone service for nine new numbers in the office. After midnight, he picks the lock on the building's phone closet, clips his orange butt set onto the spare pairs, and dials the ANA number until he locates the new numbers he's created.

Kevin stands on a chair by the phone closet, pops open a flimsy ceiling panel, and hoists himself up. He worms through the dusty ductwork a good twenty feet, the live pairs in his hand. When he's pretty certain he's reached his office, he drops down from the ceiling, and punches down the nine new lines in his office, confident Pac Bell will never know they exist. He's created flat rate residential service, and doesn't plan on making any toll calls.

Late in the seventh week, just as Kevin feared, he loses. It doesn't make sense—seven tries at a one-in-four chance—but this time luck isn't with him. And SAS won't do for the eighth and final week. The Hollywood Pac Bell office that serves KIIS-FM has only four SAS units, only enough to take out half of the radio station's lines. Fifty percent is a chance Kevin isn't willing to take.

Kevin dials one of the front end systems that feeds directly into the Hollywood switch. He already knows KIIS's contest line number—520-KIIS. He hijacks the station's main number, diverting it to another number only he knows, a process called translation. Within seconds, KIIS's contest line answers at Kevin's office on his control phone at his number—464-SUCK.

"KIIS-FM," Kevin answers.

"Could you play ..." a listener asks for a song.

"We'll play it right away," Kevin says.

Now that Kevin has funneled KIIS's incoming calls back to his office, he can implement the second stage of his plan. It's only the Friday before the last week of the Porsche giveaway. He doesn't need KIIS's lines yet. He picks up the control phone's receiver and dials 72 #, the forward command, then enters 520-KIIS. Once he hangs up his loop is complete. Every contest call will bounce to his control number, ring once, and then forward back to the original KIIS number.

———■———

Ron arrives early Monday morning and is struck by the creepiness of the building and the rank smell of the shoebox office. Once in a while, they bump into someone wandering the halls in a bathrobe, using a cheap office as an apartment. Two doors down, a heavy metal band practices at odd hours. The crusty old apartment manager says he doubles as a talent agent, and offers to take Ron's picture.

As the minutes turn to hours, they devise games and amusements to pass the time. Those careless enough to pass under their window are showered with a pail of water. They keep the front door voice monitor constantly live to eavesdrop on hookers propositioning johns. But the weirdest noise they hear seems to be coming from somewhere above their closet. At first they wonder if it's a big rat, but when Ron bangs on the ceiling space, a voice responds. "What the hell are you doing?"

The hackers soon learn that their neighbor, a recently released mental hospital patient, has built himself a bunk bed in the crawl space adjoining their closet.

———■———

Prince sings the final note, and the contest begins, each hacker manning his four phones. Ron can't win because his voice is known to the station. The agreement is that if he hears the disk jockey on one of his phones, he'll quickly pass the handset to Kevin.

The control phone starts ringing wildly, and they count the rings—five, ten, fifteen. At fifty, Kevin picks up the line and hits 72 #, canceling the forward that looped the calls back to KIIS. The next person to call will hear it ring once. Everyone else will get a busy signal.

But Kevin and Ron are ringing through. Four phones apiece, two on speakerphone, two with handsets. Once they hear a voice, they flash the switch hook to hang up, and the phone automatically reconnects to KIIS. It doesn't take long. "You're caller number ninety! You're caller number ninety-two, You're caller number ninety-three!" the voices shout in their ears.

Then, it happens. They have to put their voices on. They have to talk on the air. Kevin picks up a line.

"You're caller number—ninety-nine!"

"ARGHHH!" he groans.

Seconds later, Kevin's got another phone to his ear.

"Hello," says Rick Dees, sounding friendly. "You're caller number ONE-O-ONE!"

"SHITTTTT!" Kevin sighs dramatically

Ron lifts a phone to his ear. "This is KIIS, you're on LIVE!"

Oh my God, Ron thinks. He jams the receiver to Kevin, but he's busy on his own lines.

"This is KIIS, you're on LIVE!"

"Awwww, what am I?" the caller whines.

"What's your name?" probes Rick Dees.

"Mike."

"Do you always use this fake little talk when you talk to people on the radio, Mike?"

"No, I'm just nervous," the caller squeaks.

"That's OK. I thought you were putting another voice on. Because so many people from other radio stations have disguised their voices trying to win Porsche number eight . . . and Mike—"

"Uh huh."

"What is your last name?"

"Peters," the caller struggles, gasping for air, hyperventilating.

"Mike, eeeh, eeeh," Dees mocks the caller. "You're caller number ONE-O-TWO!"

The caller sounds stunned. "Oh, I don't believe it."

"Well, then bye, bye—" Dee cuts off the caller.

"What!" Mike screams.

"OK, caller number—"

"What?"

"Well, Mike, you said you don't believe it. If you don't believe it, then I'll have to move on."

"No. Don't," Mike pleads.

"Well, then, say 'I BELIEVE IN KIIS!'" Dees thunders like a gospel preacher.

"I believe in KIIS," Mike mutters.

"Put your hands on the radio, Mike, repeat after me . . . Say these words after me as loud as you can, and listen carefully."

Phrase by phrase, Dees forces Mike to repeat the station's call sign and name, like the marriage vow at a shotgun wedding. "KIIS-FM has put me in the driver's seat of a brand new fifty-thousand-dollar Porsche Cabriolet." Finally, Dees hits his screaming girls track and then asks the caller what he does.

"I'm an electrician."

"Don't hot-wire this car, Mike!" Dees jokes, hitting his laugh track.

The caller giggles, and Dees asks the name of his company.

The caller hesitates. "I'm unemployed right now, but that's what I do when I work."

"Well, you've got a fifty-thousand-dollar car. You can keep it, you can sell it, you can drive it off a cliff, whatever you want to do, but I would get behind the driver's seat if I were you, Mike," Dees sneers, "and I'd say, ha, ha, ha at least one time. . . . God bless you for being number one-oh two."

"Oh thank you," Mike gushes.

"Mike?"

Dees punches up a tape that sounds as if the nerdy Mike had just gulped down a mouthful of uppers and inhaled helium. "Ha, ha, ha, ha, oh, whooppeee, ha, ha, ha, I'm so happy I just wet my pants."

"That a boy, Mike!" Dees cries.

Michael B. Peters, the eighth and final winner of the KIIS-FM Porsche giveaway, is the only caller to be so publicly humiliated. But Peters holds another distinction. It seems that after all the careful preparation Kevin had worried that his voice had been heard on a couple of the final calls and pressed the phone back into his friend's hand. Ron too had feared that someone was bound to recognize that just a few weeks before he had won the second Porsche. The idea of impersonating a nerd popped into his head. Dees immediately sensed the voice was fake, but Ron hung by his impersonation, even as he listened to his voice dangerously slip back to his own.

Once the station takes Ron off the air, Kevin takes over the call, imitating Ron's nerd voice for a few seconds to ease the transition. They've come a long way from the nights they spent dueling on the Internet. Once they've both collected their prizes, they go for a joint spin, racing in the hills above Los Angeles, chasing one another, revving the powerful engines, doing what boys do. It's the most fun Kevin has had in a long time, and one night to test his car's limits, he accelerates up to a hundred miles an hour on an abandoned road, and slams on the brakes, marveling at how the high-performance sports car comes to a sudden stop without skidding.

If only the other powers Kevin has set in motion could be so easily controlled.

THE STAKEOUT

"**I** know this john who can do the phone thing," a hooker tells Detective Bill Spradley one night on the Strip in July of 1990.

"What's his name?"

"David Starr."

A couple of days later, on July 6, Spradley tells the hooker how it's going to go down. He's got a Yellow Pages number for her to turn on, an outcall massage service that he had personally busted, and a judge had ordered disconnected. It's the ideal test.

Starr tells the hooker it will cost $250, and she passes him the marked bills and the number. Across town, at his office at 1010 Wilshire Boulevard, Terry Atchley is watching. At precisely 5:30 P.M., on July 7, the outcall number mysteriously springs back to life. Atchley's computer screen gives him a big clue. Whoever turned on the Yellow Pages number called through one of Pac Bell's hundreds of dial-up ports and used Cosmos. Atchley, who took the precaution of placing a tap on David Starr's line, knows something else. The order was not made over David Starr's line.

"This is Big Brother calling," announces the man on the phone. Fine, thinks the Hollywood vice squad detective at LAPD's downtown headquarters, Parker Center, who answers the anonymous call.

"What kind of trouble would someone be in if they . . . ?" Big Brother begins tentatively. The detective listens to the elaborate, "purely hypothetical" description of Yellow Pages ads, phone numbers, and computer hacking. Sounds like the stuff Spradley is working on, he thinks. The detective keeps Big Brother on the line, and talks him into a meeting with Detective Spradley.

———■———

Terry Atchley saunters past the line of Rolls-Royces in his faded Levi's, tennis shoes, and sport shirt, drawing on a cigarette. He's never been to the Four Seasons before, never seen such a flagrant display of wealth. These people either have money or know how to fake it, he thinks. The fancy clothes, the jewelry, the Gucci bags.

Of all the coffee shops and restaurants in Los Angeles, David Starr has chosen the elegant, expensive hotel to meet Atchley, Spradley, and his partner, Megan McElroy. Amid the Casablanca setting, Starr delivers his lines as if he's auditioning for the biggest part of his career. "I want immunity," he demands as he sips on the Coke the investigators bought him at the bar.

The investigators don't reply.

"You've got to protect me," Starr harps shrilly. "If word gets out these people could kill me."

Spradley has seen a lot of David Starrs in his years on the Strip. Over thirty, short, with a paunch, Starr is just the sort of small-time flimflam man cops despise. "You're a co-conspirator," Spradley informs Starr in his clipped monotone. "You can cooperate or risk prosecution."

———■———

On September 7, Spradley hands Starr six twenty-dollar bills and requests a Yellow Pages number invisible to Pac Bell. Starr, meanwhile, continues to insist on protecting his source.

Spradley and McElroy drop their fidgety informant at Sunset and Fuller, sit back in their unmarked van, and watch him start down a familiar street. Before Starr turns up the sidewalk, Spradley and McElroy have a hunch their rat is heading for the house of Henry Spiegel. Years before, McElroy had the pleasure of busting Spiegel for pimping at the rock 'n' roll Denny's. Spradley, too, has memories. He'd served a warrant at the Martel address and been amazed at the number of phone lines leading into Spiegel's house. Spradley had returned with telephone linemen, and even after they'd clambered up the pole they couldn't sort out how Spiegel had swiped so many phone lines for his telemarketing scams.

After a short wait, Starr emerges with Spiegel and gets a ride home in the pimp's Lincoln Town Car. But after the quick Beverly Hills drive, Spiegel makes a short detour. He parks on Sunset and swings open a pair of glass doors into a private post office box service. Spying with binoculars from across the street, Spradley sees Spiegel slip an envelope into a box. Perhaps the Yellow Pages scam goes beyond Starr and Spiegel, the detective wonders. As Spradley watches an empty-handed Spiegel drive away, he radios two undercover cars for backup and turns his attention to the box. It's now 8:45 P.M. Positioned across the street, the three undercover vehicles stake out the P.O. box. Midnight comes and goes. Up since dawn, Spradley catches his eyes drooping toward the dash.

———■———

Well before Kevin pulls up at the P.O. box at the corner of Sunset and Laurel Canyon, he glances over at the Ford Bronco and what looks like a cop behind the wheel. Kevin has seen plenty of mail service joints staked out before to catch criminals, but he doubts tonight's surveillance has anything to do with him. Nor is he the least bit worried about the Bronco, though he knows that cops love the four-wheel-drive vehicle. On the drive over, Kevin scanned the FBI's channel and didn't hear any activity at all.

At precisely 2:15 A.M., Spradley rights himself and watches a thin, casually dressed man with platinum blond punk hair stick a key in the glass door. Peering through his nine-inch binoculars a hundred feet away, Spradley sees the man reach up to Spiegel's box and retrieve an envelope that looks like the one the pimp just dropped.

"We've got a pickup from the box," Spiegel radios his team.

Kevin fires up his van, then watches the Bronco quickly pull behind him to get his plate and then duck into the corner gas station. But two can play at this game. Kevin swings a U-turn, doubles back behind the Bronco at the gas station, and leans forward to memorize the plate.

Kevin chuckles to himself as the Bronco pulls onto Sunset, amazed they didn't even bother with the pretense of getting gas. He lets the Bronco go, and turns back on the same side street where he was parked, stopping a couple of blocks away to write down the Bronco's plate number.

Suddenly, Kevin sees a car several blocks back in his rearview mirror. He decides the attention must be because he glanced at the Bronco and because anybody visiting a P.O. box at two in the morning looks suspicious. Kevin revs up his old van and begins weaving and screeching through Hollywood. He even goes the wrong way down a one way street. A few minutes later he pulls over and waits, but nothing pops up in his rearview.

Time to do a little "dry cleaning," Kevin thinks. He heads over the dry hills to the Valley, takes a right at Laurel, and drives under the 101 Ventura freeway into a grid of suburban homes. Right, left, double back, kill the headlights. Wait.

But even after all of Kevin's evasive driving, a Camaro pulls into the street, slows, and then speeds away. Kevin takes off after the Camaro, pulling close enough to get the license plate. He hasn't seen an FBI Cessna or an LAPD chopper, but he's pretty sure someone up above is directing the guys on the ground. He hops on the 134 freeway, quickly gets off, and then takes the first exit in Burbank. He spots an office building to hide behind and swerves hard to make the turn, but his right tire hits the curb and explodes.

Steering the crippled van behind the building, Kevin kills his headlights. A minute later the Camaro zips by. Kevin considers his options. His van is dead. The FBI hasn't said a peep on his police scanner. It can't be related to him. Why should he worry? There's nothing incriminating in his van, unless, of course, they're looking for a hacker. Kevin grabs his black gadget bag and starts walking. A car is stopped in the street, its blinding lights trained on him.

Kevin casually approaches the open driver's window, a woman looking at him with a pinched smile. "Hey, listen," Kevin says. "As long as you guys are following me around, maybe you could give me a hand with a blowout?"

"Oh yeah?" snaps the woman.

Another car skids toward Kevin and shudders to a stop. A cop leaps out, gun drawn. "Who do you think you're fucking with?" Spradley yells, splaying Kevin against the hood and shoving the barrel of a gun against his face. "We're the fucking police!"

A cop's silver badge is waved in Kevin's face, but it's been removed from its holder, and there's no name.

"I didn't do anything," Kevin protests.

But Spradley isn't interested in talking just yet. First, he wants to ID the guy. He's got no driver's license, just a DMV learner's permit and a business card in the name of Steve Holland. The van is registered to a Jerome K. Anderson at a San Diego P.O. box.

"Where are you coming from?" Spradley asks.

"Downtown," Kevin answers.

"No you weren't," Spradley corrects him. "We picked you up in Hollywood."

"Oh yeah, that's right. I went to Hollywood."

"You were dealing narcotics."

"No, I wasn't. I met a friend of mine."

Spradley empties Kevin's tote bag. Out spills a portable police scanner, binoculars, a flashlight, and a plug spinner for lock picking. In the back of the van are two chairs and an M-16 squirt gun.

"Is this where you work?" McElroy asks, waving Kevin's fake work ID in his face. "What's your name?"

Let's see, I know my first name.

"Steve," Kevin replies dumbly.

"Steve, what's your last name?" McElroy snaps.

Ignore her. Try to look shocked.

"Oh god, oh god," Kevin mumbles, faking distress.

Finally, Spradley takes out one of Kevin's fake work ID's and waves it close. Kevin cranes forward.

"Steve, what's your last name?" McElroy snaps again.

"Holland," Kevin replies confidently.

Spradley tells Kevin they're narcotics cops, and they pulled him over because he was driving recklessly. But Kevin says they were following him.

"No," Spradley insists, "we started following you because you were driving recklessly."

"Then what were you doing at my mailbox?"

"Why do you have a pair of binoculars?" McElroy changes the subject. "Are you some kind of Peeping Tom?"

Spradley fires another question. "Why isn't the van registered under your name?"

———■———

Kevin is cuffed to a bench in a narrow holding cell with a long window in the central Burbank police station. Anyone else would be terrified in his situation, but Kevin is calm and shows no fear as he waits out the last minutes before what must certainly be his capture. He's done all he can do. Now it's a question of staying cool and hoping for a little luck.

"How much money do you have on you?" Spradley asks.

Kevin pulls five twenty-dollar bills out of his wallet.

"Why do you have a hundred bucks?" Spradley asks. "Out picking up hookers?"

"No," Kevin replies. "I just have a hundred dollars."

"Where do you work?" Spradley asks.

"RCA," says Kevin, remembering the card they showed him.

———■———

The cops take Kevin's prints at Parker Center, running them through the National Crime Information Center computers and local systems for a criminal record. Meanwhile, the company and address Kevin gave Spradley don't check out.

A uniformed cop peers through the lens as Kevin stands behind the rack of black plastic booking numbers. The hacker grins, pleased with himself, his arms hanging easily at his sides, his sport collar open and platinum hair flopped in a fashionable part.

"I'll take an eight-by-ten and two wallet-sized," Kevin quips.

A couple of minutes later, one arm cuffed to a bench, Kevin asks if he can call his lawyer. The cops will be logging the call, of course, so he phones the 800 extender number he's memorized for just such occasions, and then dials Eric's answering machine. It's the theme music from Eric's favorite TV show, *America's Most Wanted,* and it adds just the right measure of humor to his otherwise ordinary message. "I can't get to the phone right now, but if you . . ."

A cop stands next to Kevin, listening.

"Hello this is . . ." Kevin tries to remember his alias. "Steve. I've been arrested at Parker Center. They might be holding me on suspicion of stealing my van. Thought you should know. See what you can do out there."

A little after four in the morning, Terry Atchley arrives at Parker Center, careful to stay out of view of the suspect cuffed in a holding cell. They still figure the Yellow Pages man is probably a Pac Bell employee, and the last thing anyone wants is for the suspect to recognize Atchley, a coworker. Still, when they bring the man out, Atchley sneaks a good look at the punk blond, bespectacled young man. He's certain he's never set eyes on him before.

A couple of hours later, Spradley reluctantly realizes that his suspect will walk. The computers came back with nothing. Sure, he's got the marked twenties, his story doesn't wash, and he jerked them around on his wild ride. But there's no real hard crime. Besides, there could be an advantage in letting him go. Spradley has been careful to mask his questions in the guise of a narcotics investigation, and he doubts the man knows why he's been followed. If they still hope to capture the Yellow Pages mastermind that ignorance might prove invaluable.

———■———

As he walks out of Parker Center that early-September morning with Spradley and McElroy, Terry Atchley just wants to hurry home to take a nice hot shower before heading off for work. He says his goodbyes, starts up his gray Chevy Celebrity, and then sees the suspect walking alone. But by the time Atchley swings his Chevy out of the parking lot he's lost him. He swears at himself for blowing the opportunity, and circles the area for several minutes, hoping to get lucky.

He finds him over a mile from Parker Center, carrying the black bag the cops returned, the one with his police scanner, flashlight, and plug spinner. The suspect walks toward the Union 76 station on Alameda near the bustling Hollywood freeway, opens a phone booth door, and dials. Atchley wants to get closer, but he'd have to turn right in front of the booth, too much of a risk. He loops around and approaches the station from a one-way alley along the freeway. Just a twenty-second detour, he figures. But the one-way street turns out to be longer than he thought. The knot tightens in his stomach as the odometer passes one mile. Atchley guns it on the way back, then slows as he approaches the gas station.

The phone booth is empty.

THE CHASE

◼

Kevin hops out of the cab and walks about a half mile to the Sherman Oaks Galleria in the Valley. Eric is casually sipping a Coke on the top level of the crowded mall when he spots Kevin down by the mirrored elevator. A few minutes later Kevin returns his look, then approaches and passes him. Eric lags behind, and they drift with the teenagers and parents past the chain stores. Seeing nothing suspicious, Eric walks to the bank of phones next to the multiplex and leaves Kevin a voice mail, "Follow me to my car."

Kevin waits a minute or so, dials his voice mail, and picks up the message. Down in the garage, Eric unlocks the passenger door of his Porsche and starts the engine. "Duck down," Eric whispers to Kevin as he slips into the car.

Eric guns it out of the underground garage, checking his rearview mirror for a tail. Just to be certain, he jumps onto the 101 freeway and winds it up to a hundred, darting in and out of traffic. Everything looks clean, so he heads into the hills of Encino and stops at Dupar's, a coffee shop in Studio City. Over coffee and pie, Kevin tells the strange story of the surveillance, the amusing chase and capture, and the long police interrogation. Kevin sees no irony in having phoned Eric in his moment of need. He wanted someone's help to make sure he wasn't still being followed. Ron wasn't around, so he called Eric.

"I don't understand why they let me go," Kevin wonders. It's a good question. Although he'd given the cops a fake name, he couldn't disguise his fingerprints.

Why hadn't the cops' computers revealed his true identity?

———■———

Terry Atchley sits in his cubicle at 1010 Wilshire, shuffles the few notes he's written on the case, and muses about that morning a few days ago, and the turn he wished he hadn't made. Instinct had told Atchley to follow the blond guy from Parker Center. If only he had maintained his position he might have seen the car that picked him up, might have had something to go on, a clue. He's stumped because Starr has been telling them it's an inside job, that the mastermind is a dirty Pac Bell employee, a scenario that doesn't match the guy they grabbed a few days ago. But what if Starr was wrong, or simply lying? The idea comes to Atchley out of the blue. On a hunch he calls Pac Bell security in Oakland and asks about the hacker case. A thick sheaf of papers with a big eight-by-ten photo arrives the next day in an overnight pouch. No platinum blond hair, but that face, Atchley knows that face.

On September 18, ten days after the Burbank chase, Spradley and the FBI fugitive hunter pay a visit to Atchley's office. Before anyone has a chance to speak Spradley pulls out a blowup of the mug shot taken the night he'd had the blond in custody. Special Agent Beasely just about falls out of his seat. It's Kevin Poulsen, and he slipped right through their hands. That night when Spradley had Poulsen in custody and ran his prints he was told by the fingerprint department that the suspect had no criminal record. He didn't—in Los Angeles City and County. But Spradley wasn't told that the network was down and Poulsen's prints were never run on the federal and state systems in Sacramento. The FBI's most wanted hacker was saved by a computer glitch.

Long after Beasely and Spradley leave, Atchley keeps poring over the file, remembering how close he had been. It's staring him right in the face. The pay phone. Poulsen must have called a cab or a friend. Atchley checks his file for the time he followed Poulsen, and pulls up the gas station pay phone record on his computer. He's lucky this time. On the morning of September 8 there were hardly any calls made from the 76 station. He finds one call to a cab company and another to what Atchley recognizes as a Beverly Hills prefix. That's all he needs. Atchley enters the number onto another Pac Bell system and surveys the billing information: Eric Heinz, 999 Doheny, apartment 801. Atchley runs the call detail for the apartment, and sure enough, finds a call to a Cosmos dial-up number.

He remembers one of the things Poulsen had said to Spradley. Somebody would vouch for him, somebody by the name of Eric.

■

The following evening Kevin runs his Cosmos tap search and finds two Hikamin DNR units attached to Eric's line. Eric is partying at the Hollywood club X-Poseur when he gets the page from Kevin. He phones back immediately. Kevin announces he's calling from a pay phone.

"You been dialing anything interesting lately, Eric?" Kevin asks.

"Quite a bit," Eric replies. The past week he'd called the computers of TRW Credit, the Department of Motor Vehicles, even Pac Bell's Cosmos.

"Two of your lines have DNR taps on them."

That night, after the club closes, Eric reluctantly goes into "secure mode." He packs all of his diskettes, proprietary manuals, and handwritten notes, loads them into his car, and parks a couple of blocks away. He returns to his apartment and deletes everything sensitive on his computer. Then, he runs Norton Utilities to wipe his disk clean. Satisfied that he's safe for the moment, he downs a couple of beers. In the morning, he'll phone Kevin and Ron and enlist their help to move out the bulk of his computers and electronic equipment. But for now, Eric turns his attention to a little unfinished business, the Australian girl he picked up at X-Poseur.

■

Spradley and his partner, Megan McElroy, arrive in an undercover car outside Doheny Towers. The tall, white art deco style building with white canvas awnings and a circle drive resembles an elegant hotel more than an apartment complex. The Rainbow and the rock clubs the Roxie and the Whiskey are all within walking distance, however unlikely walking may be in Hollywood. Half a block down from the priciest section of the Strip, perched on the hill, Doheny Towers is clearly the address of a somebody.

The guard buzzes in Spradley and McElroy and the detectives take in the gold elevators, marble floors, plush sofas, French antiques, and chandelier. They flash their badges and slip Poulsen's eight-by-ten mug shot to the Filipino guard, who has worked at the posh complex for nearly eight years.

Last night, says the guard, nodding. He's a regular. Comes late, alone, usually at about midnight, staying for an hour or so. Always leaves alone too. Unlike most guests, he never asks to have his car parked, he just buzzes to be let in. He wears black clothes, a leather jacket, black boots. Sometimes glasses, sometimes not. His name is always different. He signed in once as Tom Cruise, another time as Magic Johnson.

Eric, on the other hand, the guard could write a book about. The first night he met him he said he worked for the phone company. Strapped around his waist hung a heavy leather belt stuffed with screwdrivers and other telephone tools, a red butt set clipped to one side. A laminated Pac Bell card dangled from his neck, and in his arms, spiked climbing boots. Several hours later, Eric showed up at the front entrance, waiting to be buzzed in, dirty and sweaty, as if he'd been to work.

But on other evenings, the guard told Spradley and McElroy, Eric dressed sleekly in a club suit or even a tuxedo. He told the guard all about his favorite club, the Rainbow, and a few hours later the guard could see the attraction. Sometime before dawn Eric returned in his Porsche with at least one new beautiful young woman. On the afternoon shift, girls would pump the guard for information. "Is he in the movie business?" they'd ask. "Is he a casting director? Does he really have big bucks?"

The guard would shrug his shoulders. Maybe, he thought to himself. Or maybe he's just a telephone man with the right hair, right car, and a good line.

The building manager across the street volunteers a vacant apartment with a clear view of Doheny Towers and the entrance to the underground parking lot. The guard tapes up Poulsen's mug shot under the Doheny Towers security desk next to the eight video cameras surveying the entrance, the parking lot, and the exits. Detective Spradley briefs his commanding officer on Kevin Poulsen's computer and phone intrusions and is given the green light to run the investigation as he sees fit—to use the entire division if need be. Kevin Poulsen, after all, is the FBI's most wanted computer hacker.

The vacant apartment becomes the command post, manned around the clock by the detective and two or three cops or FBI agents. Atchley supplies the detective, the FBI, and others working the case with cellular phones to complement their handheld radios. On the streets of Los Angeles, the detective has about thirty-five LAPD officers at his disposal, plus an eight-man FBI squad and the Pac Bell investigator. The goal is simple: get Eric Heinz to lead them to Kevin Poulsen.

On the first evening, the black Porsche growls from the underground parking lot, cuts right, and guns down Doheny, heading west away from the Strip. The late-model American undercover cars struggle to keep up, but traveling on side streets at speeds of sixty to seventy, the Porsche loses them in about a mile. On the second evening, the Porsche heads into the winding hills of Laurel Canyon above Hollywood, snaking through the hills. Undercover cars wait at the back side for Heinz and his Porsche to emerge. He doesn't.

Spradley tries a new approach. He staggers the surveillance cars at strategic points through the Hollywood hills. Six are positioned over Laurel Canyon, one up on Lookout Mountain, another up on Mulholland Drive, a couple on the back side near Ventura Boulevard, three in each direction on Sunset Boulevard—cars strung out as far as ten miles away. But the carefully woven web can't trap the black car. Eric thunders up Laurel Canyon, turns off onto one of the streets where an undercover car waits, and promptly disappears into the labyrinth of curving side streets.

It's hard to know when Eric realizes he's being tailed. He drives so fast all the time that he may have lost the cops once, even twice before he even knew he was being followed. But the late-model blue Thunderbird catches his eye. Something about the way it just flipped on its headlights as Eric approaches Sunset Boulevard. Still, he doesn't make much of it, and is about to turn into the Rainbow parking lot and toss his key to the valet when suddenly two more sets of headlights appear in his rearview mirror.

He changes his mind and continues down Sunset a few blocks before pulling over abruptly. A minute later, when he eases back into traffic, he spots the Thunderbird at a stop sign on a cross street. No reason to take chances, Eric thinks. Laurel Canyon is the next street. He hangs a left, floors it, and in a few minutes no one is in his rearview mirror.

Fifteen minutes later, Eric parks behind Denny's ready to congratulate himself on having lost them when the blue Thunderbird slowly cruises by. As if on cue, one of Eric's girlfriends drives into the lot, a Lancome girl at Bullock's makeup counter. Eric tells her about his suspicions and asks her to help to see if he's being tailed. He leaves voice mail messages for Kevin and Ron telling them about the Thunderbird, and then the Lancome girl trails Eric over Laurel Canyon in her car. Neither of them spot a tail, and Eric invites her to share a hotel bed with him for the night.

The following afternoon, Eric leaves messages for Kevin and Ron saying he's all right, and then heads for the Investigator's office on Wilshire. He tells the Investigator about his predicament, picks up a paycheck for a few wiretaps, and borrows a cellular phone. The more Eric thinks about it, the less certain he is that he was being followed. Maybe the guy in the Thunderbird thought he was a chick? It's happened to Eric before. So Eric heads back to Doheny, carefully checking for a tail. He's only going to grab some clothes. But once inside, he figures why not take a nap?

Midnight approaches and the Porsche roars out of Doheny Towers, up the hill, and right on the Strip. Eric pulls over suddenly, across from the Coconut Teaser restaurant, and watches the surveillance scatter like so many pigeons. He knows it's not his imagination and decides to have some fun. He does his typical zigzag maneuvers, and in no time he cuts back and is following his pursuers, picking up their license plates. He pulls onto his favorite boulevard, Laurel Canyon, glances over at the adjacent car, and spies a man in a windbreaker with slicked back hair and a cigarette hanging from his lip. A cop, he figures. Eric scratches down the car's license plate on a scrap of paper and floors it.

The Porsche's speedometer bounces over eighty. Signs for Hollywood and Mt. Olympus streets blur and the hills dry out as the road narrows. The houses crowd closer, stone fences and palms inches from the road, yellow and black directional signs leading the Porsche through the tight corners. Halfway up the canyon, well before Mulholland and the mansions of Jack Nicholson and other legends of the screen, Eric hangs a skidding left at Stanley Hills and takes an anonymous side street. This time somebody is watching. The airborne helicopter's observer peers through his nightscope and sees the Porsche veer toward the curb and then fade from view. The suspect seems to be under a tree. Then, the car appears to move, without headlights.

Eric hears the heavy whir of the chopper's blades overhead. In the dark he searches for what he needs. He's driving slowly now, and when he swoops down a private driveway to several houses and into a covered garage, it's as if he's driving home, except for his dead headlights. He slides quietly out of the car, and begins walking. They've lost me, he thinks, when he spots the flying machine a fair distance off, moving in a straight line at a good clip.

The blades thud closer, and he knows by the distinctive sound that it's a Bell copter. Suddenly, the contraption spins into a circle. The blades seem to beat above his head. He has to be fast. He runs well, amazingly well for someone missing the better part of a leg. He spots a pickup truck, crawls under, and slides to the front. The engine block is still warm.

Eric has discussed this very scenario before with Kevin. Normally, the chopper's infrared heat sensors would pick up the heat given off by a human body. But what if you hid under a warm car engine? Might that shield him from the high-tech eyes in the sky? He flips open his cellular phone and dials the voice mail box. It doesn't take long. Kevin is never far from a phone. Eric can still hear the chopper circling when his phone rings.

"Hello," he whispers.

"What's going on?" Kevin asks.

"I think we did it this time."

Kevin flips on his scanner and finds the LAPD's tactical frequency. Curled up under a warm engine in the Hollywood hills, Eric listens with Kevin on his cell phone for over half an hour, hearing little nuggets, such as the police in the copter asking if they're looking for a 911 or 944 Porsche.

"They're really doing it!" Kevin exclaims, thrilled by the car chase and the show of force. He warns Eric it's time to go into "secure mode," time to move everything out of his apartment and only make calls from pay phones. Eric reads Kevin the license plates he wrote down so he can run them through the DMV's computer.

Eric lies under the pickup until the pulse of the chopper's blades has faded away, and says goodbye to Kevin. He calls a few friends and a woman he plans on sleeping with later that night. His last call takes only a few seconds. The cab pulls up, and the man with one leg slides out from under the engine block and off into the night.

———■———

Kevin runs the plate numbers Eric gave him. The first two come back "no record found," which often means the FBI. The third comes back to the Pac Bell motor pool.

Kevin phones the Los Angeles Pac Bell motor pool office to social engineer some answers. "I'm calling from Pac Bell claims," Kevin lies. "I've got an accident report here involving a company employee, and we'd like to know who was driving."

"All right, what's the license?"

"2 HLX 600," Kevin replies.

The Pac Bell motor pool man hits a few keys, and breaks into laughter. It seems the man responsible for the accident is in the same division as Kevin's department.

"This is one of your guys. This is a 6DAA, the security department. Yeah, that's one of your guys all right."

The motor pool man reads Kevin the address, and Kevin is about to hang up. "Hold on, I'll give you the guy's name. Let's see, uh, Atchley."

Kevin can't resist. He knows Atchley as the security man who searched his house when he was seventeen. "Oh yeah, Terry Atchley."

"Oh, you know him?" asks a surprised motor pool man.

"Yeah, that's one of our guys."

——■——

By the day after the copter chase, Kevin has located 453.350 megahertz, the frequency on which the vice squad is broadcasting its surveillance of Eric Heinz.

"Let's go see what they look like," Kevin suggests to his associates. So what if just a couple of weeks ago Kevin was interrogated, fingerprinted, and escaped capture only by his nerves and a computer snafu? He's eager for another opportunity to size up the enemy, to see who's following Eric, and very likely searching for him.

The three hackers meet near Doheny Towers and pile into Ron's old Toyota, Kevin listening in back with his Bear Cat scanner. The trio cruises Sunset, and they spot the surveillance team up a residential street on the hilly side of the bustling avenue.

"Why don't we take a closer look?" Kevin suggests. It's a radical move, but neither Ron nor Eric protests. On the next pass, Ron hangs a left up the street and Kevin, before he ducks out of view, catches a glimpse of a bunch of guys sitting around their cars drinking coffee from Styrofoam cups. Ten feet at the most. That's all that separates Kevin from the cops. After driving up a few blocks, Kevin boldly suggests another pass by, and when they loop around, Ron narrates what he sees. He can't believe how obvious the cops are. One is even sitting on the hood of his car.

Later that afternoon, Kevin and Ron opt to help Eric move out his computers and electronic gear. Kevin feels obligated. He knows there's a good chance his recent arrest caused Eric's predicament, and despite their differences, he just can't let him move by himself.

Kevin listens to the surveillance, checking the FBI's frequencies, and then about half an hour after the transmissions stop, the hacker slips in through a back entrance, makes his way upstairs into the heavily mirrored, chandeliered hallway, and is actually talking with Eric in apartment 801. Kevin sees nothing irrational about walking right into a building under surveillance. He's brought along his Bear Cat scanner and he's watching them at least as professionally as they're watching him.

He rides the elevator a couple of times, and walks right past the guard, who has been briefed to phone LAPD if he spots the platinum blond whose mug shot is taped under the desk. If Kevin is nervous he doesn't show it. He even jokes to Eric. "You think you've got problems. I just found out that next week I'm going to be on *Unsolved Mysteries.*"

UNSOLVED MYSTERIES

———■———

SEPTEMBER 5, 1990

TIMOTHY J. ROGAN
COSGROVE & MEURER PRODUCTIONS
4303 WEST VERDUGO AVENUE
BURBANK, CALIFORNIA 91505

Dear Mr. Rogan,

I am writing to you regarding an upcoming segment of "Unsolved Mysteries" which you have already produced. Apparently titled "Dark Dante," it is said to include a dramatization of allegations that the San Jose U.S. Attorney's office has made against me. . . .

Criminal cases involving suspected unauthorized computer access, or "hacking," are frequently subject to wild, unsubstantiated, and often bizarre claims by prosecutors and investigators. In the last five years hacking suspects have been accused of, among other things: breaking into classified NSA computers, causing the January crash of AT&T's switching network, shifting the position of orbiting satel-

lites, and "threatening the safety of residents throughout the Southeast" by publishing proprietary details of Bell South's emergency
911 system. Most of these fanciful accusations have not been backed
up by formal charges and none of them has ever resulted in a conviction. In the latter case, in which a Missouri man was accused of con-
spiring to steal an eighty-thousand-dollar secret document on the
workings of the 911 system, federal prosecutors were recently forced
to drop all charges when the defense proved that not only was the
document quite harmless, but it was actually available to the general public from Bell South for a ten-dollar fee.

These outrageous claims allow prosecutors to win absurdly high
bail requirements for suspects or even no bail at all. Further, they
will often generate press coverage for what may otherwise be a de-
cidedly unnewsworthy case.

. . . What I've read about the segment you've produced is that you in-
tend on showing a Kevin Poulsen look-alike actually doing what the
prosecutor has accused me of. . . . Even after I am eventually cleared
of these ludicrous accusations involving national security, Ferdinand
Marcos, etc., the images of "Kevin Poulsen" huddled over a computer
stealing military secrets while cackling evilly will remain in the
minds of your fourteen-million viewers . . . My life and my career
will be irrevocably damaged.

From a legal standpoint, if you portray me committing crimes that I
am innocent of you will be guilty of slander . . . as well as "false light
invasion of privacy," i.e. placing me before the public in a false and
offensive light . . . Don't count on my conviction on these charges
either. The more sensationalistic charges will be early casualties
when I come to trial, if not sooner. Indeed, unlikelihoods and inconsis-
tencies in the government's claims are already beginning to emerge.
A New York Times article quoted several computer security experts
as expressing skepticism over the claim that I broke into a classified
computer system. . . .

Of course, I have not actually seen your report. . . . Perhaps your piece is an objective, or even skeptical look at the government's case, rather than a mindless parroting of its allegations. Maybe your dramatization does not act out the indictment, but rather exposes the absurdity of its claims. If this is the case then I can only apologize for what would be a presumptuous letter. However, this seems unlikely.

Finally, I have not used the pen-name "Dark Dante" since I was sixteen. I humbly offer "Dark Deception" or "Defamatory Dramatization" as more generally descriptive titles.

Sincerely,

Kevin L. Poulsen

cc: New York Times
*   Peninsula Times Tribune.*

————■————

Though the fugitive left no return address, there is one tantalizing clue, a U.S. mail postmark from Waco, Texas. The first thought that goes through the mind of Timothy Rogan, a polite, reserved young producer with *Unsolved Mysteries*, is how Poulsen got his name. The second is whether he can read the detailed demand for retraction, which includes footnotes ranging from a legal citation to articles in the *New York Times* and *Time* magazine, without smudging his fingerprints all over it.

Rogan isn't totally surprised by the letter. There had been publicity in the local papers up north when they'd done some shooting in Palo Alto and Menlo Park. Rogan and his staff had been in touch with Poulsen's parents and childhood friends and talked with employees of SRI. Word was bound to have gotten back to Poulsen, though Poulsen's knowledge of the impending broadcast, scheduled five weeks away, is intimidating, especially considering that he's the FBI's most wanted hacker. Rogan remembers when the FBI had first contacted the top-rated, NBC show and suggested they profile the fugitive hacker. Who cares about the phone company, he thought, as long as our calls get through? Where's the victim in the story? Rogan wondered. It was only when the government told him what Poulsen was capable of that he saw the appeal.

The letter and envelope, which he would turn over to the FBI—who would promptly consider the relevance of the Waco, Texas, postmark and examine the documents for fingerprints—is the first public statement by the hacker in the year he has been underground. The footnotes and legal citations make Rogan wonder whether Poulsen consulted an attorney. NBC doesn't have to worry only about slander, it seems. Simply by invading the hacker's privacy, the network might be liable.

But the letter of an accused man says most about its writer, and Kevin's letter is most revealing for what it does not say. The letter he researched with hacked access codes to Lexis and Nexis and sent through a remailer in Waco, Texas, is silent about the facts of his documented wiretaps, his break-ins to countless Pac Bell central offices, and his knowledge of FBI and spy wiretaps. Kevin is in control of this game. When the government finally lives up to its past offer to grant him bail if he self-surrenders in court, Kevin will face down his accusers, prove the absurdity of their claims in a court of law, confident that his latest crimes will never be discovered.

The Watchman, the one who has the power to watch and listen to scores of intimate secrets, seems to have an intense wish to keep his own life and alleged criminal exploits private. But then Kevin doesn't believe he invades the privacy of others. He wiretaps to expand his technical knowledge and defend himself against his enemies. If he wiretaps a friend or two in the process and uncovers a few dozen spy taps, those are unfortunate minor casualties. Kevin has no problem distinguishing his grossly exaggerated Northern California activities from his more serious Southern California deeds. He sees nothing ironic about arguing his innocence in Northern California. He was innocent. Then.

Kevin has a point about the government's unimpressive record on prosecuting computer crimes. Ignorant of the technical subtleties of computer hacking, the government's indictments and attempted prosecutions resemble a hapless comedy. The Hacker Crackdown has turned into a public relations disaster. The Secret Service raided a maker of fantasy role-playing games called Steve Jackson Games and seized a manuscript and delayed the publication of a science fiction book, mistaking it for a manual on digital crime. In general, the government's cases have lacked hard evidence, and when it has seized upon something, like the Bell South 911 emergency document referred to in Kevin's letter, it often has proved to be a red herring.

Hackers know better than almost anyone that the government has no idea how to prosecute computer crime. The bloodless, anonymous, and often victimless nature of hacking leaves few traces. Computers seized are often wiped clean, and phone records, even when they aren't altered, hardly excite a jury. The government appears outmatched, lacking the know-how, technology, and laws to fight what it perceives as a growing menace.

Kevin has thrown down the gauntlet in his letter, publicly challenging what he terms the government's "ludicrous accusations involving national security, Ferdinand Marcos," and the stealing of "military secrets." Kevin believes the government is fighting with press releases as much as it is with indictments and convictions. The fight against the mob died out years ago. The Red menace has faded. In the ensuing vacuum, hackers have become the latest threat to American society, and Kevin Poulsen is falling into the government's crosshairs at exactly the wrong time.

———■———

"I guess I could knock out Channel Four," Kevin proposes to his fellow hackers.

Kevin has asked for their advice about the impending *Unsolved Mysteries* broadcast, and though his idea is a bit extreme, both Eric and Ron know it's possible. Kevin knows where the junction points are for the transmitter towers up in the hills. Cut the right cable at the right time and *Unsolved Mysteries* won't be broadcast in Los Angeles.

"Sure." Eric laughs. " If you want to guarantee a repeat appearance on every segment of *Unsolved Mysteries.*"

———■———

The secretary takes the call at the discreet Tudor-style Burbank offices of NBC's *Unsolved Mysteries* a little after three on October 10, 1990, a few hours before the scheduled broadcast of the Dark Dante episode. She receives hundreds of calls every day, and would likely have forgotten that particular one, except that after she rattles off the number she thinks it odd. The caller doesn't leave a tip or make an inquiry. All the man wants is the toll-free number for that night's show, the same number that he could get on his television screen later that night when it airs.

———■———

Hours before the broadcast, Kevin scouts out a small kitchenette unit at a Super 8 Motel northeast of Los Angeles to hide out for a couple of weeks after the *Unsolved Mysteries* episode airs. He decides to have someone else check in for him under a phony ID. Kevin realizes that the show might air Ron's photograph as one of his known hacking associates, so he asks Eric to check in for him and pay two weeks' rent in advance. It's not a question of trust. Kevin just figures that Eric won't turn him in when it would be so obvious.

That afternoon, Kevin parks his van away from his apartment in case it's mentioned on the broadcast, and returns in his Fiero to his stripped-down apartment, already emptied of anything that might be sensitive. That evening, right on schedule, the show begins, and after a few minutes he hears a promotional blurb, "Coming up next, 'Dark Dante.'" He walks into the apartment complex's utility closet and lashes the breakers into the off position with thick phone cables, killing power to the whole building.

———■———

Richard Beasely of the FBI, sitting in the *Unsolved Mysteries* telecommunications center in Sherman Oaks, seems pleased with the advance screening of the Kevin Poulsen episode he's just seen. The time is about a quarter past four on October 10. In approximately an hour and fifteen minutes, at roughly 5 P.M. Pacific time, NBC will begin broadcasting the episode, beaming the top-rated show, according to Kevin Poulsen's letter, into the consciousness of 14 million viewers.

David Rajter, the show's phone center manager, is surprised at how tight-lipped Agent Beasely is. Usually, in the minutes before a broadcast about an FBI fugitive, the agent would open up to him and tell him little intriguing tidbits of the case to pass the time. But this guy won't say a word.

Rajter is hoping for a good batch of tips that night. The Sherman Oaks telecommunications center, which keeps its exact location secret as a security precaution, has thirty operators on duty to take the calls, raising red cards when they've received what seems a valid tip. Beasely is on hand to monitor the best of the tips and, if a caller seems to have particularly valid information, he's prepared to take over the call himself.

On schedule, NBC plays the show's eerie theme music followed by a quick preview of that night's episodes. The first segment that afternoon is about a mob hit, "The Man Who Knew Too Much." Rajter sneaks glances at the bloody mafia murder, while he continues to try to strike up a conversation with Beasely.

Then, in a matter of seconds, everything changes. "I'm dead!" calls out an operator, peeling off her headset. "Me, too!" another cries, and then like an angry flock of blue jays the voices squawk. "I'm dead! I'm dead! I'm dead!" Rajter looks at his watch: 5:10 P.M. Every phone line in the thirty-operator telecommunications center is dead.

He's worried about this scenario before. Much of *Unsolved Mysteries'* appeal is based on the premise that viewers can help solve crimes, and indeed, the FBI long ago realized that the show often reaps results. But without operators to take tips the show might as well not have aired as far as the FBI is concerned. It's a little like performing for an empty house.

Rajter phones MCI to report the emergency. Ten minutes pass, and still nothing. Every line in the center dead, without dial tone, as if thirty cords had been yanked at once. Another five minutes, and still nothing. The Dark Dante episode will air any minute. "Is this Kevin Poulsen?" Rajter nervously probes agent Beasely. The FBI agent says nothing, but

Rajter can tell by the look on his face that he too is waiting for word to come back that this has been the work of his nemesis.

———■———

Kevin drives off in his Fiero, a tiny black-and-white television plugged into his car lighter, the reception cutting in and out. For a moment he sees the image of *Unsolved Mysteries'* host, Robert Stack, and then his own, and though the picture is fuzzy, the voices are clear. He stops at a pay phone at a Van Nuys car wash and pages Eric, asking if they aired the photo of him as a blond. Surprisingly, they didn't.

Kevin returns to his Super 8 room in Canoga Park with a couple of weeks' worth of groceries he picked up at Hughes Market and the stray cat that showed up on his doorstep a few months before. Eric arrives a little later with a care package: a scanner, antenna, and tape recorder to monitor law enforcement frequencies, and, of course, a VCR and a tape of that evening's show. They watch the tape together perched on the edge of the bed, Kevin's nameless cat clawing Eric's boots.

"WANTED" flashes across the motel TV screen, followed by Robert Stack striding through what Kevin suspects is the PBX in NBC's basement.

"Inside the labyrinth of a telephone company's huge computer system one feels a sense of insignificance," Stack booms in his imposing voice, looking impressive in a detective's mackintosh. "It seems impossible that any single person could jam up these sophisticated works. Yet think of it. All the interactive computers across the country are linked by telephone lines. Both private citizens and classified government operations can be vulnerable to a computer genius run amok."

Tentative plucks of a harp play as Kevin's face engulfs the screen. A voice-over picks up the narrative, gently telling of the death of Kevin's mother and his painfully shy childhood. An actor resembling Kevin begins tapping away on a computer in a darkened room, as the narrator quickly describes how Dark Dante began to explore the Arpanet. "He liked the idea of having power," notes Sean Randol thoughtfully on-screen, her blond curls cut short. "He wanted to have power over the people he saw as being beneath him."

Wearing a suit and tie, Von Brauch, the bullnecked Pac Bell investigator, is shown rummaging through Kevin's locker. "We found a storage locker that contained pieces of electronic equipment, a printout of the unpublished number of the Soviet embassy in San Francisco," Von Brauch tells the camera. "That's not the type of material that one would buy at a swap meet."

Sitting in his motel room, Kevin grimaces as Von Brauch mischaracterizes the capabilities of the old telecommunications junk that filled his Menlo Park apartment, and wonders why the TV producers moved things into his "room" that weren't there before. He groans at the photos of him picking the lock of a telecommunications trailer and sitting before a phone company terminal. But he enjoys the dramatization of him breaking into a central office. He looks cool.

To the FBI it's all proof of a dangerous conspiracy. FBI Supervisory Special Agent William E. Smith, a black man with a red tie and a blue suit, asserts that Poulsen's secret clearance and cracking of a U.S. military computer spells trouble. "Kevin Poulsen had allegedly infiltrated U.S. military computer transmissions, obtaining classified Army information," the voice-over continues. "Authorities also believe he obtained classified information about the FBI investigation of overthrown Philippine president Ferdinand Marcos ... his possession of the unlisted Soviet number led the FBI to believe that Kevin Poulsen might be engaging in espionage."

Now, 14 million people think I'm a spy, Kevin thinks. The voice-over summarizes the indictment against Poulsen, Lottor, and Gilligan. Snippets of newspaper headlines flash on the screen: "HACKER'S RAMPAGE ALLEGED," "COMPUTER ACE INDICTED," and finally, photos of Kevin, as the voice-over gives his physical description for the audience. "Kevin Poulsen is twenty-five years old and five foot eight inches tall, with a slim build. He has used the surnames "Drake," "Locke," and "Cooper" as well as the aliases "Walter Kovaks" and "John Anderson." The FBI's information on Poulsen is that he may be living in the Los Angeles area and driving a white late-seventies van. He is an expert in the computer operating system called Unix and may be working in that field."

The camera returns to Stack, his eyes hard and remote. "One can only speculate at what motivated Kevin Poulsen. Those who knew him before he fled agree that he is an unusually talented and bright young man, possibly a genius. But now he is a wanted man, facing up to thirty-seven years in prison. If you have any information about Kevin Poulsen, please contact the FBI at our toll-free number. 1–800–876–5353."

———■———

How could Kevin not laugh at the melodrama? The stone faced G-men droning on in Bureau-speak about the next great new danger to national security, and, of course, that wonderfully evocative phrase, "a computer genius run amok."

Humor aside, there are some very odd things about the broadcast. The show claims Kevin was "accessing sensitive government and military computers" for more than a year, when as far as Kevin knows, he never cracked a government or military computer. "It's a frame job," Kevin tells Eric, who isn't sure what to think of the broadcast. "I had nothing to do with the military."

Still, Kevin realizes it could have been worse. They could have aired his new platinum blond booking photo and publicized details about his suspected associates. To Kevin's relief, NBC largely ignored this new information, and his letter too, broadcasting instead only old photos. All in all, Kevin and Eric agree that the night was more or less a success. And though Kevin mocked most of the broadcast, he found the scenes of his television double sleuthing about a real, modern central office surprisingly hip. It had taken a federal indictment and a year underground, but Kevin had finally become a television star.

"Play it again," Kevin insists, and Eric dutifully rewinds the tape. Four more rewinds later, at about midnight, Eric heads over to the Rainbow, where he meets Grant Straus, and they talk excitedly about the show. "It's strange," Eric confides to his friend. "I'm the only person in America who knows where this dangerous fugitive is hiding out."

MUSICAL CHAIRS

———■———

The strange calls to LAPD division headquarters only make Spradley and company more dedicated in their search for Kevin Poulsen. One anonymous caller tells the cop who answers the phone that he knows all about the surveillance at Doheny Towers. He casually mentions a Hollywood coffee shop where the officers met before setting up the evening's surveillance, the blue Oldsmobile and red Pontiac that couldn't keep up, and the officers' radio call signs. Before hanging up, the caller adds a personal message—"Say hi to Bill and Megan for me"—using Spradley's and McElroy's first names. Other calls are less friendly. Threats that the officers' credit will be ruined, and not so subtle warnings of the electronic havoc that will follow if the investigation doesn't stop.

To Spradley, the failure of physical surveillance reflects what they're up against. FBI agents sent to interview Poulsen's parents and friends have uncovered precious little. Even if Spradley could find Eric, he knows it's unlikely he would lead them to Poulsen. By now Poulsen must know he's the target of a full-fledged manhunt. Spradley doesn't think for a minute that Poulsen would be so foolish or bold as to make physical contact with Eric or Austin or even distant friends. If he's really the cyberfugitive that the feds make him out to be, he knows this is the time to be invisible, to hide in the world of electrons that he understands.

———■———

Spradley and Atchley switch the focus of their investigation to electronic terrain. Spradley is amazed at the volume of traps and traces Atchley places on lines—twenty-five to thirty at a time, all without a single court order. Though no one raises the question, some might wonder why, with the parallel FBI investigation of Poulsen, Pac Bell isn't required to get court orders for the surveillance. Nevertheless, draped on the lines of Poulsen's parents, friends, and associates, the traps bring in the numbers of voice mail boxes, pagers, and pay phones. That's where Spradley comes in. Each time a pay phone number is caught calling a suspicious, trapped number, Atchley alerts Spradley, who promptly sends out an unmarked car to put the phone under surveillance. Van Nuys seems to be the prime location.

Atchley combs through thousands of calls looking for patterns. Besides traps and traces, he does number searches, checking every person who ever called anyone who might possibly have a tangential connection to Poulsen, Eric, or Austin. The work is tedious and exhausting, and even when Atchley finds a pay phone that may have been used by Poulsen he never knows whether the call to a voice mail box had actually been made from that particular phone or had simply been made to appear as if that phone had been used.

———■———

Kevin has packed carefully for his two weeks in the Topanga Canyon Super 8 next to a Midas muffler shop. He's brought Stephen King's *The Dark Half,* and for digital entertainment, he made a special purchase of the Nintendo game Super Mario Brothers II. He's got a couple weeks' worth of clean clothes, plenty of Top Ramen dried noodles, Kraft macaroni and cheese, and canned food, and more than enough New York Seltzer iced coffee to stay wired. His cat will provide companionship.

Kevin vows not to venture outside or touch a computer for a week. He looks on it as an act of discipline, proof of his commitment.

He hangs the DO NOT DISTURB sign outside room 205, and each morning when the determined maid phones asking to clean, Kevin rolls over and says no. When he rises a few hours later the room is still dark from the shades. Cats aren't allowed and Kevin can't think of a good reason to open the shades, so he keeps them drawn day after day, held down by thumbtacks. His only view is through the tiny peephole in the door. Located just off a busy intersection, his second-floor motel room hums with the continuous stream of cars and trucks. From his bed, his world is four paces over the green carpet to the windowless kitchenette, three to the TV, and three to the bathroom with the plastic drinking cups. He hooks up his video game to the motel's color TV and soon excels at Super Mario Brothers II.

But Kevin is working too. Twenty-four hours a day, he tape-records the vice squad's surveillance, the police scanner crackling with field operations like the daytime soaps. Often vice is just following some random hooker, running plates and bantering back and forth in cop lingo. Kevin listens as the hookers enter a hotel room, responding to an ad he knows was placed by the LAPD. The operation seems geared toward developing dossiers on the major escort services, and at one point, Detective Spradley himself comes on the air and describes the girl his team is supposed to tail. "She's got blond hair, but it's not really natural blond," Spradley says.

Kevin passes his days and nights keeping a log of the transmissions of the investigators following Eric. He tracks the key players in a steno book, noting their call signs and what they say. There's no doubt that the investigation is being run by LAPD vice—with Spradley and McElroy the main players. One afternoon, while playing his video game, Kevin hears street names that sound vaguely familiar. He dials American Voice Retrieval without the slightest worry that a trap on a mailbox might reveal his location. As always, he dials a random box and then skips over to the box he actually wants to leave a message in. There's nothing to trace.

Ever since the initial surveillance at Doheny Towers, Ron has tired of Kevin's incessant round-the-clock pages. Often Kevin simply hears a co-incidence, a nearby surveillance operation that invariably is centered on a hooker, not a hacker. So Ron is perhaps understandably irritated one afternoon when he receives yet another "*99" emergency message on his pager. He dials his voice mail and listens to Kevin's message, something about, "If you live on . . . you've got some problems. Turn on your radio." Ron hasn't lived in the Woodland Hills apartment long enough to know the streets outside his apartment. He flips on his radio just in case.

"I've got this entrance blocked over here on . . ." snaps one cop over the radio. "I'm over here on Oxnard," replies another.

At that instant, Ron looks out his apartment window and sees a car exiting the parking lot.

"Is that him?" asks one of the cops. "No," says another.

Ron turns up his radio, and learns to his amazement that between the LAPD, Terry Atchley of Pac Bell, and the FBI, all four exits to his complex are surrounded. How could they find his apartment so fast? He'd rented it only weeks ago under a false identity. But then he remembers the call he'd made to Eric at Doheny Towers before Kevin had learned traps had been placed on Eric's line.

Ron sits tight and waits, hoping they'll leave when their shift is up. He thinks of a friend's place where he might be able to hide out for a few days, and then tries to sort through the puzzle. First they tried to use Eric to lead them to Kevin, and now him. How long before they'll be on Kevin's trail?

■

"Listen, we have to get in there and clean," says an irritated Super 8 motel manager early one morning on the phone, a few days before Kevin's two weeks in hiding are up.

Kevin quickly gathers his stuff and cat and leaves before the maid arrives, driving a few miles before checking into a Vagabond Inn. Kevin is stubborn. He has to finish his two weeks. A couple of days later, he parks down the street from his apartment and tunes in the vice and FBI frequencies. After a slow drive by, he returns to his apartment, sees nothing amiss, and then proceeds with his security plan. He brings a snake toilet plunger to the building manager's apartment. The manager had admired it a few weeks ago, and Kevin figures it will make a good pretext for stopping by. He offers it to the man, notices nothing unusual about his demeanor, and then quickly retreats to a safe distance in his car. After several hours of monitoring vice and FBI frequencies, Kevin is satisfied that all's clear. He can return home, blond hair and all.

———■———

A week later, after listening to his scanner long enough to be sure that the coast is clear, Ron returns with a truck to clean out his apartment, none too happy about having to forfeit his last month's rent and security deposit. He's finding that the life of an underground hacker has its financial and emotional costs. It's a pain to worry constantly about where he makes every phone call and who might be following him. As he carts his furniture and belongings down to the truck, he keeps his police radio on, just in case. So far, all he's heard is routine surveillance, interrupted by another random hooker case code named "Lollipop."

His pager buzzes and he looks down to see the familiar "*99" emergency code. A few minutes later, he's got Kevin on the phone. "They've got him under surveillance in Beverly Hills," Kevin says matter-of-factly.

"What do you mean?"

"Lollipop," Kevin says flatly. "That's Eric's plate."

Amazed, Austin realizes that Kevin is right. Eric stored his Porsche with a friend and has been driving a Mazda RX7 with the amusing license plate LOLLIPOP. Security precautions and countersurveillance aside, the cops seem to be moving fast. Kevin, of course, had warned Eric about the traps on his line and voice mail and made him promise that when he moved into his new apartment he wouldn't call any number he'd called in the past. The precaution wasn't idle. Since Atchley had Eric's phone bills, it was likely that he'd put traps on every number Eric called regularly.

Eric is angry when Kevin gives him the bad news. He's tired of being watched like a caged animal and chased all over Hollywood, forced to abandon one apartment after another, all simply because he's the closest the cops and feds have gotten to Kevin. A couple of days later, after the LAPD tires of watching the empty apartment, Eric returns in the middle of the night and loads up the last of his furniture. The night before Eric leaves town he meets a blond named Shannon at a Hollywood party and enjoys his last one-night stand in Los Angeles at a hotel. The next day he loads up his Porsche and begins the long haul to Texas. It doesn't take long. At 3 A.M. the next morning out on an empty desert freeway, Eric hits 160 miles per hour. He's free.

THE OFFICE

The *Unsolved Mysteries* episode convinces Kevin that it's time to take extra precautions. He isn't about to make the same mistake twice. No storage locker slipups, no apartment stuffed with computers and telephone memorabilia they won't understand. No, this time he'll do it right. If hacking and phones really are his life, then like other people with a calling, he needs a place to hack. If he were an artist it might be a warehouse studio, filled with air and soft light, and if he were a writer, it might be a lonely cottage, looking out on the sea. But he's a hacker. Kevin wants four walls, a place to plug in his computers, and as many phone lines as he can swipe.

Kevin finds what he's looking for near the 101 freeway in North Hollywood, at the corner of Van Nuys and Victory. Peep shows and pawnshops crowd the district. Graffiti-strewn bus benches advertise legal services for one-hour bankruptcy, evictions, and divorce. Steel bars line the windows. Down the street at Tommy's World Famous Hamburger, the Mexican gangs hang out, and anybody with any sense knows that Victory and Van Nuys isn't a smart place to be alone at night.

The eight-floor building towers over the neighborhood, a 1960s statement in angled concrete and glass. He parks in the back lot, by the bank on the ground floor, the worn facade of the adjacent building colored with faded murals advertising diapers, soap, and sanitary napkins.

Even if Kevin arrives late at night, all he has to do is sprint from the car to the locked metal gate near the bank door. From there it's only twenty feet to the elevator, up to the fourth floor, past the line of worn brown doors with missing placards to the end of the blue-carpeted hall. Next door is a small travel agency, and down the hall, a detective or low-rent lawyer. Most of the offices have been empty for months, a fact Kevin finds all the more attractive since his digs are about ten feet from the floor's phone closet.

———■———

With his radio prize money, Kevin has bought a Sun workstation with two terminals, an IBM XT, a fax machine, and a laser printer. He hangs a framed sign he swiped from a central office, "PACIFIC BELL, A NEW BEGINNING."

On a white board above his computers, Kevin pens simple instructions with a black felt pen marker on how to make an untraceable phone call. He still makes his calls through a trunk test set, changing the route index, bouncing the calls back and forth between random trunks to disguise their origin. But in the shadow of increased surveillance, Kevin is further bolstering his defenses.

Kevin makes a late-night visit to his local central office, and connects a pair of phone lines from the ESS computer to the frame, cleverly hiding the new line that will run to his office among the spaghetti of wires. Every fifteen minutes, the raw output from the ESS computer at the central office refreshes his Sun's screen with an updated list of traps and traces. Before Kevin or Ron make any calls, by phone or computer, they check the on-screen list.

But Kevin wants a real-time connection to the switch. He wires his Sun workstation into all five of his office's phone lines, and attaches relay switches to each line. He hacks out a program that continuously searches the ESS computer for the trace command. The millisecond a Pac Bell technician keys the trace command the Sun anticipates the electronic pursuit, the relay switches snap, and the phone lines go dead. At most, they'll locate one of thousands of anonymous trunks.

Encryption is Kevin's last defense. Scrambling his files so that if all else fails, if they trace one of his calls, capture his number, and raid his office, they'll find only random ASCII characters and digits, the 128 character computer alphabet. Encryption transforms files into a non-recognizable form—ciphertext—by scrambling them with an encryption algorithm. But first Kevin needs to create a key, his ten-character password, to begin the encryption and later to reconstitute his ciphertext into plaintext. It can't be a common name because that would be too easy to crack, but he isn't willing to have a completely random key. Then, he might have trouble remembering it, and write it down, which would defeat the whole purpose.

So Kevin thinks about letters that mean something only to him, and comes up with the keys he strikes on his test trunk to make an untraceable call and the extra letters on a sixteen-button phone. Though it's not random, to anyone but Kevin KPfofip0ST is pretty unique. For encryption, Kevin uses Sun's and IBM's versions of DES, the Defense Encryption Standard, a fifty-six-key technique used by federal agencies and thought to be virtually uncrackable. But Kevin doesn't take any chances. He knows his pseudo-random key makes his files less secure. He encrypts his files twice, three times, and occasionally five times. When he wants to read a file, it's a guessing game. He just keeps decrypting over and over again, until the curtain of ciphertext on his screen lifts and reveals intelligible words and numbers.

———■———

Ron surveys his Hollywood apartment and smiles. In the few short hours he's been gone his bathroom has been transformed into a beauty salon. Spread around the sink are five spray bottles, two bottles of mousse, two blow dryers, and a couple of wood-handled brushes.

Eric had phoned from Dallas and asked if he could stay at Ron's apartment for a couple of days, and now, after spending the night with his girlfriend, Ron is back surveying the wreckage for the first time. Ever since Eric left for Texas things have been surprisingly quiet. For months, nothing much has happened. Kevin and Ron have picked up no tails, found no security memos on-line, and where once they could count on regularly following LAPD's surveillance, they've found themselves pushed off the airwaves.

In short, life in Los Angeles has become dull without Eric. He's been back for a couple of brief visits, and a few weeks ago the three of them had actually met down at the Rainbow on a busy weekend night. Eric had gotten the two of them in for free, and Ron was amazed at how relaxed they all were. There seemed precious little of the jangled nerves from the days when nobody trusted one another. Watching Eric do his club thing, smiling casually at the scantily clad girls who paraded by, Ron couldn't help but think that maybe Eric wasn't such a bad guy after all.

Eric was in a chatty mood, and once they'd firmly established that the investigation had ground to a standstill, he began holding forth. He sipped on a vodka cranberry and spoke in reverential terms about Texas, a new frontier for hacking. He told of a state wide open, central offices without locked fences, without locked doors. Southern sex, he boasted, wasn't bad either. In L.A. everybody already knew his act, and even for Eric, things had gradually slowed. But when he moved to Texas, he was pleasantly surprised by the strong rock scene and the bustling, upscale stripper trade. It was like being the new guy in town. He'd already bedded several strippers, a *Playboy* lingerie model, and even had a regular thing with a schoolteacher.

"You should move down there too," Eric suggested to Kevin in a friendly tone. "We could check out COs together." Kevin was noncommittal and quiet, and while they didn't stay long enough to order drinks, the meeting had a friendliness that surprised Ron. The three of them had actually all met together for once without worrying about who might be being tailed or pressed to rat out the others.

———■———

The next day Ron returns to his apartment, and immediately notices a scanner tuned to a North Hollywood police frequency. "Yeah," Eric explains nonchalantly, "I've been listening to this police frequency all day expecting to hear something on a stolen car."

Eric tells the story matter-of-factly, as if recounting the dry details of an ordinary day. He'd gone out to the Valley to test-drive a 944 Turbo he fancied and taken it for a spin. After a few minutes, with evening setting in, he asked the seller in the seat next to him if he could see it in the light. The man said sure and they pulled to the side of the road, under some streetlamps. They circled the car together, and then suddenly Eric jumped back in and floored it.

"He was standing there stunned," Eric says with a smile, perhaps sensing the irony of his crime. Ron and Kevin had hacked their Porsches through computers and phone lines, while Eric, partial to less technical solutions, had simply driven his latest conquest right out from under its owner's nose.

Before Ron can ask any questions, Eric returns to the bathroom to take his evening shower and freshen up. Ron is listening to the Van Nuys frequency for any mention of a stolen Porsche when Kevin shows up.

"Why is there a Porsche down there with Eric's plate?" asks Kevin.

Ron is impressed by Kevin's powers of observation. Sure enough, Eric had simply taken the plate from his old Porsche and placed it on his new white Porsche.

Ron smiles. "Just ask Eric."

———■———

"Meet me at the Rainbow at about 2 A.M.," Eric suggests.

Kevin knows what that means. Maybe he'll go along with his plan, or maybe he'll go along with whatever turns up at the Rainbow.

Later that evening when Kevin pulls up outside the club's teeming parking lot at the designated hour, he's thinking how Eric has always claimed his obsession with sex is an addiction that he'd like to kick. Kevin has never taken the claim seriously. How could he? The idea of Eric not scamming women was about as likely as Kevin quitting tapping phones. Then, Kevin sees the ordinary-looking girl Eric has on his arm.

The three of them walk together toward Eric's car, Kevin making cryptic remarks about his plan for later that evening. Eric, however, remains undecided. Kevin tells Eric where he's parked, returns to his car, and waits. Eric pulls up behind, tells the girl he'll just be a minute and steps into Kevin's Fiero. Eric wants to know how sure a thing it is, how confident Kevin is that it will work out. Then he leaves Kevin, returns to his car, and talks with the girl awhile, asking similar questions. How sure a thing it is, how confident she is that it will work out.

A few minutes later, Eric returns to Kevin's car, a serious look on his face. "Well, I don't know. She's being pretty convincing."

Kevin pauses a minute and then makes his pitch. "Look, Eric, go back to your car, turn on the interior light, and take a good long look at her." Then, like a good friend, Kevin reaches in his wallet. "Here's ten dollars. You can call her a cab."

Eric pockets the ten, and Kevin watches as he opens the car door and leaves it ajar so the interior light stays on. Eric and the girl talk a few minutes more.

Eric walks back and holds out his palm. "A cab will cost twenty."

———■———

After all the months of car chases, traced numbers, and close calls, it has finally come down to 1010 Wilshire Boulevard, security headquarters for Pacific Bell. It's not exactly the sort of place you'd expect a wanted FBI fugitive to plan a late-night burglary. But then, Kevin is unlike any fugitive the FBI has ever encountered. He'd told Eric that it was time to go to the source and find out what Pac Bell, LAPD, and the feds had on them. Why operate in the dark, stupidly running from some unknown entity, if you have the power, and more importantly, the nerve to investigate the investigators?

This time the stakes are higher. They aren't talking about an unmanned central office. A guard sits in the front lobby of the high-rise on the busy boulevard, a video camera trained on the door. The risks aren't simply capture and whatever the feds might piece together about their past activities but the additional federal charge of obstruction of justice. Tonight, it won't do simply to pick the lock or use one of Kevin's Pac Bell keys.

Eric boosts Kevin up a wall alongside the building and tosses him a backpack with a scanner, flashlight, and lock picks. Kevin yanks him up, and they thread their way down a narrow passage to the rear of the building. Climbing up on on Eric's shoulders, Kevin grabs for one of the rails of the fire escape ladder hanging from a balcony. A flock of pigeons scatters suddenly, and he slips and then regains his grip. Once firmly up he takes a look at the door.

"EMERGENCY EXIT ONLY. OPENING DOOR WILL SOUND ALARM."

Kevin whispers down to Eric what's written on the door. They both know that Pac Bell often posts such warnings when they don't want to pay for an alarm.

Eric shrugs. "Go ahead if you want to take the chance."

Kevin mulls it over, and then decides to check around first. He traverses the terrace and spots a video camera pointed toward the knot of freeways and off-ramps. The second door he finds has no sign and is unlocked. He returns to the balcony and reaches down a hand for Eric, who's been passing the time listening to a Bear Cat scanner tuned to the LAPD's frequency. So far, it's been quiet.

The door opens into what appears to be a cafeteria, and they waste little time in finding the stairs. On the sixth floor, they tiptoe to the office. Kevin has known of the office since he was a teenager, finding it when he'd bring up a security agent's number in Cosmos or read a Pac Bell security memo on-line. Before coming over tonight, just to be sure, he'd checked it again in Pac Bell's directory.

Eric drops to his knees with a screwdriver and a flashlight, a bit fuzzy from the vodka. A couple of minutes later, the door swings open to a large room with partitions. Kevin hits all the light switches. Flashlights aren't a good idea when burglarizing an office building with a wall of glass. He wants it to look like they're working.

"Which is Atchley's desk?" Eric wonders out loud.

Kevin doesn't hesitate. He picks up a phone and dials Atchley's extension, and listens to it ring more than a hundred feet away. A minute later, he picks the lock on the desk, slowly pulls open the drawer, and there staring up at him like a bad dream is an eight-by-ten mug shot of himself.

"Oh my god!" exclaims Eric.

Till then, they hadn't really known for certain just how large a target Kevin might be. Everything had been circumstantial, bits and pieces here and there. But the celebrity-sized photo is clear. Atchley wants to remind himself of Kevin's face every time he reaches for a pencil.

Kevin thinks it's kind of funny, this Pac Bell security man obsessed with his capture. Now that he's found his desk, he can return the favor and investigate the investigator. He finds catalogs of spy equipment and high-tech surveillance. Invisible powder to spread on equipment that later could be viewed under blue light to see if hands had been where they shouldn't. Video cameras and recording equipment. Secret phone company radio frequencies to carry out surveillance.

Eric is impressed by the stacks of manuals on the company's investigative procedures. Books with block diagrams discussing how to wiretap phones legally and set up DNRs, written in such a manner that Eric figures any idiot could understand. But it's the files they've come after. The Kevin Poulsen file. Files with Ron's and Eric's phony names, phone bills, DNR printouts and scraps of paper with the Investigator's name. They stay until the sun rises, Kevin making trips back and forth to the copy machine, only leaving when they hear the groan of a delivery truck arriving outside.

———■———

At Ron's apartment, Kevin holds up a stack of copied documents at least five inches thick. "You wouldn't believe the stuff we found." In his hand are the phone bills of virtually every person Ron or Eric has called in the last year: Austin's girlfriend, his girlfriend's grandparent, Eric's girlfriend Frecia, the Investigator, his secretary, even Henry Spiegel. Poring over the bills, they're impressed at Atchley's thoroughness. The Pac Bell investigator had apparently run everyone who had ever phoned these disparate individuals through a database to see if the billing might by chance come back to a Kevin, any Kevin at all, on the faint hope that he hadn't changed his first name.

Amid the phone bills are DNRs on Eric's lines and Ron's voice mail numbers and random hand-scrawled notes about the vice investigation and the FBI. The whole picture is coming into focus, and as far as Ron is concerned it isn't good. The next morning he tells Eric to gather up his beauty products and leave. First the stolen car, now the break-in to Pac Bell's security office. It's all getting to be a little too much. After months of calm, Ron suddenly has two wanted criminals hanging out in his apartment and a freshly swiped Porsche sitting down in the parking lot.

But Kevin is just getting warmed up. The following evening he's back at the Rainbow, trying to persuade Eric to leave that night's catch for another night of traipsing around Pac Bell security headquarters. Kevin pleads, reminding Eric that they both stand to gain, and that the window of opportunity is likely to end after the weekend. The first break-in had been on a Friday, and Kevin knows that once Monday arrives, Atchley will find signs of the burglary.

None of these arguments sway Eric, his arm firmly wrapped around the slim waist of a young, attractive stranger. Besides, what more could they possibly find? They know Atchley has it in for Poulsen, that he's stuck DNRs on every line imaginable, and that the vice squad and the feds have been chasing them all over town. This isn't just a routine visit to the nearby central office. Kevin is talking about scouring the office of Pac Bell security two nights in a row.

"I need a boost to get in," Kevin pleads on the phone later that night to Ron. Dismayed that Eric turned him down for some anonymous girl, Kevin is counting on his old friend to help him out. They drive separately, parking on a side street with a view of the building, and Ron is secretly happy when Kevin tells him that he can climb up alone with the rope he's brought and won't need a boost after all.

He hands Ron a radio and asks him to listen to the police scanner and radio him in the building if anything sounds amiss. Ron sits in his dark car while Kevin clambers up the wall. Watching him disappear, Ron knows that he isn't ready to do what Kevin has asked. Without Eric, Kevin will take chances, and Austin knows that the odds are that he'd be in for a long wait, several hours at least, stretching past dawn, at least until Kevin might have a greater chance of getting caught. After about ten minutes, Ron flips off the radio and drives away.

HOUDINI

—■—

Terry Atchley keeps chipping away, doing traps and traces, checking phone numbers. Finally, he spots something interesting, calls to Eric's voice mail from a private investigator's office on Wilshire Boulevard.

Detective Spradley pays the Investigator a visit and asks him to make one more call to Eric's voice mail. The Investigator isn't happy about the hacker carelessly leading the cops to his business. When Eric returns his voice mail he tells him matter-of-factly that the police are looking for him. "They want you to call here and talk to them," he says. "Tuesday, four P.M. They'll be at my office."

Eric knows damn well Atchley will be tracing the call, but he's still gotta know what they're offering. He calls through three different 800 numbers and then dials the Investigator's number. The conversation is barely audible, but Eric already knows their script. "We know you're involved with Kevin Poulsen, and that you've been breaking into Pac Bell computers," Spradley stiffly informs him as Atchley tries to trace the call. "We're going to proceed with criminal prosecution against you."

Eric interrupts the cop and gets to the point. "Poulsen knows your every move," he says in his toneless voice. "He knew where you were when you were tailing me. He even knew your first names."

"I'm sure we can work out some kind of deal," Spradley softens. "The guy we want is Poulsen."

———■———

Atchley traces Eric's U-Haul truck to the apartment of one of his friends, but it's Special Agent Beasely who does all the interviewing when they drive out to the address in the Valley. Atchley sizes him up as a musician type, hair dyed black, full leathers. The guy knows Poulsen, and claims to have even seen him recently late at night at a Hughes Market in Van Nuys.

Atchley and Beasely both make trips to the Hughes Market, bringing along Poulsen's blond LAPD mug shot. A couple of boxboys say they recognize Poulsen, but add that he hasn't been in for a few weeks. The phone investigator and G-man leave the mug shot and their phone and pager numbers. It's a lead, all right, but neither man is too optimistic. Eric left town months ago, and they figure that if for some reason Poulsen hasn't already left, he's too clever to shop at the same market twice.

But shortly before midnight on April 9, Brian Bridges, the Van Nuys night manager, sees the man in the mug shot enter the store. Bridges wasn't on duty a month or so ago, when Atchley and Beasely had dropped off the photo. He only knows that the man in the photo is wanted, and that if he comes in they're supposed to call the numbers. The man is neatly dressed, wearing a black leather jacket, Levi's and round wire-rim glasses, but it's the dried-out, platinum blond hair that catches Bridges's eye. He runs to the upstairs windowed office that overlooks the aisles. "He's in the store," he whispers to another employee, alerting her to call the FBI. Bridges follows the man's movements, while the woman dials the Bureau's numbers. When no one answers, she tries 911, but the skeptical 911 operator wants to know what the man is wanted for. Incredulous, Bridges watches the man collect his change and calmly walk out the door with his groceries. He grabs the phone in frustration and shouts angrily, "He's driving away now!"

———■———

The last few weeks have raised the hopes of the authorities. Eric has decided to help the FBI catch Kevin and has been in regular phone contact with Terry Atchley and the FBI, passing on whatever information he has. Bob Gilligan, too, has decided to betray his old friend. Kevin's onetime boss at SRI, who led Kevin back into phones and computers when the hacker had a chance to go straight, has agreed to plead guilty to the conspiracy charge in the indictment. Gilligan's deal is simple. The government will drop all the counts in the indictment except for the conspiracy charge and accept a plea that will likely result in a $25,000 fine and no jail time. In return Gilligan will help the government apprehend the "fugitive defendant Poulsen."

But on the evening of April 10, Kevin is unaware of how his old friends have turned against him. Alone at his office, programming, Kevin's scanner is tuned to 800 megahertz, Pac Bell's frequency, when his arch-enemy, Pac Bell security investigator Terry Atchley, comes on the air.

"Have I gotten any calls?" Kevin hears Atchley quietly ask his boss.

"No."

"Did those new number searches come in?"

Kevin keeps listening to the conversation and then suddenly realizes what's so odd. There's none of the ordinary background noise of a car engine or traffic. It sounds as if Atchley is just parked somewhere, waiting for something to happen.

———■———

Atchley sits in his gray Chevy Celebrity in an unlit corner of the lot with a clear view of the entrance. He's decided to stake out Hughes Market, and though the boxboys say the night owl usually doesn't shop till midnight, Atchley arrives at 9 P.M., hoping to see the Pontiac Fiero with the busted headlight they spotted Poulsen driving off in the night before. He figures on staying past four in the morning, a seven-hour stint, not so long that he won't be able to grab a couple of hours' sleep before going to the office. He's got a cell phone, a police radio, coffee, and plenty of cigarettes. He'd like to read something to pass the time, but that isn't what surveillance is about. He has to sit there, looking, doing nothing, letting his tired eyes scan the area.

Ten minutes before midnight, a black Pontiac Fiero swings into the lot, and Atchley watches one headlight blink shut and the other stay open. Out steps the man Atchley saw seven months before at the Union station pay phone. Atchley considers paging Beasely, but there isn't time. He hops out and runs anxiously to the corner of the building, about ten feet from the Fiero. He wonders if the night manager has done as he instructed, paging Beasely and phoning LAPD.

Suddenly, an excited security guard runs out the front, yelling, "We got him! We got him!"

"Get Bridges!" Atchley shouts back, worried that everything is happening too fast. Atchley had hoped to arrest Poulsen in front of the market, but a couple of Hughes boxboys took the law into their hands, tackling Kevin as he picked up a few cans of soup. A minute later the guard runs back, breathing heavily. "We've got him in a storeroom in the back."

His arms are cuffed and he seems extremely surprised. He looks quizzically at the Pac Bell security man. "Who are you?"

"Get off it, Kevin!" Atchley shoots back. "I'm the guy whose desk you sat in front of."

Atchley replaces the security guard's cuffs with his own and pats down Kevin for weapons. "You know me better than that," Kevin says.

"I know," agrees the phone investigator.

"So how did you know I'd be here?"

Atchley isn't going to tell him, but he also can't resist snapping back with a smart reply. Kevin asks again, and Atchley plops him down on a milk crate. The last thing he's going to do is give Kevin the satisfaction of knowing how he'd finally been caught. But as the hacker continues to try to strike up a conversation with the investigator, Atchley begins to wonder when Beasely and LAPD will show. He isn't a cop and he'd appreciate some professional assistance.

"My contacts are bothering me," Kevin complains.

Atchley ignores him for a few minutes, but the hacker persists. "Can I take them out?"

The hacker asks again. Maybe this isn't another one of his tricks, Atchley thinks. Maybe there is something wrong with his contacts.

"You could go out to my car, get a black bag out of the front seat," Kevin continues. "It's got my contacts case. Search it if you like."

"Watch him," Atchley instructs the boxboys, and takes the key from Kevin and trots out to the car. He isn't gone for more than a couple of minutes.

Back in the storage room, Atchley uncuffs Kevin and takes the glasses out of the case and hands them over. Atchley watches his hands. Kevin pops each contact into his palm, and then Atchley lets him put the contacts in the case. His movements are slow and deliberate. Then, the hacker puts his round, wire-rim glasses on. Finally, Atchley puts the case back in the black canvas bag.

At about 1 A.M., roughly an hour after the capture, Special Agent Beasely arrives at the storeroom. "Thought you'd never catch me," Kevin greets the G-man.

A few minutes later, Atchley's beeper buzzes.

"Uh, your beeper went off," Kevin observes, standing up and taking a step. Atchley, busy with his beeper, doesn't notice. Or hear the slight clunk.

"What did you just drop in that trash can, Kevin?" Agent Beasely asks.

Kevin says nothing, and the agent walks over and calmly fishes his wallet out of the can. "What do you have in this wallet that you didn't want us to see, Kevin?"

Deep inside the wallet, the agent pulls out a folded list of what appear to be four car licenses. "Whose licenses are these Kevin?"

"I don't know," replies the hacker.

Atchley takes a closer look at the license numbers of his work vehicles, personal vehicles—even his wife's car. His mouth tightens.

"Oh, *he* knows whose plates these are," Atchley says.

A few minutes later, Beasely and his partner move off to talk for a minute. Atchley squats down in front of the hacker, his face inches away. He takes the cigarette out slowly and chews the words.

"Listen to me, you motherfucker," Kevin claims the phone investigator warned him. "If you ever fuck with me or my family, next time there won't be enough of you left to put in jail."

Atchley refuses to confirm or deny that any such conversation took place.

Led out into the crowded parking lot, amid the circus of flashing lights and squawking police radios, Kevin chats amiably with Beasely and another agent. Bridges, the Hughes night manager, is surprised by the scene. This mysterious guy in black, who a moment ago had been wanted by the FBI, now seems to be engaged in shoptalk, casually discussing the particulars of his police scanner and the other gizmos the Bureau found in his black bag. Later, when the last of the police and the FBI leave, Bridges and the boxboys return to their routine, all thinking the same thought. Somehow, somewhere, the FBI would find a way to use the hacker.

———■———

Kevin Poulsen relaxes in the back of the car on the drive down to the Los Angeles Metropolitan Detention Center, listening to music on the Sony Walkman Beasely has given him, and realizing with growing confidence that all is not lost. He encrypted his computers twice, three times, sometimes five times, just to be sure, and while the FBI may have finally captured him, they still don't have his data or his secrets. He's prepared for this too. In America, even the most wanted criminals are allowed at least one phone call.

Debbie Poulsen is upset when the stepbrother she loves calls and tells her the inevitable has happened. But she does as she's told. She gets a pen and a piece of paper and writes down the strange elliptical message. She doesn't understand it, but that's the way Kevin wants it.

Ron arrives the next afternoon as usual at the office, expecting to see Kevin. He rewinds the voice-activated tape recorder they left hooked up to the scanner. It doesn't take long. He catches a reference to "6Y64 Adam," Lieutenant Spradley's call sign, and then, over the crackle of the radio static, hears the simple message, "Your boy has been taken."

Ron calls his voice mail and hears a young woman's voice. He isn't sure who it is, but combined with the vice recording there's little doubt in his mind that Kevin has been arrested. "This message is for Ron Austin. I was captured last night at Hughes Market," says the woman, sounding as if she's reading a script. "Do what you can." It's the rest of the truncated message that confuses Ron, something about the authorities having found Kevin's address and arresting him with his credit and ATM cards and a grand total of forty-four dollars cash.

———■———

In the glasses case Kevin asked Atchley to retrieve from his black bag of tricks, tucked away in a hidden compartment, Special Agent Beasely finds a tool inspired by Kevin's idol, the legendary Houdini, a tiny handcuff key.

Then, he finds a clue.

"I've got this orange parking stub," Beasely tells Atchley on the phone a few days after the bust. "I can't figure out where it's from."

Atchley gladly accepts the invitation to do a little gumshoe work. "Van Nuys Parking," says the stub, which seems like a clue, except that after a dozen or so phone calls Atchley discovers eight parking lots by that name in Van Nuys, California. By checking the serial number on the stub, though, Atchley gradually eliminates one lot after another, until about a day later he finds himself standing in the actual lot, near the corner of Victory and Van Nuys.

Where would he have set up shop? Atchley wonders. Clutching his mug shot of Poulsen, Atchley canvases the neighborhood. The shoe repairman has seen him, and so have plenty of other local shopkeepers. Returning to the parking lot, mug shot in hand, Atchley spies the adjacent office building. Fidelity Federal Bank occupies the first floor. It fits, Atchley thinks. Who would ever look for a hacker in a bank building? A couple of minutes later, Atchley finds the building manager. Sure enough, he too recognizes the man in the photo. He rented a suite on the fourth floor.

The Bureau moves in for surveillance, and Atchley, too, joins in the waiting, spending a few more afternoons and nights in his Chevy, smoking and sipping coffee. But from the outset they fear they might be too late. When the manager first showed Atchley the office, the investigator found no computers, no modems, no proprietary Pac Bell manuals, none of the evidence the government needed to build a solid case against Kevin Poulsen. All that remained of the headquarters for the nation's most wanted hacker was some ordinary used furniture, and in the middle of the floor, as if to leave a message, a Pac Bell phone bill.

EPILOGUE

———■———

Two months after Kevin's capture, on June 21, 1991, Eric was summoned from the bed he was sharing with a model and arrested by county sheriffs at his Dallas apartment. By October, the federal government had obtained his release from a Texas jail, and he was back in Los Angeles, working as a paid informant for the FBI. The G-men paid him several hundred dollars a week in cash and covered his thirteen-hundred-dollar-a-month rent at Oakwood Apartments at 3636 South Sepulveda. The FBI supplied Eric with a cellular phone, a lineman's test set useful for wiretapping, a computer, a modem, and a thin, flat tape recorder to plant on his body. They also gave him back his SAS wiretapping manuals. But Eric Heinz had to earn his government pay. His assignment was to find Kevin Poulsen's computers, for without them the government didn't have a case against the hacker.

That fall, Eric phoned Ron and they met at Norm's, the famous greasy spoon in West L.A. As Ron approached the restaurant, he heard what sounded like the static of encrypted FBI transmissions on his scanner, but he relaxed when he found Eric already seated, his own scanner on the table. After moving to another restaurant, the static faded, and Ron figured it had just been a coincidence. Eric eased into his pitch. He was looking for a new crime partner.

Ron ignored the invitation for a moment, and the two reminisced about their days on the run. When Eric finally mentioned Kevin's computers, Ron realized that he'd been waiting, indeed hoping he'd ask. He'd been worrying about the cache of computers, encrypted files, and manuals ever since he'd boxed them up that April day. On the drive over to the locker, Ron didn't pick up a bit of surveillance on his scanner. Eric rummaged through Kevin's things for an hour or so, and then announced that it was too much to go through all at once. The next day he asked if he could borrow Ron's laptop, and they arranged to meet later at a nearby Taco Bell on Sepulveda.

As Ron turned the corner toward the restaurant, he spied Eric across the street, exiting a tanning salon. How fitting, Ron mused, as Eric waved back. Hacking had always seemed just a sideline for Eric, a way to scam a buck and be cool.

At the restaurant, Ron opened his laptop, but the Hollywood man seemed more interested in a burrito, leaving Ron at one of the outdoor tables next to the parking lot as he slipped in to order.

Ron first heard a car door opening, and then a barrage of discordant sounds. Cars careened in from every direction, bounced over curbs, and squealed to within inches of the tables. Somebody shoved him and grabbed his hair, but what he remembered most was the muzzle of a gun pressed against his head.

———■———

It wasn't until his court hearing a few days later, when his attorney showed him some documents referencing secretly tape-recorded conversations, that Ron realized he had been set up by his friend.

Ron soon agreed to plead guilty to computer fraud, wiretapping, and other charges, but he got his revenge. While out on bail, he pieced together Eric's crimes from the hacker's garbage, built a dossier, and handed a copy to the FBI. When the government confronted Eric, the hacker fled and planned an even larger crime. Those bank codes he had found with Kevin came in handy. Not long after going underground, Eric hacked into the computers of Heller Financial, in Glendale, and fraudulently transferred $150,000 to a local bank, phoning in a bomb threat to distract attention from his activities. But before he could withdraw the money, the bank was onto his scheme and froze the account. Soon he had Ron to worry about too. Within a couple of weeks, Ron spotted Eric's car parked in front of a stripper's apartment, phoned the FBI, and assisted in capturing the fugitive. There was no doubt who won this hacker showdown. Ron's plea required that he volunteer several hundred hours of community service; Eric was sentenced to forty-one months in jail.

———■———

Several months after Kevin's capture, a stranger showed up unannounced at Rob Crowe's door on the third floor of the San Jose U.S. attorneys' office. He introduced himself as Scott Harper, an FBI foreign counterintelligence agent. Without skipping a beat, he informed the prosecutor that he was working on the Poulsen case, understood that classified information was involved, and needed a complete review of the evidence and the charges.

Crowe grumbled that he was fed up with the FBI and rattled off his complaints. The FBI's misinformation had led Crowe to bring the bogus Masnet Army network charge, and Crowe had wasted months trying to build an espionage charge against Poulsen, partly because the FBI couldn't get a straight story from the military.

But Harper was no ordinary FBI agent. Harper knew the people in power. He could get answers from the military in a day that would have taken Crowe weeks. Suddenly John Dyon, the FBI's head of Internal Security, was calling Rob Crowe and offering his assistance. The reason was simple. Scott Harper was known among a very tight knit group of top FBI and CIA agents as a first-rate counterintelligence agent. He'd worked some of the biggest cases in the last decade, including the John Walker spy case.

Accompanied by an attorney from the Justice Department's Internal Security section, Harper set off cross-country, interviewing nearly a dozen SRI employees, and everybody he could find with knowledge of the Caber Dragon air tasking order. At Fort Bragg, North Carolina, Dave Borchert, head of the SRI field office, told Harper that Poulsen had been on the Caber Dragon 88 exercise. He even remembered him acting suspiciously one night at the base. And he was ready to testify in court.

But there were still a couple of significant hurdles. It wasn't merely that a computer hacker had never before been charged with espionage. As far as they could determine, no one had ever before been charged with espionage merely for obtaining classified information.

———■———

The FBI set about decrypting Kevin Poulsen's computer files. Officially, the government would not comment on the attempt. The reason for secrecy was simple. Publicly, the government had maintained for many years that it was impossible to crack the Defense Encryption Standard.

A Department of Energy Cray supercomputer was used by the National Security Agency to perform a "brute force" attack on Kevin's encrypted files, blasting every possible key at the computer, one after another, a task that consumed several months at an estimated cost of hundreds of thousands of dollars. Though Kevin's key was not random, by encrypting his files several times, he had increased the difficulty of cracking the code.

Several months after the computers were seized in the fall of 1991, Rob Crowe was informed that the NSA had successfully decoded Kevin's files. Kevin had meticulously kept files documenting his activities, everything from the wiretaps he had discovered to the dossiers he kept on his enemies. The government printed out nearly ten thousand pages of material. There was evidence Kevin had examined the credit records of the law enforcement agents pursuing him, and his file for Bill Spradley, the LAPD vice detective who pursued him for turning on the Yellow Pages ads, was titled "Dickhead."

———■———

On December 4, 1992, a superseding indictment was filed in the Northern District Court in *United States of America v. Kevin Poulsen and Mark Lottor.* Gone were Crowe's 1989 charges that Poulsen had accessed the Masnet Army network or stolen an FBI wiretap printout related to an investigation of Ferdinand Marcos. There was no longer any claim that Poulsen had wiretapped Pac Bell security employees. Trimmed of the major technical mistakes and exaggerations of the first indictment, the superseding indictment nevertheless included one serious new blow, "Count Twelve: (18 U.S.C S 793 (e)—Gathering of Defense Information)." Kevin was alleged to have had unauthorized "control over a document and instrument relating to the national defense, namely, a computer magnetic tape containing a United States Air Force air tasking order classified 'Secret.'" Scott Harper's efforts had been successful. Kevin Lee Poulsen had just become the first computer hacker in history to be charged with espionage.

———■———

On April 21, 1993, the second shoe dropped. David Schindler, a Los Angeles assistant U.S. attorney, filed an additional indictment against Kevin based on the crimes he had committed in Southern California while running from his original charges. Schindler issued a press release announcing that the *Unsolved Mysteries* hacker had been indicted on nineteen counts of computer fraud, wiretapping, money laundering, and obstruction of justice.

Kevin and his unnamed coconspirators were charged with fraudulently winning two Porsches, $22,000 in cash, and at least two trips to Hawaii. Schindler's indictment alleged that Kevin had hacked into Pac Bell's computers and learned of "a court ordered wiretap of telephone service provided to Splash restaurant and Ronald Lorenzo." Still another count charged that Poulsen's hacking had revealed FBI front businesses and telephone numbers.

But the government attempted to keep the full extent of Kevin's crimes secret. The indictment was silent about Kevin's discovery of dozens of consulate wiretaps and wiretaps near the Concord Naval Weapons Station, and his extraordinary ability to wiretap remotely by computer with Pac Bell's SAS. But even without charging Kevin for these serious national security violations, the government estimated that if convicted of all counts, the hacker would face $4.75 million dollars in fines and a maximum of one hundred years' imprisonment.

Being forced to fight two indictments in two separate jurisdictions against two separate assistant U.S. attorneys was only the beginning of Kevin's legal problems. In the spring of 1993, the government threatened to hamstring his defense by informing Paul Meltzer, Kevin's Northern California counsel, that because of the espionage charge, the entire defense team would be required to undergo fifteen-year background checks. Meltzer thought about complying, but found the idea repugnant. What would happen if Kevin's defense team simply refused to comply with the order?

Nothing. "We got and saw and did everything without the rigmarole of the Classified Information Procedures Act," said Meltzer.

For Kevin and his attorneys, the espionage charge dictated everything. A guilty plea was impossible for two reasons. First because the espionage charge carried a penalty of from fourteen to eighteen years, and second because Kevin believed he was innocent. Once Kevin realized the federal guidelines were going to figure prominently in his cases he dove into them like Pac Bell manuals. "He read them cover to cover with total comprehension," recalled Meltzer. "He was well versed in the law and not just of computer fraud and access devices, but general law." Kevin would prepare notes and graphs in triplicate for his attorneys, showing things like the differences in grand jury testimony by witnesses.

Kevin was also getting lots of practice with the federal guidelines on his Los Angeles case. On June 14, 1994, Assistant U.S. Attorney David Schindler issued a press release that the *Unsolved Mysteries* hacker had pled guilty to seven counts including computer fraud, interception of wire communications, mail fraud, money laundering, and obstruction of justice. Poulsen, the government said, faced up to forty years' imprisonment and a fine of $1,750,000.

In the fall of 1994, Kevin's attorneys prepared for trial in the Northern District of California. He had already spent three and a half years in jail, easily the longest prison term ever for a computer hacker. A successful defense motion to suppress the evidence seized in the Menlo Park locker search had been reversed by the Ninth Circuit. A lot was on the line. An espionage conviction could easily keep Kevin imprisoned until he was in his forties.

His attorneys focused on debunking the espionage charge, dispatching a detective to interview the SRI managers who had directed Kevin to modify the program that had used the air tasking orders. Meltzer believed he could prove that Kevin's job required that he handle the military documents.

As trial approached, Meltzer had hundreds of exhibits ready and twenty witnesses from SRI and other entities. But just days before the trial was set to start, Rob Crowe contacted Meltzer and offered to dismiss the espionage charge if Kevin would plead guilty to several felonies that would amount to a sentence of roughly two years. Why did Crowe dismiss the espionage charge? Crowe later said it was a combination of factors, ranging from the successful Los Angeles prosecution to the five years that had passed since the 1989 Northern California indictment. Meltzer implied that the government was no longer confident that it could successfully prosecute Poulsen for espionage. But the end was still not in sight for Kevin. He still hadn't been sentenced in Los Angeles.

On February 9, 1995, Kevin wrote to his sentencing judge in the Los Angeles case, admitting that he had used his considerable talents to "break the law" and must now "live with the consequences."

The letter did not impress Judge Manuel Real. On April 10 Judge Real exceeded the assistant U.S. attorney's recommendation and sentenced Kevin to a term of fifty-one months. "I think there are matters that have not been considered by the Sentencing Guidelines here," the judge explained, seeming to speak to the uncharged crimes the government was unwilling to discuss "in that there was a very fair—at least, very potential danger to law enforcement, not only in this country but also in other countries, where this man had hacked into information on foreign intelligence security matters."

Judge Real was also concerned that the government "had to change their whole operations." A source within the Justice Department revealed that the FBI's secret communications "tech center in Los Angeles had to be moved. Poulsen had the address. The San Francisco center was moved too." The centers were the equivalent of Q's super gizmo workshop in the James Bond movies. FBI agents would go there when their cars needed to be modified for electronic surveillance or they needed to have a wire fitted on their body. Federal wiretaps were also often monitored from the secret locations—the San Francisco center was disguised in what appeared to be a dilapidated building.

———■———

The political stakes in keeping secret the scope of Poulsen's intrusions were high. As the hacker's case was being played out in the courts, the FBI was waging a public battle to expand its wiretapping powers in the digital age. In the early 1990s, the FBI had begun lobbying for new, increased capabilities to monitor digital telephone and computer communications. The Bureau wanted to install software directly inside phone company switches to expand its eavesdropping powers. After one congressional rebuff, the proposal became law with the passing of the Digital Telephony Act in 1994. But when the Bureau's true plans became known, they sparked a public outcry. The FBI announced that it needed the extraordinary power potentially to wiretap 2 percent of the phones in major metropolitan areas.

Kevin's command of Pac Bell's computers seemed to dramatize the potential danger in placing that power in phone company software. If the FBI was proposing moving the entire wiretapping process directly onto the switch, what would stop hackers like Kevin from eavesdropping on the FBI and its targets?

From 1989 to 1991, Kevin had access to nearly every federal and national security wiretap in California. He had this extraordinary ability because he could hack the computers of Pac Bell, considered by hackers to be among the most secure in the telecommunications industry. Pac Bell, through its spokesman, "special" investigator Kurt Von Brauch, confidently explained that the vulnerabilities Kevin had exploited had been closed. Physical security at the company's hundreds of buildings had been tightened, the number of dial-up lines had been greatly reduced, and a product called "Secure ID" was being used to restrict unauthorized access. Pac Bell employees had to use a tiny card that contained a unique algorithm synchronized with a computer. Every thirty seconds the card would create a new random number, and if the number didn't match up with the computer, the holder was denied access.

But despite these improvements, other present and former Pac Bell employees told another story. In an age of fierce telecommunications competition, Pac Bell's security budget had been cut, and the number of investigators reduced. Kevin himself noted that he had seen no evidence that Pac Bell had improved the physical security at its buildings. And there was something else that Kevin had told me years ago. He had stolen a manual to Secure ID and hinted that for him the miracle card Pac Bell was counting on to protect its systems was no more than a difficult password, hardly a challenge for an elite hacker.

Underneath all this, there was the possibility that Kevin may have stumbled onto some dirty secrets. According to Mark Lottor and others who had direct knowledge of Kevin's activities, some of the federal wiretaps Kevin uncovered may not have been authorized by court order. The FBI declined all comment on Kevin Poulsen and wiretapping in general; Kevin, too, was elusive on the ticklish subject. "I learned some interesting things, but I tended to put my interest in the technical over the social," he told me during a jail visit. "I can't confirm or deny what I did or didn't know, whether I discovered interesting taps. We live in a country where the army used a U2 spy plane to watch Martin Luther King, where Nixon was tapping the phones of his rivals. Nothing could shock me."

But we do know this: Kevin learned firsthand that phone companies can wiretap the first two minutes of anyone's phone call without court authorization, a fact that Pac Bell acknowledges. And simply by the force of his hacking, Kevin proved that the communications infrastructure that we rely upon for banking, commerce, and even national security is far more vulnerable than we imagine.

———■———

I visited Kevin on several occasions while he was in Santa Clara County Jail and in the federal penitentiary in Pleasanton, California. I also talked to him for hundreds of hours by telephone.

Upon his release on June 4 of 1996, after more than five years in prison, I met Kevin at his parents' home in North Hollywood and spent an evening talking to him and visiting many of the sites of his crimes. We drove past the rundown Hollywood office where he pulled off his Porsche radio scam, and walked outside the Sunset central office where he discovered the SAS wiretapping system and sabotaged Eric. Finally, we visited the hotel room where he hid out after the *Unsolved Mysteries* show, and I watched as he deftly picked a door lock and revealed the kitchen where he had prepared meals.

After a decade of hacking and half a decade in jail, was he truly ready to quit? There was no doubt in my mind that Kevin was still angry. He wouldn't talk about the countless county and federal jails he'd been shuttled between, the weeks he'd spent in solitary confinement, the years he'd spent preparing his defense, playing Ping-Pong and chess, chain smoking, and reading books. But he made certain I understood that he wanted to bring a RICO racketeering suit against Pac Bell for what he called the false charges brought against him.

There were signs that he was renewing old acquaintances. Just before Kevin's release, the government dismissed its nearly six-year-old indictment against Mark Lottor, stating that he was the "least culpable of the three defendants." Kevin's former roommate put up a World Wide Web page for Kevin on his site, entitled, "The Switchroom," protesting the "bullshit charges" that kept him in jail for five years. It was a far cry from his repentant letter to Judge Real. He quoted the nineteenth-century Russian aristocratic anarchist Bakunin, who believed that through "anarchism, collectivism and atheism" and the overthrow of existing states and institutions, men would achieve complete freedom: "Does it follow that I reject all authority? Far from me such a thought. In the matter of boots, I refer to the authority of the bootmaker; concerning houses, canals or railroads, I consult that of the architect or engineer."

After five hard years in jail, Kevin continued his battle against the system. As part of Kevin's three-year probation, Judge Real had ordered that he not have any access to computers. Despite the nature of his crimes, it seemed an unrealistic condition in an age when nearly every job requires some computer use and you need a computer to find a library book. In the years Kevin had been in jail, the Internet had leaped from obscurity to a general tool that promised one day to be as ubiquitous and useful as the telephone. Networking had gone mainstream, and Kevin was being ordered to stay on the sidelines and watch the revolution pass him by. Since computer programming was Kevin's only marketable skill, the government also seemed to be making it all but impossible for him to pay back the over $70,000 he owed in restitution to the radio stations and the court. Nevertheless, his probation officer ordered that his parents put their home computer in storage and suggested that Kevin start with a job at McDonald's.

Kevin enrolled at Pierce Community College and planned to study English literature with an eye toward eventually earning a degree in computer science. This didn't please his probation officer, who asked to meet with him to clarify matters. Barely a week had passed since Kevin's release and already he was in a tussle with the federal government. His probation officer told him he couldn't attend school full-time and would have to begin working immediately. Furious, Kevin wrote a letter to his probation officer, saying, "You ended the meeting on a cautionary note, warning me that there were outside agencies that would like to see me back in prison as quickly as possible. I asked if it was possible that such an agency had contacted your office, and you acknowledged that it was possible."

Kevin took his fight to the media, and on August 18, 1996, Keith Stone of the *Los Angeles Daily News* wrote a front-page article about the hacker and the government's harsh probation terms. Kevin described himself as a hacker who had performed a public service "by spying on the government and phone company" in a time when these institutions wielded tremendous, unchecked powers. The article was picked up by the Associated Press, and even the *Philadelphia Inquirer* did a front-page piece on Kevin's predicament, headlining the story, "A Hacking King Without a Realm." Kevin played up the irony of the government's prohibitions, telling the *Inquirer* that he asks librarians to look up books for him, and was considering applying for one of the few jobs open to him, a boot salesman in a western clothing store. In the media rush, Kevin was invited to talk on a Los Angeles radio talk show. The first caller shouted, "Have I won, have I won?"

It was Ron Austin, playing an inside joke.

———■———

Having investigated Kevin's exploits for several years and talked to him for three, I took his public statements with a grain of salt. I found Kevin to be be polite, friendly, and manipulative. Over the years I came to enjoy his ample sense of humor and respect his reputation for investigating those who got too close to him. He was as clever with people as he was with computers, but I wasn't convinced that he was hacking for the public interest.

On collect calls from jails all over the state, Kevin lectured me for hours on end about the importance of the hacker ethic, the ideal that he said had dictated his every act. Kevin had the power to come closer to that ideal than anyone who had ever hacked, but he seemed to have broken his own code. Drawn to the seductive power of Pac Bell's computers, Kevin became an old-fashioned master burglar and then threw his lot in with Eric, a hardened criminal. Kevin had hacked for profit, pimped electronically, and eavesdropped on his friends. He had thrown away numerous chances for redemption, especially his once promising jobs with SRI and Sun Microsystems. Even the first Northern California indictment was a warning, an opportunity to go straight, for there was a good chance that if Kevin had immediately given himself up the charges would have amounted to no more than probation or a few months in jail. Looking back on the first thirty years of Kevin's life, I and many others who knew him were struck by the waste of intellect, if not genius. Who knows what Kevin might have achieved if like Steve Jobs or Steve Wozniak or other hackers he'd learned to apply his obsession to legal ends.

Kevin talked of the service he and his kind provided for society but appeared oblivious to how his own actions jeopardized privacy and national security. Today, the federal government is continuing its public fight against hackers, rightly arguing that public safety and national security must be preserved. But some hackers also honestly believe they provide a service for society. For instance, hackers recently risked punishment to make a political statement, tarring the Justice Department's World Wide Web site with graffiti to protest the government's controversial efforts to ban obscenity on the Net. Freedom of speech was at issue. Were they dangerous criminals deserving of several years in jail or unruly protesters who spat on opposition placards in a virtual Hyde Park?

Kevin is correct that hackers have the potential for good as well as evil, and this is certainly a time when contrasting views might be beneficial to society. The explosive growth of the Internet, the passing of the Digital Telephony Act, and government attempts to control encryption should all be viewed with caution by those who believe that privacy and freedom are essential to democracy.

I would like to believe that there are hackers who might perform the checks and balances that Kevin talked of, but his criminal and personal motives clouded whatever good intentions he may have once had. Kevin knew he was a danger to national security, and that his most serious crimes had taken place after he moved to Los Angeles. When I met with him in his hometown, I asked him about the espionage taps he'd discovered on consulates and near the Concord Naval Weapons Station. Kevin only smiled. There were things he could never discuss.

As a condition of his plea in Southern California, Kevin had agreed to be polygraphed by the government in perpetuity. Neither the FBI nor the U.S. attorney's office would comment on what seemed an extraordinary demand. Nor was there any policy about what might happen if he failed the test. But when I asked him whether he was worried about the prospect of indefinite polygraphs the hacker played it cool. Kevin had never failed a polygraph, and he saw no reason why he would fail one in the future. I had to agree, and not only because I doubted Kevin would ever talk about the national security aspects of his case that might get him in trouble.

If anybody could beat a polygraph, it would be Kevin Poulsen.

AUTHOR'S NOTE

———■———

I first began following Kevin Poulsen's electronic exploits in January of 1990, shortly after he became a fugitive from the FBI. Three years later, as Kevin awaited trial on charges of espionage that could keep him in jail for more than a decade, I wrote an article about him for the *Los Angeles Times Magazine* titled "The Last Hacker."

In early 1994, I set out to write this book and began by spending several weeks in Los Angeles and on the San Francisco Peninsula researching Poulsen's story. Angry about my *Los Angeles Times* article, the hacker initially refused to talk to me, but I interviewed his childhood friends, his mother, his teachers, and many of his coworkers at his former workplace, SRI International, in Menlo Park. Ron Austin, Kevin's longtime friend and fellow hacker, was generous with his time and knowledge, and met me often in Los Angeles, on a few occasions actually pointing out the scenes of some of their celebrated crimes. In April of 1994, Poulsen's other main confederate, Justin Petersen, then a wanted fugitive, phoned me in the middle of the night from a pay phone and began to tell his story. A few weeks later, another fugitive called, the soon to be legendary Kevin Mitnick.

In August of 1994, Kevin Poulsen finally broke his silence and phoned me from the Metropolitan Detention Center in Los Angeles and gradually revealed his story. The warden refused to let me visit him, but Kevin called me several times a week, often talking until his evening meal, when I'd hear his jailers shout just before the phones would suddenly go dead. He had a good memory for details and dialogue and helped bring to life some of his most spectacular escapades.

Then Kevin Mitnick's world suddenly came crashing down. In February of 1995, the hacker was tracked down by the security expert Tsutomu Shimomura, and I jumped a red-eye for Raleigh, North Carolina, the scene of the arrest. When I returned home a few days later, my editor at Little, Brown, Roger Donald, agreed with my suggestion that I write a Mitnick book first. Six months later, I finished *The Fugitive Game: Online with Kevin Mitnick—The Inside Story of the Great Cyberchase.* I took a short break and returned to my Poulsen manuscript. By then, Poulsen had been moved to a federal camp near my home in the San Francisco Bay Area. I trekked out to the penitentiary several times and we sipped Cokes I bought from the vending machine and talked for hours at a time. I had already interviewed the other main characters in the story at length; the government prosecutors, Robert Crowe and David Schindler; Kurt Von Brauch, the Oakland Pac Bell investigator who first built a case against the hacker; Bill Spradley, the LAPD detective who chased Poulsen around Los Angeles; and Terry Atchley, the Los Angeles Pac Bell investigator who captured Poulsen.

This is a journalistic work. I've tried to offer my perspective on the social phenomenon of hacking and the underlying legal and privacy issues, but at heart this is a true story of three young men on the edge of technology and the law. I interviewed Kevin Poulsen for hundreds of hours and spent dozens of hours talking to Ron Austin and Justin Petersen. I visited many of the places described in this book, interviewed over a hundred people, and reviewed thousands of pages of court filings, grand jury transcripts, and miscellaneous documents. The dialogue in the book is based on interviews, court or police transcripts, and movie, television, or radio broadcasts. I was fortunate to have had the opportunity to interview both the hackers and the pursuers thoroughly enough to sort out the points where individual memories conflicted.

Thank you to my good friend Rusty Weston, who encouraged me to write this story in the present tense and proved a gifted book editor. My friend Deborah Radcliff, an able journalist and writer, helped edit too. Roger Donald, with his broad sense of the story, sparked me to blend the narrative with the action. My agent, Kris Dahl of ICM, secured an excellent publisher and generously read early drafts. Finally, my father shared his usual good advice.

Writing two books in three years was both challenging and exhilarating. I had some tremendously exciting times on the trail of a good story, and I won't forget the collect calls from jail, the late-night conversations with fugitives, and the mysterious trips around Hollywood. I'd like to thank Kevin Poulsen and all the others who made this book possible.

October 15, 1996
Mill Valley, California